A Place of Springs

In this book Grace Jantzen constructs a Quaker spirituality of beauty as a theological–philosophical response to a world preoccupied with death and violence. Having mapped the foundations of western cultural violence in the Greco-Roman period and the Judea-Christian tradition in *Foundations of Violence* and *Violence to Eternity*, she now offers her alternative vision. This vision is an original and creative feminist reading of the Quaker tradition, considering George Fox and the writings of Quaker women, exploring the themes of inner light and beauty as alternatives to violence and the obstacles to building such an alternative world. After showing how seventeenth-century Quakers offered a different option for modernity, she maps the philosophical and ethical implications of engaging with the world through beauty and its transforming power. Written for everyone interested in contemporary spirituality, it explains how Quaker ideas can provide a way to transform our violent world into one that celebrates life rather than death, peace rather than violence.

This work is the second of two posthumous publications to complete Grace M. Jantzen's *Death and the Displacement of Beauty* collection, which began with *Foundations of Violence* (Routledge, 2004).

The late **Grace M. Jantzen** (1948–2006) was Professor of Religion, Culture and Gender at Manchester University and a widely respected feminist philosopher and theologian.

Jeremy Carrette is Professor of Religion and Culture in the Department of Religious Studies at the University of Kent and is the author of *Selling Spirituality* (Routledge, 2005) and *Religion and Critical Psychology* (Routledge, 2007).

Morny Joy is University Professor in the Department of Religious Studies at the University of Calgary. She is author of *Divine Love: Luce Irigaray, Women, Gender and Religion* (2007).

A Place of Springs

Death and the Displacement of Beauty, Volume 3

Grace M. Jantzen

Edited by

Jeremy Carrette and Morny Joy

Routledge
Taylor & Francis Group

LONDON AND NEW YORK

First published 2010
by Routledge
2 Park Square, Milton Park, Abingdon, OX14 4RN

Simultaneously published in the USA and Canada
by Routledge
270 Madison Ave., New York, NY 100016

Routledge is an imprint of the Taylor & Francis Group, an informa business

Typeset in Sabon by
Taylor & Francis Books
Printed and bound in Great Britain by
CPI Antony Rowe, Chippenham, Wiltshire

British Library Cataloguing in Publication Data
A catalogue record for this book is available from the British Library

Library of Congress Cataloging in Publication Data
A catalog record for this book has been requested

ISBN13: 978-0-415-46999-9 (hbk)
ISBN13: 978-0-203-87079-2 (ebk)

To Tina, Beloved Beauty

'They, walking through the bitter valley, make it a place of springs: the autumn rain covereth it with blessing.'

Contents

Preface

A Place of Springs is the third and final volume of Grace Jantzen's multi-volume study *Death and the Displacement of Beauty*. It is a response and answer to the first two volumes examining death and violence in the Greco-Roman (Volume 1, *Foundations of Violence*) and Judaic-Christian traditions (Volume 2, *Violence to Eternity*). The original project was to have been a six-volume study, but this third volume completes the unfinished material that had sufficient shape for publication and which Grace Jantzen left before her death in 2006. It leaves the incomplete studies of the modern and late-modern period to the remaining inferences in the completed works.[1] While the multi-volume project will always be marked out by its unfinished potential, this volume is nonetheless a suitable point at which to finish Grace Jantzen's feminist philosophical studies because it returns to the heart of her own lived and politically engaged Quaker spirituality. It brings an analysis of beauty from non-violent feminist and Quaker consciousness and reveals a theology and spirituality that opens beauty as a central place for life and living. After exploring the genealogy of violence in western civilization, and showing how violence and its conceptualizations were constantly suspicious of beauty, this volume brings philosophy to the beauty of life. It was, as Jantzen explained, a 'happier task of showing the significance of beauty' as an alternative to violence. Beauty is the opening to a new spirituality built from old Quaker resources and shaped by a critical feminist and post-structuralist concern. It completes a long journey in her life and work to find an alternative symbolic to the dominant western preoccupation with death.

Grace Jantzen's (1948–2006) journey from her Mennonite background in Northern Saskatchewan, Canada, to Professor of Religion, Culture and Gender at the University of Manchester, England, was one of shifting the dominant paradigms in the philosophy of religion through a critical feminist consciousness and a Quaker sensibility of peace and justice. After her studies at the University of Saskatchewan she completed double doctorates in philosophy and theology: first at the University of Calgary, with Terry Penelhum and Kai Nielsen, and then at Oxford University, under the direction of John Macquarie and Basil Mitchell. This provided her with a strong background for rethinking old debates in the philosophy of religion and eventually brought her a post at King's College, University of London in 1980. Here she established her scholarship on feminism, philosophy of religion and medieval mysticism. Her first work, *God's World, God's Body* (DLT, 1984) explored the theological–philosophical problem of God's embodiment in the world – a question from her graduate days – and its theme arguably returns in her final work in recognizing how vital conceptions of the divine and transcendence/immanence are to the understanding of beauty (see Chapter 5). Following her first philosophical study, she wrote – perhaps her most popularly successful work – *Julian of Norwich: Mystic and Theologian* (SPCK, 1987; 2nd edn 2000). This study was to become a key reference within the field and a guide for many outside academia who were inspired by this female mystic.

Her next study brought a new political development in the field of mysticism by linking it with feminist and Continental philosophical thinking. In her major work *Power, Gender and Christian Mysticism* (Cambridge University Press, 1995), she showed how the category and construction of mysticism was determined by gender politics, not least by showing how women mystics who lacked access to the Latin text brought about an authority through visions and how the female body was displaced and abused in the construction of the mystical. The courage of her thinking was to work with Continental and feminist philosophers in a theological world dominated by male analytical philosophy. Such an engagement brought her much personal suffering and deep misunderstanding in some of the places where she worked. Her feminist identity had been a challenge to many in conservative religious and academic institutions, but her ability to think outside the constraints of the system brought healing and liberation to many caught in similar oppressive regimes. Despite the challenges, her intellectual perspective was held in such high regard that she was asked to become part of the Canadian Royal Commission on New Reproductive Technologies between 1989 and 1993; the two-volume final report, reflecting on genetic engineering and new reproductive technologies, was partly adopted in Canada, the World Health Organisation and various United Nations organisations.

The next stage in Grace Jantzen's thinking, during her time at the University of Manchester, brought about a radical reshaping of the philosophy of religion from French feminist theory. She developed her own distinctive feminist philosophy of religion, creating an internationally acknowledged philosophical perspective to counter gendered analytic thinking. These ideas appeared in two works in her own Manchester series, Religion, Culture and Gender: her own innovative work, *Becoming Divine: Towards a Feminist Philosophy of Religion* (Manchester University Press, 1998) and *Forever Fluid: A Reading of Luce Irigaray's Elemental Passions* (Manchester University Press, 2005), a study completing the work of her doctoral student Hanneke Canters, who also died of cancer some years before. Her study, *Becoming Divine* brought the work of Irigaray, Lacan, Foucault and Derrida to feminist theology and the philosophy of religion and challenged the preoccupations of the male western philosophy, which she saw as driven by a concern with death, or what she termed necrophilia. Recognizing the problems of critique without alternatives, she constructed a philosophy of religion built on natality and birth. While not denying the reality of physical death, this sought to correct the neo-Platonic idea of the eternal realm and the preoccupations with the afterlife with a valuing of this life process in its own embodied terms, such that eternal life was seen as living fully or flourishing in the present moment, rather than something after life. Her aim was to offer different ways of imagining life outside the patriarchal symbolic of western thinking.

The first phase of her work, rethinking medieval women mystics, and the second phase, mapping French feminism and the philosophy of religion, set the ground for what was to be her final – and perhaps most significant – contribution: an anticipated six-volume study on *Death and the Displacement of Beauty* in western philosophy. This was a working through of her understanding of natality and necrophilia in an extended genealogical examination of western thought. It was not simply a critique of the problem, but a radical and inspired opening of the alternative options. The first volume, *Foundations of Violence* (Routledge, 2004), sought to show how Greco-Roman philosophy created a foundational symbolic of violence and death, linked to a devaluing of women and creating a cultural ideal which resulted in the modern world of conflict and warfare. The work was an original search for an alternative symbolic and, as in the case of the French philosopher Michel Foucault – whose ideas shaped the work – her death brought an end to a potential multivolumed project. The second – posthumous – volume *Violence to Eternity* (Routledge, 2009), examined the religious roots of death and violence in the Jewish and Christian traditions, which underlined contemporary values and actions. She showed how these religious constructions of violence were always gendered and how man's fear of women and the female is often implicated in religious violence. In her critical genealogy of the Hebrew Bible and the Christian New Testament she examined a range of themes that show the western preoccupation with necrophilia (a fascination with death and violence). She examined the relation of death to the Jewish covenant, the nature of monotheism and Holy War, the obsessions with blood and sacrifice, and in the Christian tradition, the link between death and the new covenant. Jantzen recognized that the violent concerns in the Greco-Roman and Judaic-Christian foundations of the western world reflected a choice, not a given, and that submerged beneath them are traces of an alternative world of beauty, creativity and life, which this final volume maps out.

In order to appreciate the journey that Grace Jantzen made in her project *Death and the Displacement of Beauty*, it is worth noting her original mapping of the multi-volume work in Volume 1. In this volume she stated that she wished to show 'how the attraction of beauty can inspire resistance and creative response, and can draw forward desire that is premised not upon lack or death but upon potential for new beginning' (p. viii). Her project sought to bring 'healing and hope' and to 'enable human flourishing' (pp. viii and 3). It was an attempt to find ways of thinking and living differently and a 'path to the healing of the western psyche' (p. 4). The extended genealogy of western thought – in Foucault's sense of a critical exploration of what was displaced and marginalized in history – was a corrective exercise to bring a new 'balance of attention' (p. 6). The 'hope for life' was to move away from preoccupations with death and violence to the hidden order of beauty (p. 6). However, as this volume shows, the move towards beauty requires some understanding of the reasons why beauty creates such anxiety in a male-dominated world of violence. This final volume is her 'redemptive imaginary' (p. 17). It returns us to primary location of the maternal body and female sexuality at the foundations of life itself.

This volume also brings a focus on the Quaker tradition and shows the extent to which, according to Jantzen, Quakers were 'disrupting the social symbolic of early modernity' (see Chapter 5). Jantzen's account of the Quaker tradition also reveals something of the power of women's voices as part of that challenge, but not without a critical concern about early Quaker attitudes. The Quaker tradition becomes the heart of Grace Jantzen's solution because it bridges spiritual and political worlds, a feature of its emergence in the political turbulence of British seventeenth-century society and something carried in its continual link of corporate mysticism and social transformation or, what Benefiel and Phipps, in a volume to which Grace Jantzen contributed her own separate essay, called 'practical mysticism' (Benefiel and Phipps 2001: 129). The Quaker peace testimony for contemporary Quakers includes a statement of gender equality and it provides the force of critique to the violent symbolic of western culture. As Jantzen states in this volume: 'Quakers won through to an acceptance of gender equality (without the distinction between spiritual and temporal) far more thorough-going than most other non-conformist denominations (except the Unitarians) and far in advance of the established church, where sexism is still deep seated.'

The importance of the Quaker tradition is found in the fact that it offered an alternative to violent modernity, and through ideas such as the 'inner light' challenged the existing orders of power. As Jantzen contends, 'rediscovering the contours of an alternative symbolic at the cusp of modernity may give us resources for thinking and living otherwise'. This volume is thus, as Jantzen suggests, an invitation to 'choose life' through a feminist Quaker vision of beauty, linked to a long line of alternative forms of spiritual engagement. Beauty is the counter-memory of the masculinist, necrophilic western psyche, it is the choice that was continually rejected, but which always remains an option. Beauty 'is life giving and life enhancing' and it requires a substantial material change to the world. As Jantzen realized at the beginning of her multi-volume project, the work is 'highly optimistic' and it shows that the 'present is not inevitable' (Volume 1, p. 20–21). This volume offers the corporate spiritual challenge to rethink the symbolic order of a violent world that Volumes 1 and 2 carefully detailed. It brings together the voices that 'urged other choices, voices which were silenced and repressed but which could yet offer resources for freedom and newness' (Volume 1, p. 21).

Grace Jantzen's multi-volume study began with the 'pleasure of the Lake District' (Volume 1, p. vii) and this final volume begins with the same appeal to its beauty. The southern Lakes of the north of England inspire the text and reveal the material and lived world beyond the words. It conveys a delight in the beauty of landscape, the beauty of music and – ultimately – a love of life. Grace Jantzen's philosophy is a philosophy of 'hope for life', even as her own life was cut short by death, but life – as Jantzen understands – is bigger than any one individual and demands choices that give birth to beauty as a collective response to the western preoccupation with death and violence. Jantzen's work was, in her own mind, a 'therapy of philosophy', an attempt to heal the symbolic order, and her alternative imaginary is the womb of social transformation. It is a philosophy and spirituality of transformation and renewal and one that 'invites creativity and imagination' (see Introduction). Grace Jantzen's legacy is precisely to awaken new forms of imaginative thinking that can change the embodied and gendered world so that justice can flourish. This volume is a celebration of beauty and life and a hope for change – a hope for life.

Jeremy Carrette and Morny Joy
May 2009

Acknowledgements

This project has always been marked by loss and honours Grace Janzten's request that we complete as far as possible her remaining volumes for *Death and the Displacement of Beauty*. It has been a journey of meetings in various parts of the world and extended e-mail exchanges to discuss different versions and editorial questions. It began in the Lake District, England – the place that so inspired Grace Jantzen with its beauty – and ended with editorial meetings in the Russell Square area of London. In editing the work we have sought to remain as close as possible to Grace Jantzen's original intentions, but the task was complicated by working with different versions and selections of chapters. The final version is an integration of two different versions of the volume. We have amended chapters to avoid excessive duplication, and for cohesion of the argument we have also rearranged material into some new sections and included material from published articles and chapters produced in the final years of her work. Although there is some repetition of her basic ideas on the moral imaginary in the final chapter, entitled 'On changing the imaginary', it has been included because it is only here that Jantzen specifically addresses the imaginary in relation to questions of religion today, and the repetitions could not be removed without distorting the meaning of the chapter. The selection of additional essays gives witness to Grace Jantzen's unfinished project, yet indicates the directions in which she had hoped to go. The title of one remaining chapter that she had intended to write, but did not even begin, was 'Engaged contemplation'. No doubt this would have developed further certain spiritual aspects of her explorations. Our hope is that these extra chapters that reveal the immensity of the task that she had undertaken – nothing less than attempting to develop an alternative philosophical and theological vision for the contemporary world – will inspire others to follow in her footsteps and honour her challenging and transformative legacy. The final editing also required solving the problem of some incomplete references. We have attempted to do deal with these issues to the best of our knowledge, but accept that some errors may have occurred in the process. The final version is nonetheless the closest we could come to the intended volume and provides a final gathering together of the remaining material of Grace Jantzen's inspirational philosophical project.

The completion of this book would not have been possible without the support of Grace Jantzen's partner, Tina Macrae. She gave us hospitality and warmth while we both worked on Grace's original documents in 2007 and her personal encouragement and support has been essential in helping us complete this project. The continued commitment to the project by Routledge has been central. Lesley Riddle – who by chance commissioned Grace Jantzen's first work at DLT in 1984 – has been a tremendous support. Her devotion to completing the project has enabled us to rescue as much as possible of the original six-volume work. Amy Grant has been extremely helpful in guiding us through the final stages of editing and permissions.

We hope that these volumes will be a tribute to our friendship and our appreciation of Grace Jantzen's philosophical insights, and will reflect as far as possible something of her vision for life and justice. Jeremy would like to thank the British Academy for a small grant to support travel and administrative assistance for his part of the project. Morny would like to thank John King for his generous help in editorial matters. Finally, we are grateful to a number of journals and publishers for permission to include material that enabled us to complete the unfinished parts of this volume. The first two were originally intended for inclusion by Grace Janzten, and the others were then selected to extend and enhance the argument. Chapter 7 originally appeared as 'Before the Rooster Crows: The Betrayal of Knowledge in Modernity', *Literature and Theology*, Vol. 15, no. 1 (March, 2001): pp. 1–24. Chapter 5 originally appeared as 'Choose Life! Early Quaker Women and Violence in Modernity', *Quaker Studies*, 9/2 (2005): pp. 137–155. Chapter 10 originally appeared as 'Flourishing: Towards an Ethic of Natality', *Feminist Theory* 2/2 (2001), pp. 219–232.

Introduction

It has been my immense privilege, during the past several years, to live with my partner in the heart of the beautiful English Lake District. The happiness and tranquillity of our home, full of pets and flowers, music and books, is paralleled by the ever-changing delight of the fells as the seasons pass. Day by day as I sit at my desk the light falls differently on Todd Crag across the valley, clear shining after rain, russet in the winter glow of bracken, luminously green in springtime. Day by day as I walk with Button, my happy spaniel, beside the rivers or up the hillsides, there is the endlessly various beauty of water rippling over stones, a rainbow arching across a mountain top, primroses along the banks, dippers or heron in the water, sunlight or rain in the old oak and beech woods. And when we get back home, there is Tina and warmth and loving companionship: most beautiful of all. It is indeed immense privilege.

It is also sacramental. As the beauty of it all has shaped my outlook and my soul, it has become clear to me that beauty must play a very large part in any account of spirituality. This is sacred if anything is. The slant of light, the delicate orchid, the curlew's cry mediate the divine more surely, more immediately, than words or doctrines. More people feel that they encounter God in nature than in creeds, let alone in philosophical arguments. Considering the significance of beauty for spirituality, Christendom, at least in modernity, has paid astonishingly little attention to it. Why not? What shape might theology and spirituality take if beauty were given a central place?

And yet beauty is not the whole story. In our own home there is not only loveliness and delight but serious illness and impending loss and mortality as I live with cancer. Further afield, monsoons and hurricanes, earthquakes and tidal waves engulf hundreds of thousands of people; many are killed and more have to struggle to live with their loss in appalling conditions. If the beauty of nature mediates the sacred, what about its violence? A theology or spirituality that ignored death and destruction and focused only on beauty would be consolatory sentimentality, neither persuasive not strength giving. If the snowdrops beside the pathway are an epiphany of the divine, what about the movement of the tectonic plates which causes the earth and sea to heave and the mountains to fall on schools full of children?

Just as worrying as the violence of nature is the incalculable violence inflicted deliberately by people upon one another. The recent past has seen escalation of wars large and small, most notably the 'war on terror', an elastic concept that can be used to justify the bombing of whole cities, prison camps beyond the reach of international law, torture and execution. Suicide bombers go to their deaths in the name of Allah; self-satisfied western politicians, full of moral certainty, send out troops and authorize massive force, much of it falling on civilians. God bless America. How could a spirituality of beauty possibly respond to this? What would it be worth if it did not? Unless it is precisely to a spirituality of beauty that we could look for alternatives to violence?

It is obvious that a merely consolatory focus on prettiness, averting the eyes from the manifestations of greed and fear and hate that wrack the world, can be of little use. But it is equally obvious that a religion of doctrines and creeds, where true belief is given greater emphasis than sensibility or compassion, lends itself all too readily to the justification of violence upon those who have the audacity to think otherwise. How many wars have been fought to enforce a point of view held to be the 'truth', whether overtly religious or its thinly veiled secular offshoots of so-called democracy and free-market economy? Perhaps if theologians – and thinkers of every kind – put as much emphasis on deepening sensitivity to beauty, on creativity and delight, as we have for centuries put on beliefs and truth, we would begin to find alternatives to violence, would be less willing to destroy the beauty of a landscape or the lives of children. It is at least worth exploring; and in this book I propose to do so.

But from what standpoint can such an exploration take place? In view of the ways in which religion, especially dogmatically held religious beliefs, are invoked to justify violence, it might plausibly be argued that the best stance is one which dispenses with religion altogether. Only a resolutely secular perspective could confront the injustices brought about by those who are confident that they are acting in the name of God.

However, although I have a good deal of respect for such a morally engaged secularism, it is not a standpoint which I can adopt. One of the reasons for this is sheerly biographical. Spirituality and the sacred have shaped my life from its earliest days, and there would be no integrity in my writing as if that were not so. There have been major changes in *how* I have thought about God or the divine, but *that* I have thought about God, and tried and failed and tried again to live consistently with those thoughts, is what has made me, for better and for worse, who I am. Such insight as I can bring to issues of beauty and violence must therefore be rooted in a religious standpoint if they are to be rooted at all.

Much more important than this autobiographical comment, however, is the fact that religion itself is getting a tighter grip on the world of the twenty-first century than might have been expected by the proponents of the secular Enlightenment. Until relatively recently, many thinkers in the west took for granted that religion was declining. Although individuals might be personally devout, this was held to be a private matter and should not be allowed to intrude on science, economics, or issues of public policy. Many thinkers welcomed this secularism; some deplored it, but most accepted that it was so.

Events since the turn of the millennium have shown that things are very much more complicated. The violence that erupted with the destruction of the Twin Towers is overtly religious, as I have already noted. But the thundering violence of aircraft and bombs and military interventions occurs against a background noise of violence which is also, often, justified by appeal to religion or its ideological offshoots. The economic system that promotes global capitalism would be impossible without the support of the religious right in America, the same religious right that upholds the death penalty and that opposes abortion. Burgeoning domestic violence, rape and sexual and physical assault by men on women and children is partly an expression of centuries of patriarchy sustained by a Christendom which taught that men were superior to women and had a right to dominance and mastery, by force if necessary. All these trends are increasing in strength and in their overt religiosity in the west, as is also the appeal by western political leaders, especially in the USA and the UK, to religious or moral imperatives to impose western-style democracy and economics anywhere in the world, using whatever degree of violence is necessary to achieve their aims.

Along with all this is the burgeoning of spirituality. In any bookshop can be found a considerable selection of volumes on 'Mind, Body and Spirit'; and the sales of such books and associated products are enormous. Spirituality in this sense is often contrasted with religion. Its adherents or practitioners might distance themselves from churches or creeds or institutionalized religion, and be loosely grouped as a 'New Age' movement, a label that often indicates greater esteem for aromatherapy and yoga than for volumes of systematic theology. Because of its anti-intellectualism and its privatization of religion it is easily turned into a commodity at the service of capitalism (see Carrette and King 2005) and often disparaged by theologians.

One thing that the growth of spirituality demonstrates, however, is that religion (in this looser sense) is not about to disappear. Church attendance may decline (in Europe, but not in North America), and fewer people might accept the confessions and creeds of Christendom, but this does not mean that the west is becoming more secular. It is in fact typical of this development for people to respond to questioning with, 'No, I'm not religious: but I would consider myself spiritual ... ' Whether or not this is intellectually sound, or plays into the hands of global capitalism, or simply pacifies people to put up with the difficulties of life rather than work to change them, it is at least obvious that this is not atheism. The sacred is taken deeply seriously.

Given that religion (broadly understood) shows no sign of withering away anytime soon, given the ways in which it is used to justify violence and political and economic ideology, and given the cultural hunger for religion as non-institutional spirituality, it is immensely important to rethink religion, not to ignore or abandon it. Those who appropriate religion to underpin violence cannot be allowed to have it all their own way; and those who look to spirituality for sustenance deserve better than to be told that their sincere aspirations are rubbish. What are the resources within religion (rather than against religion) which could deepen spirituality, work for justice and peace, meet the hunger of body and emptiness of soul which shape the struggles of the world in the twenty-first century? Once again I circle back to my starting point: might a much deeper appreciation of beauty play a significant role in discerning those resources?

I have used the broad terms 'religion' and 'spirituality', but it is obvious that I am writing from within the historical context of western Christendom. This is not meant to imply that other religious traditions do not also incorporate strands of both violence and beauty: of course they do. One need only remember the emphasis on the warrior among Sikhs, or the blue and gold glory of the mosques of Damascus and Samarkand. Once again, however, it is within the western Christian tradition that my biography places me; more importantly, it is urgent that the west looks to its own violence, and resources for alternatives to violence, before pointing fingers elsewhere. Not all of the violence and oppression that shapes the world as we know it can be attributed to Christendom and its secular progeny, but a great deal of it can be; and it ill behoves the oppressor to speculate on the sins of the oppressed. Similarly, it is not only within Christendom that resources can be found in beauty and in spirituality for creativity and compassion; but unless these *are* found and used to reshape western attitudes and actions, its destruction of the world will continue.

Like other world religions, Christendom has many different strands, some of them standing deliberately at an angle to the structures of theology and power that characterize its major institutions. It could be argued that its very inception was such a stance, as Jesus and then his disciples, especially Paul, took a radically reforming position toward their Jewish faith. As Christendom became established, especially after the conversion of Constantine in the fourth century, men and women moved out to the desert and adopted a life of extreme asceticism over against the growing wealth and comfort of the church. Throughout the Middle Ages there were movements of reform. Some, like the Cistercians, developed in a monastic context and emphasized simplicity and austerity in contrast to the magnificence of the Benedictines. Others, like the Franciscans and later the Beguines, placed compassion, caring for the lepers, the outcast and the poor, at the heart of their spirituality. Some of these movements lost their early vision and reverted to the luxury and power against which they had at first protested. Some were branded heretical by the institutional church while others were taken into its heart. Whatever the case, however, these movements and the significant individuals within them were not seeking to destroy Christendom but to refashion it, usually by recalling it to what they perceived to be its roots in the compassion and love of its founder, the Prince of Peace. They were not wreckers; they were the loyal opposition, with at least as much emphasis on loyalty as on opposition. The last thing they wanted was to be outside the church. As for being outside of Christendom itself, it is hard to see how that could even be conceptualized, unless it meant converting to Judaism or, in medieval Spain, adopting the Muslim faith. But this would have been an option only for very few; and in any case, it is not from them that resources for rethinking Christendom could come. The point is that in the reforming movements themselves, sometimes taken up into the mainstream, can be found ways of thinking and living that challenge the gender and power structures prevalent in Christendom and look for creative alternatives, sometimes with a sensitivity to beauty that was largely lost in the theologies of modernity.

In modernity too, however, there are many strands, most obviously deriving from the Protestant Reformation and the responses to it by the Catholic Church. Especially in what is sometimes called the Radical Reformation – the Anabaptists and later the Quakers and other Dissenters in Britain – there is a discernible effort to draw upon the spiritual and theological resources of Christendom while also subjecting it to a thorough critique, not omitting continuous self-criticism. These Dissenting movements have historically been at the forefront of social reform, ranging from the abolition of slavery and work for racial harmony, to universal suffrage, gender equality and campaigns against poverty and toward ecological concern. Some of them, especially the Mennonites and the Quakers, are known as the 'peace churches' because they corporately renounce violence and make the work for peace and justice central to their self-identity. In this respect they stand at odds with many larger denominations which have supported what they have considered to be 'just wars'; in other respects the Dissenters draw on a shared heritage of Christendom, even while claiming the right to reinterpret this heritage for our times.

The standpoint I take in this book is that of a Quaker, having been born and brought up as a Mennonite on the Canadian prairies and via a formative decade or so in the Church of England. These are two respects in which this standpoint is particularly relevant to what I am trying to achieve. The first of these is the Quaker peace testimony, already referred to:

> We are called to live 'in the virtue of that life and power that takes away the occasion of all wars'. Do you faithfully maintain our testimony that war and the preparation for war are inconsistent with the spirit of Christ? Search out whatever in your own way of life may contain the seeds of war. Stand firm in our testimony, even when others commit or prepare to commit acts of violence, yet always remember that they too are children of God.
>
> (British Yearly Meeting 1995: 1.02.31)

This is much more than denunciation of violence; much more, too, than personal or corporate refusal to participate in it. It is rather a commitment to live in a manner that seeks to remove the *occasion* for violence, the injustice that generates desperation, the fear and hatred and oppression that ignites conflict, the ugliness which subverts the value of peace. It is also a commitment to seek out alternatives to violence, paths of beauty and fulfilment that make peace worth pursuing. Quakers are of course not the only ones who can take this stance; but a Quaker perspective is the one that informs this effort towards resources for peace.

The second respect in which a Quaker standpoint has a special bearing on this work is the centrality to it of spirituality, waiting on God in silent worship or spoken ministry, while sitting lightly to any particular doctrinal formulation. Quakers emphasize receptivity to the 'inner light' and obedience to its promptings. This idea is not without problems, and I shall explore it more fully in the following chapters. However, a preliminary sketch of some of its facets can show how it is important for this book.

First, emphasis on the inner light, or 'the light in their conscience', as early Quakers often put it, places Quakers in a long tradition of Christian spirituality. A standard description of spiritual progress used the terms purification, illumination and contemplation, or again used metaphors of the soul as a mirror filled with the divine radiance and reflecting it back to the world. There have been those who have argued that Quakers drew their spiritual teaching from medieval and early modern mystics and spiritual reformers (Jones 1914, 1971 [1923]), sometimes giving the impression that there is a single line of authentic spirituality that can be traced through the ages from early Christianity (or before) to which Quakerism is the heir. This argument must, however, be heavily qualified. In the first place, there is no single 'tradition of Christian spirituality', but rather, complex and often conflicting strands in which issues of power and gender, institutional authority and individual sanctity all played an often tangled part (Jantzen 1995). Second, even where similarities of themes and ideas stand out, it is hard to see what the actual historical linkage could have been. For example, it would be highly instructive to study the comparisons and contrasts between Teresa of Avila and Margaret Fell, often considered the mother of Quakerism, or between Meister Eckhart and George Fox, Quakerism's founder; but while striking similarities can be found, there is little reason to think that Fox could have read Eckhart and it passes belief that the radical English Protestant Margaret Fell could have known the work of the Spanish Catholic or shown any interest even if she had heard of it. Nevertheless, although actual historical connections are doubtful at best, similarities of themes remain, and (with due caution) invite exploration of their meanings.

A second aspect of Quaker emphasis on inner light, again connecting it to older themes in Christian spirituality, is the relation between light and beauty, a crucial theme for this project. As Umberto Eco has shown, medievals loved light and colour: 'the beauty of colour was everywhere felt to be beauty pure and simple' (Eco 1986: 44). Moreover, unlike the neglect or disparagement of beauty characteristic of theologians since the Reformation, light and beauty were important themes in medieval spirituality, often with a direct link between physical and divine light. Hildegard of Bingen, for instance, wrote:

> I [God] am that living and fiery essence of the divine substance that glows in the beauty of the fields. I shine in the water, I burn in the sun and the moon and the stars.
>
> [Quoted in Eco 1986: 47]

Quite what the relationship is between inner light and the beauty of the world remains to be explored; and again there are conflicts and complexities. But at least on the face of it there are parallels between Quaker ideas of inner light and the beauty of the world, and ideas such as those of Hildegard of Bingen: for example, in the exasperated response of Margaret Fell to the proposal that all Quakers should wear uniform grey dress:

> We must look at no colours, nor make anything that is changeable colours as the hills are, nor sell them, nor wear them: but we must be all in one dress and one colour: this is a silly poor Gospel. It is more fit for us, to be covered with God's Eternal Spirit, and clothed with his Eternal Light, which leads us and guides us into righteousness ...
>
> (British Yearly Meeting 1995: 20.31)

This passage raises many questions: about God, about beauty, about inner light and outer colour, about the literal and the metaphysical. But at least it *does* raise them, *does* indicate that there is more to religion than doctrines and rules, recognizes the significance of light and colour and beauty for spirituality. It will be a central theme of this book.

Third, in Quaker thought the theme of inner light is directly connected with the peace testimony which I have already mentioned. If the inner light is available to illumine everyone, then in that fundamental respect all people are equal. It is from that basis that Quakers have refused to recognize social conventions that demand hierarchies of class, race or gender, and have worked for social structures that treat everyone with equal dignity as 'children of God'. As George Fox famously put it, 'walk cheerfully over the world, answering that of God in everyone' (British Yearly Meeting 1995: 1.02.42). Such an 'answering' is incompatible with violence. Again, the questions are glaring: what happens when the 'inner light' illumines people or groups in incompatible ways? How can one discern genuine illumination from self-deception or wishful thinking? And if there is 'that of God in everyone', it would also seem obvious that there is also in everyone (emphatically including Quakers) that which is *not* of

God: hatred, greed, malice, bitterness ... all the seeds of evil and violence. Whatever we might mean by God or the divine, this is not part of it. How, then, shall it be confronted, in ourselves and in others, individually and in societies and between nations? As the world careers into escalating violence, often in the name of religion, these questions must not be evaded.

Finally, the theme of the inner light, among Quakers and in Christian spirituality more generally, shifts the centre of gravity from questions of doctrine to issues of obedience. From a Quaker perspective, it is incomparably more important to live with integrity according to the light that one has than it is to arrive at certainty or even at precise formulation of doctrines. One can be perfectly comfortable in a Quaker meeting without being able to affirm the creeds, or knowing what one means by the divine, or even whether there is a God at all; but one would be increasingly uncomfortable if one did not care about poverty or oppression, or supported war, or held racist or sexist attitudes. This does not mean that Quakers are anti-intellectual, or even that they are uninterested in beliefs. It does mean that Quakers intend a great deal more by 'truth' than mere accuracy of doctrinal formulation, that living in the truth involves moral and aesthetic dimensions. Beauty and goodness are central.

The contrast with most other Christian denominations is obvious. Many branches of Christendom define themselves in terms of what they believe, the items of doctrine which they hold to be true. Often they construct their identity by contrasting their beliefs with those of other denominations. Thus, for example, some denominations insist that the bread and wine of the sacrament become the body and blood of Christ when they are consecrated by the priest; others hold that they do not, but rather are tokens of remembrance. Some believe that God has pre-determined who will be saved, while others stress human freedom. Many believe that it is beliefs, correct beliefs, which are essential to salvation.[1] In most churches recitation of the creed – a sequence of statements of belief – forms an important part of their regular services. Indeed so fully identified is religion with belief, in everyday thought, that a 'believer' is thought to be a religious person, while a nonreligious person might be described as an 'unbeliever'.

All this is different from Quakerism. Quaker origins are rooted in Christian history, more particularly in the Puritan conflicts of seventeenth-century England; and most early Quakers probably took mainstream Christian beliefs about God, Christ and salvation for granted (Moore 2000: 111). Many Quakers today continue to hold some or all of these traditional beliefs. But then as now, it is the *place* of beliefs that is the issue: what is, out of comparison, more important than whether or not particular beliefs are held, is openness and obedience to the 'light'. We can observe the interplay of traditional beliefs and echoing biblical language, while still emphasizing the priority of light, in many early Quaker writings: this example is from William Smith, writing in the 1660s.

Whilst the Lord is visiting thee in tender mercy, harden not thy heart gainst him, nor reject his counsel, but be diligent, and ready to receive, and in the quietness of thy mind attend to the word near thee, which is in thy heart, and in thy mouth, that thou mayst obey it, and do it; for it is God's gift unto thee, and stands a witness for God in thy conscience; it is the life, and the life is the light, and the light breaking forth in thee, and making manifest the secrets of thy own heart.

(Quoted in Moore 2000: 212)

It is this light which must be attended to and obeyed; and this attention and obedience matters in a way that specific beliefs and doctrines do not.

In this respect again, Quakers have affinities with spirituality, both in its history in mainstream Christendom and in its current 'New Age' variants. Among the practitioners of New Age spirituality there are many who would disclaim having traditional beliefs (which are associated with churches and institutional religion) while looking instead for inward direction. Among the mystics and spiritual giants of Christendom, too, we find an emphasis on contemplation and illumination, attention to the vision of God in their souls. Time and again, this emphasis put them at an angle to traditional beliefs, even though their intention was usually to be faithful to the church: thus Julian of Norwich questioned the idea of hell and eternal punishment; Meister Eckhart was in trouble with ecclesiastical authorities for his teaching of the union of the soul with God; Marguerite Porete was burned at the stake for her mystical teaching of the direct illumination of the soul; Teresa of Avila sailed very near the wind and was investigated by the Spanish Inquisition, and so the list goes on. There has been endless debate about whether or not these various mystics were heretics or somehow managed not to fall foul of orthodoxy after all. Surely the more important point is that, if it came to a choice between their own experience of God, the illumination they felt they had received, and orthodox Christian beliefs, it would be their own illumination that would take priority. Of course this still leaves all the questions about illumination or inner light to be considered: questions of subjectivity, conflicting illuminations, individual and collective insight, and so on. I shall address some of these in Chapter 2, where I shall show parallels between these questions and questions about the subjectivity of beauty. The point here is that the Quaker emphasis on attention and obedience to the inner light is not idiosyncratic, but is rooted in a long history of Christian spirituality.

One further aspect to be noted here, however, is the way in which the priority of the inner light puts Quakers at an angle to the usual technologies of power of mainstream Christendom. The emphases on tradition and scripture characteristic of Catholic and Protestant denominations must give way to a different kind of authority. How that authority should be constituted is another question, and generates problems of its own which I will consider later. But what is immediately obvious is that the refusal to acknowledge the ultimate authority of ecclesiastical structures meant that Quakers were, from their inception, in a position of resistance to the structures of power of church and state. They were considered a threat to national security. The early history of Quakerism is a history of persecution and suffering, with imprisonment in such dire conditions that many early Quakers died in prison. The story has often been told, and I shall not repeat it (Moore 2000; Punshon 1984; Braithwaite 1955, 1961). What I want to point out is the way in which this period of persecution inevitably gave Quakers a different perspective on power and its exercise, and on questions of violence more generally, than would be held by those who were in positions of control. The connection between the inner light and the resistance to power and renunciation of violence was based for Quakers in their historical experience; its conceptualization was hard won.

The intention of this book, therefore, is to explore further the issues raised by these themes of light, beauty and alternatives to violence. It will do so with constant vigilance to issues of social justice, especially gender: it is perhaps the first feminist theology of beauty. And it will do so from the perspective of a Quaker and of spirituality more broadly: in that sense it could also be seen as a Quaker theology, though with all the caveats about beliefs and doctrines in place. Although it is written for a wider readership, and will therefore explain Quaker ideas in ways that Quakers themselves might not find necessary, I hope that Friends also may find that it speaks to their condition.

Editorial summary of chapters

The work is divided into three parts. The opening part sets the scene for the entire study. It begins in Chapter 1 by rethinking how we tell the fairy story of Beauty and the Beast. This opens a consideration of the ambivalences in Christendom towards beauty, gender and violence and the close relation of these ideas. The importance of the Quaker response, while not entirely over-coming these ambiguities, is then unfolded. This entails a consideration of George Fox and Margaret Fell, as well as other early Quakers, and the differ-ences between early and contemporary Quakers are shown in relation to gender and the peace testimony. Chapter 2 is a consideration of the theology of beauty and why the subject is neglected. It sketches Edward Farley's three reasons for explaining why beauty is ignored in Christendom. The focus then shifts to considering why questions of truth have displaced concerns of beauty and how this reflects a belief–practice duality. By taking the Quaker idea of inner light, the chapter concludes by showing how beauty can inspire a new and engaged spirituality.

Part Two considers the Quaker tradition in more depth and shows how it offers an alternative spirituality of beauty. Chapter 3 opens the exploration of the relation between spirituality and beauty. The starting point for a spiri-tuality of beauty is 'recognition', recognizing that which nourishes and opens creative political and social engagement, but such recognition also requires what Quakers have understood as 'discernment'. This discernment required a training and receptivity to the 'inner light', which the following chapters examine in greater depth. Chapter 4 explores in detail George Fox and the idea of inner light in Quaker thinking. The inner light is seen to illumine conscience and requires honesty, right action and integrity. Chapter 5 considers Margaret Fell and Quaker women, not least because gender and equality among early Friends were quite different from those in society at large. The chapter shows how Quaker women shifted the symbolic order and how they were choosing life and peace. This is shown through three key issues, the authority of Quaker women, the concern with the after-world as part of justice and integrity in *this* political situation, and the symbolic shift away from violence in the notion of the Lamb's war and peace. This shift is seen to be located in a different understanding of the divine as something within, rather than exterior, as seen in Margaret Fell's convincement. This shift offered modernity a different symbolic order, which if chosen would have made a different world order of peace. The validity of the idea of inner light is considered in Chapter 6 through an examination of the eighteenth-century dispute between Fanny Henshaw and William Law. It shows the struggle between integrity of the inner light and the obedience to authority, it shows the importance of discernment and inner light. The case of Fanny Henshaw is seen to show the opening to a spirituality of beauty and an alternative modernity and those, like John Locke, who reacted against such 'enthusiasm'. The final chapter in this part, Chapter 7, explores the different options within early modernity by considering the gendered epistemology of John Locke and Margaret Fell as representatives of a choice between life and death. It shows that in the writings of 'enthusiasts', in particular the Quaker Margaret Fell, a life-giving and life-affirming knowledge was offered. However, this was repressed by Locke in terms of gender and in terms of its (related) understanding of the divine, so that modernity was structured upon a gesture of death.

Part Three maps out the philosophical and ethical implications of a spirituality of beauty. Chapter 8 is concerned principally with seeking to stop a decline in aesthetic sensibility. It traces the beginning of this tendency back to the Enlightenment, with its emphasis on rational knowledge and preference for proofs and truths. This decline is related to the emphasis on abstraction and objectivity, devoid of emotion and modes of non-rational apprehension, which can lead to a neglect of beauty. This neglect is seen as being responsible for a growing lack of generosity of spirit and hence a heightened tolerance for violence. In contrast, the chapter proposes that an increased exposure to beauty and the positive effects it produces can promote a greater aesthetic awareness and sensitivity. The western mindset can be modified through the promotion of a disposition of receptivity to others rather than a negative one of hostility and violence.

Chapter 9 addresses the place of the body in the philosophical recuperation of beauty. The body has an integral connection to the appreciation of beauty – both as subject and as object. As subject, the body's senses are the means by which beauty is experienced. As object, it is the body that is revered in all its sensual beauty. What is alarming is the antagonistic attitude towards the body that has pervaded western philosophy from Plato onwards. Augustine's conflicting views on sensuous beauty are considered. Sensuous beauty, so often related to women and sex, is regarded by Augustine as intrinsically earthly and of a material nature, and thus excluded from God's spiritual domain. In response, a new appreciation of an interactive model of transcendence and immanence is developed and the body is considered beautiful – as opposed to evil. The body is seen as a manifestation of God's love for the world.

In Chapter 10 beauty is recuperated as an antidote to violence, through a reformulation of the nature of desire from a feminist perspective. Desire is thus aligned with a positive impetus that arises from plenitude rather than from a lack. Desire, then, does not need to have connotations of possession and control. Instead it can be appreciated as an expression of creative expansion and affirmation which have distinct resonances with beauty. The traditional model of desire, from Plato to Lacan, and René Girard's model of mimetic desire, are all questioned. These versions of desire lead inevitably to violence in the urge to possess and dominate. Considering the absence of desire in traditional Christian doctrine, finding instead a theology that celebrates the beauty of creation is proposed, in the same manner that the creator, God, is recorded as confirming the goodness of the created world. Such a theology would be one that fosters human flourishing, appreciating life in this world as an outpouring of God's own love and plenteous desire.

In Chapter 11 there is an outline of the moral imagination, a key element in the diagnostic programme for the needed change in the western mindset. Indeed, it is a vital contribution, concerned as it is with replacing modernity's fixation on mortality and violence with a therapeutics of beauty. In order to help clarify the prescribed method, Pierre Bourdieu, psychoanalysis and a Foucauldian genealogical enquiry are employed to challenge the death instinct that has been displayed so often in recent events – from death camps and genocide to the exclusion of minorities. The aim is to dislodge the strong influence of the trope of death on the modern imaginary so as to allow a space for alternative ideals. It is only by bringing unconscious or self-deceptive defences to consciousness, on both a personal and a cultural level, that there will be an opportunity to introduce beauty and its affirmative orientation as a substitute for violence. It is only in this way that a flourishing worldview that endows human existence with a sense of wonder and love can begin to be cultivated. Chapter 11 originally appeared as 'On Changing the Imaginary', in Graham Ward (ed.), *The Blackwell Companion to Postmodern Theology* (2001) pp. 280–293.

Finally, Chapter 12 explores further ways of changing the imaginary to overcome the modern preoccupation with death. This chapter encourages an appreciation of beauty as inspired by the metaphoric notion of natality with its innovative and creative well-springs. Beauty both attracts and provides a positive impetus to create, not just in repetitious imitation, but in exploration and expression of the expansive awareness it promotes. Such receptivity and openness to the unknown lessens the threat of a close-minded protectionist response that would induce violence. The chapter ends with a call to be vulnerable to beauty.

Due to the combination of posthumous and previously published material in this volume, there are inevitably some repetitions. We have preserved these in order to honour the original context of their expression.

Part One

The anxieties of beauty

Chapter 1

Beauty and the Beast
Ambiguities and openings

Once upon a time, so goes a variant of the old fairy tale, there was a wealthy merchant who, by a combination of bad management and ill fortune lost all his possessions. He fell into the hands of a Beast, who offered to rescue him from his impoverished state on condition that he would give his youngest daughter, Beauty, to be the Beast's wife. Beauty loved her father and agreed to marry the Beast. At the time appointed, she moved to the Beast's house, only to find that although she was given lavish food and accommodation and all her wants are satisfied, she was never permitted to see the Beast, who came to her only in the darkest hours of the night. At last she decided to go back home. She dreamed, however, that the Beast was pining for her; so she rushed back and kissed him, brushing away the great tears that were rolling down his cheeks. And behold, before her stood a handsome prince, released by her tenderness from the frightful beastliness in which he had been trapped ...[1]

Now, those with feminist consciousness will be quick to point out that, as the story stands, it reinforces all the old gender stereotypes: the beauty and compassion of the virgin daughter, the improvident father who is willing to treat his daughter as an object of exchange, the violent ugliness of the beast/ prince from which only a woman's love will permit him to escape. But feminism has taught us more than how to recognize stereotypes. It has also encouraged us to use our imagination to look at things from another point of view, to retell old tales from another perspective: the story of Ariadne's web, say, or of Penelope's weaving, from Greek mythology, or the biblical stories from the point of view of Eve or Hagar or Bathsheba. How if we were to retell the fairy tale of Beauty and the Beast? It might go something like this.

Once upon a time there was a spoiled brat of a prince who was very confused – so confused that he hardly knew it himself. He was strong and handsome and deep down he wanted to be good; but in his social world he had learned that to be a real he-man prince he had to growl and swagger and use his big muscles to assert his power and be generally beastly. Especially, he had to compete with other men for beautiful women. So when the improvident merchant fell into his hands one weekend between his many wars, he jumped at the chance of taking his beautiful daughter, whom the cowardly old fool was willing to sacrifice to save his own skin. The beast's first impulse was to kill her and gobble her up, even though he knew that her brothers might come and fight him in revenge: he loved big fights where he could prove that he was bigger than all of them. But when he saw the girl and noticed how very beautiful she was, he was disturbed and her beauty made him even more confused. Up to now he had always had what he wanted; but he could not have his bride and eat her too. Instead of telling her what was the matter, he hid his real self from her and became more and more morose. At last he sat down and began to cry. Beauty could see, of course, that he was being a great baby, but she came over to him, kissed him, and appealed to his deep-down goodness: 'Oh, do grow up! Can't you see that there are better ways of being a man than strutting around competing with other men and generally being beastly?' And very gradually the good in him responded to her beauty and he became a truly handsome prince. He still growls a lot, and sometimes struts about, but he has become much less likely to eat people. Best of all, he doesn't need to be constantly fighting to prove that he is a man.

(But as for Beauty's father, what can be done about a man who is willing to exchange his daughter for the sake of saving his own skin?)

The retelling obviously does not escape all the stereotypes. The gender characteristics of Beauty are still conventional: the pure and lovely female effects the salvation of a brute of a man. Also significant, though less often noticed, is that the tale (both in its original form and in its retelling) is, like many western stories, rather hard on beasts: why should animals be made the repository for what are, after all, human faults? Most importantly of all, the moral of the story should come with a health warning: women held in captivity by brutal men should not feel it their duty to try to transform them by love and kisses, when they have every right to escape. It is all too easy for the fairy tale to be used as yet one more story that implicitly condones male violence against women, who should bear it patiently as they try to win over their mixed-up men.

Nevertheless, the fairy tales and old stories of any culture are sediments of that culture's attitudes and values, often at a barely conscious level. They can be examined in many different ways, turned over in the mind to reveal ways of thinking that we might otherwise not have recognized. Bruno Bettleheim, for instance, has offered an analysis of some of the best-known fairy tales of western culture from a psychoanalytical perspective, the story of Beauty and the Beast among them (Bettleheim 1989: 303–10). In religion, too, myths and stories are used to convey multi-faceted ideas. Biblical writers piled story upon story to give an account of the beginning of the world, the early life of Israel, or a portrait of Jesus whom they named as Christ. Centuries of biblical scholars have solemnly debated the historicity of this or that account, but in the popular imagination it is not the historical accuracy so much as the pictorial representation that has formed the symbolic universe of western consciousness.

One of the many ways in which the story of Beauty and the Beast can be interpreted is as a tale of the constellation of violence, gender and beauty. The father of western discourse, the *nomine Domine* of its religious lineage, has given up beauty, trying to protect its bankrupt identity by abandoning beauty and turning all its attention to beliefs and truth claims. As I shall show in a moment, Christian theology in modernity takes very little interest in beauty. On the other hand, as we are becoming increasingly aware, the symbolic universe of the west is filled with the imagination of violence, a violence which erupts with escalating intensity and devastation. Moreover, masculinity is constructed in relation to this violence. To be a man, not a wimp, is to be in control, to master or dominate a situation, whether a woman or a war. However, the growling and posturing and violence of the world will not, I suggest, be overcome by fighting it: violence begets more violence. Rather, if we hope to bring about change, to deal with our monsters, to transform relations between sexes and between nations, to bring newness into the world, then I suggest that we must look to beauty. Beauty has transformative power, power to heal and nurture and make new; and it is high time that theology reconsiders its relation to beauty, especially because of the importance of beauty for spirituality.

Theological ambiguities

The most frequently bought item of jewellery in Europe and the Americas is still, in the twenty-first century, a cross or crucifix. It is simultaneously an item of beauty and a symbol of violent death. Not everyone who wears a cross spends time thinking about its significance, of course. Nevertheless, the ambiguity of its beauty and its violence is suggestive of the ambiguities of Christendom itself: on the one hand, its possibilities for beauty, natality and flourishing, and on the other hand its investment in death and violence. Both these alternatives, moreover, are imbricated in gender construction.

The initial contours of the ambiguities can be quickly sketched. Beginning with beauty, it is evident that Christendom has been the impetus for every variety of artistic expression, from the exquisite mosaics of Venice and Ravenna to the soaring cathedrals of Cologne and Salisbury, from the music of Bach and Vivaldi to the paintings of Giotto and Rembrandt and the poetry of Dante and Milton. The art and literature of the west cannot be understood without Christendom; our aesthetic sensibilities have been shaped by its teachings. Moreover, the spirituality of millions, from Augustine to the present, is profoundly affected by the beauty of nature. It is in the slant of light upon the hills, the glory of dappled things, the fragile primrose and the starry heavens that the presence of the divine is felt; in the roaring of wind and wave or the tranquillity of sunrise. Even those who are disaffected with churches and doctrines feel that they meet God in nature if they meet God at all. The importance of beauty for spirituality can hardly be overstated.

And yet how important, really, is beauty to Christian theology? Though artists through the ages have expressed their faith in their work, and countless people encounter the divine in the beauty of the world, religious writers and theologians, with a few exceptions, have little to say about beauty. As Edward Farley has observed, with significant exceptions, 'when we closely consult the standard expressions of piety in the prayers, liturgies, sermons, journals and letters of the ages, we find beauty largely absent'. He continues:

> On the whole, beauty is a rarity in 2000 years of Christian interpretation of the Gospels ... All the types [of theology], (historical, practical, philo-sophical, systematic) and approaches (neo-Reformation, apologetic, fem-inist, African-American, liberationist, correlational) share at least one thing in common: a disinterest in beauty.
>
> (Farley 2001: 7)

Indeed, Farley goes so far as to identify beauty *as* the beast for theology: a threatening presence that could gobble up proper faith and practice. But why? How is it that theology needs to be so defensive? What is going on when the aesthetic and spiritual sensibilities of people which on the face of it one would expect theology to nurture as its greatest ally are instead squashed or ignored? I shall return to these questions in Chapter 2. Here, I wish first to consider further ambiguities with which I believe issues of beauty are closely interrelated.

The first of these is the ambivalence in Christendom about gender. It can hardly be denied that the teaching and practice of the churches has been the most powerful force of patriarchy in the west. Women were seen as daughters of Eve who brought sin into the world: they were conceptually linked, in theology and in popular story, with the body, sexuality and temptation. Their voices were silenced, their place in society constructed in relation either to husband, home and family or to the convent and the spiritual father-in-God. Women were defined not as people with individual abilities or careers, but in terms of their sexuality: virgin, mother or whore. Thousands – perhaps millions – were executed as witches by zealous witch-hunters using criteria set out by monks and theologians. Even today, it is the church, especially the Roman Catholic church in strange partnership with increasingly popular fun-damentalist Protestantism, as seen for instance in Bible-belt North America, that resists gender equality and liberation for women, crusading against abor-tion, contraception (even as a means of preventing the spread of HIV/AIDS) and the ordination of women to the priesthood. At the same time, masculinity is constructed as dominant and powerful. The male, whether he likes it or not, is to be the head of the household, and the male priest is the representative of Christ on earth. Indeed, the male is in an impossible position. On the one hand he is conceptually linked with rationality and spirituality, in contrast to women's rootedness in the body and materiality, yet on the other he is also to use his superior physical power to maintain his position of mastery.

All this being so, it is nevertheless also true that it is from within Christendom, as well, that women and men have found the resources to fashion gender differently. Women were among the first followers of Jesus, and shared with men in the establishment of early Christian communities. Although some of his writings placed women in subordinate positions, St Paul famously wrote that in Christ 'there is neither Jew nor Greek, there is neither slave nor free, there is neither male nor female; for you are all one in Christ Jesus' (Galatians 3.28). From the early days of Christendom, women and men renounced compulsory heterosexual marriage and childbearing, and chose instead the celibate life of the desert or monastery, developing gender constructions at odds with the surrounding society. Whatever the distortions (and there were many) the convent offered opportunities for empowerment for women like Hildegard of Bingen and Gertrude of Helfta, while men like Francis of Assisi and John of the Cross developed patterns of masculinity quite different from prevalent models of dominance. Protestant reformers, by rejecting monasticism and celibacy, brought a re-evaluation of gender roles which gave women significant roles in the household. Quakers held to gender egalitarianism from the start; and other Dissenters also accepted women ministers. It was from their religious commitment that early feminists like Elizabeth Cady Stanton in the USA and the Pankhurst sisters in Britain worked for women's suffrage; and it is not in spite of their religious stance but because of it that many women and men today are working for gender justice in Africa and Latin America, often drawing upon the figure of Mary for inspiration.

The ambivalences of Christendom in relation to beauty and to gender constructions are repeated in relation to violence. The Christmas angels sing of 'peace on earth, goodwill towards men'. Jesus is represented as the prince of peace, the one who brought healing and hope, and whose kingdom will be conflict free. The early church was pacifist; and later drew up a theology of 'just war' not to promote warfare, but to limit it as much as possible. Throughout Christian history, Christians have drawn upon their faith to work for peace, resolution of conflict, and alternatives to violence. Francis of Assisi, for example, went to the Sultan and tried to convert him and thus remove the occasion for the Crusades. The peace churches of the Radical Reformation, which continue today as Mennonites and Quakers, are committed not only to refuse to participate in war but to do all they can to promote justice and peace so that war becomes unnecessary. Movements of non-violent resistance such as that led by Martin Luther King in the USA and Desmond Tutu in South Africa, while owing much to the teachings of Gandhi, also drew deeply upon Christian resources.

Nevertheless, Christendom has been involved in more violence and wars than can be counted. The biblical writer exhorted Timothy, his addressee, to 'fight the good fight' (1 Timothy 6.12); and whatever was meant by that passage, the language and action of Christendom has been filled with spiritual and literal warfare. Since Constantine claimed his military victory, armies have marched under the banner of the cross backwards and forwards across Europe and beyond. From the Crusades to the Wars of Religion, and up to modernity when, in two World Wars, both sides claimed divine aid to slaughter one another, the military violence that has been done in the name of the prince of peace is incalculable. Even ostensibly secular societies whose rhetoric includes separation of church and state invoke God's name for their warfare: how many times have American presidents finished their addresses with 'God bless America'? Nor is the violence of Christendom restricted to warfare. Slavery, economic injustice and colonialism have all been sanctioned by the churches, as has the domestic violence in which women and children are abused and killed, with, too often, only muted protest by religious leaders.

None of this is at all new: the ambivalences of Christendom are plain for all to see. The point of rehearsing them is to see them side by side, and notice how they mirror one another. It is my suggestion that the ambivalences in Christendom towards beauty, gender and violence are in fact closely related. The displacement of beauty is connected, in Christendom, to distrust of the body and desire, especially gendered bodies and sexual desire; and the heart that hardens itself to beauty and its invitations to involvement is a heart whose defensive fear easily turns aggressive. The sediments of violence that shape western consciousness are connected to constructions of masculinity partly inherited from Christendom's (similarly ambivalent) Jewish provenance and from classical sources, but significantly reshaped into ideals of 'men of God' who 'fight the good fight'. In an ongoing project, I am tracing the genealogy of violence in western civilization, and showing how at every turn violence and its conceptualizations were connected with ideas and suspicions of beauty (Jantzen 2004). What I wish to do in this volume is the happier task of showing the significance of beauty and its resources in alternatives to violence, from within a perspective of feminist consciousness and broadly based religious sensibility.

Spiritual openings?

As I indicated in the Introduction, my perspective is that of a Quaker, but drawing upon the resources of the tradition of Christian spirituality. What resolution can this perspective bring to the theological ambiguities of beauty, gender and violence? It would be pleasant to think that a clear and positive response could be given. Unfortunately, that is not the case. In Quaker thought, as in the history of spirituality, the same ambiguities are to be found as I have already outlined. Nevertheless, it seems to me that it is also possible to discern openings through which it is possible to move forward.

Early Quaker comments on beauty were often at least as dismissive or outright negative as those of the Puritan ethos in which they moved. George Fox, for instance, rarely mentions beauty in his writings, and when he does it is usually to quote the biblical phrase, the 'beauty of holiness', which he contrasts with outward beauty (Fox 1831: 304–5). He rails against those who oppose godliness, accusing them of 'playing the harlot' and trusting in their own beauty 'with garments of diverse colours' (Fox 1657a: 20); and he denounces the wickedness of London and its priests, warning that its beauty will be defaced by divine punishment (Fox 1657b: 6). The one instance when he recorded a positive response to beauty was of his enjoyment of the beautiful coastline along the scenic route of a journey to Cornwall in 1656, but even this was restricted to a private letter (Ingle 1994: 133).

Even more alarming is the account of Solomon Eccles, a professional musician and instrument maker who lived in London and became a Quaker in the late 1650s. He felt that God required him to give up music. He made a bonfire of his instruments on Tower Hill,

> 'virginals, fiddles and all' and when the crowd tried to prevent him 'I was forced to stamp on them and break them to pieces [because I saw] a difference between the harps of God and the harps of men'.
> (British Yearly Meeting 1995: 21.31; cf. Moore 2000: 121)

Extreme as this is, it indicates the lengths to which early Quakers would go in their anxiety about beauty and artistic expression.

Even in those early years there were, however, voices that subverted this refusal of beauty. I have already cited Margaret Fell's words in appreciation of the beautiful colours of the Cumbrian hills among which she lived. Another major figure was James Naylor, one of the most articulate early Quakers and (until the disaster that befell him in 1656) perhaps as prominent as Fox in the leadership of the movement. In some of his pamphlets Naylor shows a positive evaluation of beauty, even though it is mostly predicated only of Christ and reserved for the world to come.

> In the greatest Floods keep your eye to your beloved Beauty ... In all things keep with him, let his joy be strength unto you in all, and the appearance of his Beauty will refresh you ...
> (Naylor 1661: 2)

This is hardly a ringing endorsement of aesthetic sensibility; but at least it indicates an awareness of the significance of beauty for spiritual strength, rather than the disparagement or neglect characteristic of Fox and many other early Quaker writers.

Their anxiety and dismissal of beauty had long roots in the tradition of Christian spirituality, where it was often a part of a larger sense of threat about bodiliness and sexuality, as I shall argue in later chapters. Although there were also positive motivations for asceticism, there are many instances where asceticism is explicitly conceived as a renunciation of the attractiveness and beauty of the world of nature and art, frequently connected in male writers with renunciation of women and the aesthetic and sexual pleasures of the female body. Thus, for example, Bernard of Clairvaux, in a passage bristling with denunciation, says,

> We who have turned aside from society, relinquishing for Christ's sake all the precious and beautiful things in the world, its wondrous light and colour, its sweet sounds and odours, the pleasures of taste and touch, for us all bodily delights are nothing but dung …
>
> (quoted in Eco 1986: 7)

It is no coincidence that in another passage Bernard speaks of a woman's body as 'a bag of shit' (Leclercq 1989: 121; see also Jantzen 1995: 131): anxiety about beauty is insistently gendered.

And yet this very anxiety about beauty shows how seriously it was taken. Beauty was a far more major theme in medieval theology and spirituality than it has been in modernity; and although it evoked plenty of hostility, as we see in the above quotation of Bernard of Clairvaux, this hostility was not the only or even the most dominant response. Medieval thought inherited from Plato and neo-Platonism the idea that Ultimate Reality must be characterized as the Good, the True and the Beautiful: insofar as Christendom took this as referring to God, beauty must be given equal status with goodness and truth. When this was qualified by Christian ideas, including the doctrine of creation, the beauty of the world was held to be a manifestation of the divine. As such, it would obviously be significant for spirituality. Thus, Augustine famously exclaims: 'Late have I loved you, O Beauty, so ancient and so new, late have I loved you!' (Augustine 1984: 144; *Confessions* x. 27). In Chapter 9 I will explore the contortions and contradictions which Augustine bequeathed to Christian spirituality in his attempts to reconcile his love of beauty with his anxiety about gendered bodies; but the point here is that beauty, so far from being dismissed, is recognized as an opening to the divine. This attitude makes possible a deeply positive evaluation of art and beauty which runs through medieval spirituality, even when qualified by worry and hostility, which was largely abandoned as modern theology made beliefs and truth claims the central focus of its attention.

When contemporary Quakers emphasize beauty in nature and in art, they are therefore abandoning the negative attitude of early Quaker writers and placing themselves within this older current of Christian spirituality. The rejection of music and other arts that led Solomon Eccles to destroy his instruments has been explicitly renounced (British Yearly Meeting 1995: 21.31); and in its place has come a celebration of beauty of many varieties.

> There is a daily round for beauty as well as for goodness, a world of flowers and books and cinemas and clothes and manners as well as of mountains and masterpieces … God is in all beauty, not only in the

natural beauty of earth and sky, but in all fitness of language and rhythm, whether it describe a heavenly vision or a street fight, a Hamlet or a Falstaff, a philosophy or a joke: in all fitness of line and colour and shade, whether seen in the Sistine Madonna or a child's knitted frock: in all fitness of sound and beat and measure, whether the result be Bach's Passion music or a nursery jingle. The quantity of God, so to speak, varies in the different examples, but his quality of beauty in fitness remains the same.

(British Yearly Meeting 1995: 21.28)

The quotation raises many theological and aesthetic questions which I shall leave until later in the book. What it does show unmistakably, however, is a whole different orientation to beauty than that of early Quaker hostility. Beauty is taken as an opening to spirituality. How to go through that opening, and how it can offer resources for alternatives to violence, is what this book is about.

If in the case of beauty Quakers find it necessary to reach back behind the negative comments of early Quaker writings to the more positive attitudes of medieval spirituality, it might be thought that in the case of violence the theological ambiguities were quickly resolved in early Quaker practice. To a certain extent this is true. Quakerism began in the troubled years of civil war in the seventeenth century and would on the whole have positioned itself with Parliament and Oliver Cromwell rather than with the king. Although initially some who became Quakers were in the Cromwellian army, gradually the conviction grew that violence was not the way to bring in the Kingdom of God; and they hoped for nothing less. One of the first was William Dewsbury, who wrote of his experience in the army in the early 1650s:

The word of the Lord came unto me and said, put up thy sword into thy scabbard; if my kingdom were of this world, then would my children fight ... which word enlightened my heart ... that the Kingdom of Christ was within; and the enemy was within and was spiritual, and my weapons against them must be spiritual, the power of God. Then I could no longer fight with a carnal weapon against a carnal man ... and the messenger of the Covenant ... caused me to yield in obedience, to put up my carnal sword into the scabbard, and so leave the army.

(quoted in Moore 2000: 12)

For some time the renunciation of violence was patchy among Quakers, some of them serving in the army while others felt that they could not, in conscience, do so.

In 1660, with the restoration of the monarchy, Quakers hoped for a cessation of the persecution which they had endured in the latter days of the Protectorate. To that end, Margaret Fell wrote a pamphlet, signed by George Fox and other leading Quakers, which she delivered personally to the king. In it she explained Quakers' disavowal of violence in positive terms: the motive is not simply to avoid war but to bring justice and peace. She wrote:

> We are a people that follow after those things that make for peace, love and unity ... We do deny and bear our testimony against all strife, wars, and contentions that come from the lusts that war in the members, that war against the soul, which we wait for, and watch for in all people. We love and desire the good of all ... Treason, treachery, and false dealing we do utterly deny – and false dealing, surmizing, or plotting against any creature upon the face of the earth ...
>
> (Fell 1992: 54–55)

Fell's pamphlet is much more than a simple refusal of Quakers to bear arms; it is a public commitment to work for good.

The king was initially sympathetic (though the same cannot be said of all his advisers). In January, however, a group of radicals known as Fifth Monarchists attempted an unsuccessful coup. Quakers were not involved, but were widely suspected, and many thousands were rounded up and imprisoned. To distance themselves from the uprising, George Fox wrote another pamphlet, again signed by leading Quakers, in which he articulated what has become the core of the Quaker peace testimony:

> Our principle is, and our practices have always been, to seek peace and ensure it ... seeking the good and welfare and doing that which tends to the peace of all ... All bloody principles and practices, we ... do utterly deny, with all outward wars and strife and fightings with outward weapons, for any end or under any pretense whatsoever ... The spirit of Christ, which leads us into all Truth, will never move us to fight and war against any man with outward weapons, neither for the kingdom of Christ, nor for the kingdoms of this world.
>
> (Fox 1952: 399–400)

It was this statement, premised on the earlier pamphlet of Margaret Fell, that became the basis of subsequent Quaker work for peace, even though at the time it did not succeed in its aim of regaining the king's sympathy.

Perhaps one of the reasons for the king's continued suspicion was that this ostensibly straightforward peace testimony is more ambiguous than it appears, and some of the ambiguities are still with us. Historically, the statement was 'distinctly economical with the truth', as Rosemary Moore points out (2000: 181), because Quakers were still in the army and Fox could not speak for all of them. Moreover, although Fox rejected violence for himself and his followers, he never took the view that others should not be violent if necessary on their behalf: he expected magistrates to do their job and took for granted that the state would have an army for self-defence even though Quakers would not

fight in it. But what integrity is there in refusal to participate in violence ourselves, while expecting others to do so on our behalf? Modern Quakers continue to struggle with this question, on the whole taking a more radical stance
than did Fox and working to persuade not only Quakers but the government
itself not to engage in warfare; Quakers are also active in movements for
justice and reconciliation and efforts towards conflict resolution. Yet contemporary Quakers pay their taxes, in the knowledge that a considerable portion of it is spent on 'defence'. Although there is disquiet about this, Quakers
have not united in the civil disobedience of withholding a proportion of taxes,
or even in arranging for it to be diverted to peaceful uses or relief efforts.
Whereas early Quakers were willing to be imprisoned or have their property
confiscated for their refusal to comply with what they considered unjust laws
and customs, Quakers in modernity have chosen to remain respectably within
the law. Thus, while the modern stance is more radical in its testimony against
all war (not just in personal refusal to participate), it is on the whole a less
costly stance and arguably even more ambiguous.

Although early Quakers renounced violence, moreover, they were quite
capable of using highly belligerent language. Even by the standards of the time,
Quaker writings by both men and women indulged in vituperation that would
turn modern ears red. To take only one example (by no means the most
extreme), here is the beginning of a piece by Esther Biddle, a prominent
London Quaker writing in 1662 against the established church, which she
conflates with Roman Catholicism:

> Oh! Woe be unto you Bishops, Priests, Deacons, Friers, and Jesuits, and
> all other Officers under you, for the Lord is risen in power, yea, he is risen
> in dreadful and terrible wrath; Oh! I have seen this night, the dreadful
> flames which the Lord God will cast you into ... the Lord [will] make you
> howl and lament bitterly, insomuch that the earth shall be astonished, and
> your downfall shall be so great, that nations shall fear and tremble before
> our God ...
>
> (Garmen *et al.* 1996: 135–36)

And so it goes on (and on). It is hard to read these pamphlets without a sense
that their writers took considerable pleasure in the thought that God would
bring calamity upon their enemies. They professed the peace testimony (and
lived by it to their cost) but they indulged in plenty of vicarious violence.

Even when they were speaking of peace they frequently used the language of
war, the 'Lamb's War', fought with spiritual weapons. 'All wars and fightings
with carnal weapons we do deny, who have the sword of the spirit ... ' (Fox
1952: 404). Their development of the biblical metaphor of a 'sword of the
spirit' could be taken to frightening lengths, especially in a social setting of
actual civil war. Edward Burrough, for example, wrote to encourage his fellow
Quakers:

> Put on your armour and gird on your sword, and lay hold on the spear, and march into the field, and prepare yourselves for battle, for the nations do defy our God ... Stand upon your feet, and appear in your terror as an army with banners ... cut down with thy right hand and slay on the left, and let not your eye pity, or your hand spare.
>
> (quoted in Moore 2000: 71)

It was all very well for Fox, Fell and others to insist that Quakers would not engage in violence. With writing like this, who could be sure, when metaphor passed over into literal language and 'the Lamb's War' became involvement in civil strife? It is not surprising that their enemies were sceptical about Quaker intentions, and not beyond belief that some Quakers were engaged in much more violence than one would guess from the writings of Margaret Fell and George Fox.

In their use of military language Quakers were of course echoing the Bible, especially the Pauline letters, and were not markedly different from many who wrote in the intervening period. Their peace testimony itself had precursors in Christian spirituality, notably in Francis of Assisi; others, however, like Bernard of Clairvaux, who preached the disastrous Second Crusade, took a very different view.

The crucial question underlying these ambiguities, and which gives them their bite, is the question of the relationship between spirituality and politics; and it is at this point that the discussion of beauty and violence also gets its purchase. I shall take some time over this ambiguity, first in relation to historical Quakers and then to its roots in Christian spirituality, since at one level it sets the problematic of this project: what is the connection between personal spirituality, which could be expressed in terms of the enjoyment of beauty or, in more conventionally Christian terms, the contemplation of God, and changing the world from violence to justice? It is my contention that the displacement or refusal of beauty in modernity is directly related to the escalation of violence (and so also is its privatization and commodification); or, put the other way around, renewed engagement with beauty provides resources for justice and peace. For this contention to be clear and persuasive it is necessary to develop a political spirituality of beauty. This is the task of the following chapters. It will help to lay the groundwork to consider some of the ways in which contemplation and the political have been theorized historically.

In the political and religious ferment of the seventeenth century in England, early Quakers believed that Christ would literally return to earth and set up his Kingdom. He would bring about a society of justice and peace, perhaps having his throne in London. Many early Quakers supported Oliver Cromwell, but they did not want him to take on the role of kingship (since that would usurp the place reserved for Christ) and they wanted him to govern in a godly way to prepare the nation to welcome Christ when he arrived. Quakers considered themselves to be in the vanguard of the coming of Christ's Kingdom on earth. Their worship was in anticipation of his coming. Although they wanted to be ready for his arrival, they did not think that they could do anything to bring it about: Christ would arrive in God's good time, and set up the Kingdom of God on earth without human intervention. Quakers were not alone in this anticipation: other radical groups, like the Baptists, also expected the literal, imminent advent of Christ (Underwood 1997: 62; Moore 2000: 61). Even Oliver Cromwell encouraged the idea that the Kingdom of God was arriving. Addressing the opening session of the Barebones Parliament in 1653, Cromwell said: 'You are called with a high call; why should we be afraid to think that this may be the door to usher in the things that God hath promised?' (quoted in Moore 2000: 61). Quakers (and many others) saw the coming Kingdom of God very much in terms of social justice. The 'new heaven and the new earth' would abolish the great divisions between wealth and poverty, would clean up political and religious institutions so that they would no longer be corrupted by greed for money or power, and would reform laws and public morals. Benjamin Nicholsen, for instance, wrote:

> O all ye powers of the earth, God is coming to overturn, overturn, overturn your power, and give it to him whose right it is: Jesus Christ shall have rule and dominion over all nations ... Instead of covering the naked, and feeding the hungry, you set out laws to punish them ... if a poor creature steal a horse, ox, or sheep, he is either put to death or burned in the hand; but you never consider how many horses, oxen or sheep you steal from the Lord ... O you great men of the earth, it is along of you that there is so many thieves, for you hold the creation in your hands, and by all means go about to defraud the poor ...
>
> (quoted in Moore 2000: 63)

All this would be rectified when Jesus was on the throne in London; and the Quakers would be ready to carry out his will.

It was not long, however, before their hopefulness began to be replaced by disillusionment. Already in 1653, James Naylor realized that the reforms he had hoped for from Cromwell were not forthcoming, and that Jesus had not appeared to set things right. 'O England! How is thy expectation failed now after all thy travails? ... as power hath come into the hands of men it hath been turned into violence, and the will of man is brought forth instead of Equity' (quoted in Moore 2000: 65). Others warded off their disappointment for a while, but gradually it became clear that the political resolution they had looked for showed no sign of happening. Oliver Cromwell, not Jesus Christ, was the Lord Protector of England; Quakers were undergoing persecution and imprisonment; and although some clung to the hope that Jesus would suddenly return to earth, others dealt with the situation differently. James Naylor had pointed the way: the Kingdom of God was not political but spiritual:

> You have been seeking without, but it is within you, and there you must find it ... and the way to the Kingdom is within you, and the light that guides into the way ... is within.
>
> (quoted in Moore 2000: 66)

The passage is reminiscent of Augustine in the *Confessions*: 'and behold, you [God] were within me and I was outside, and there I sought for you ... ' (Augustine 1984: 144; *Confessions* x. 27); and from Augustine onwards the theme of the inner light was immensely important in Christian spirituality. I shall discuss its ambiguities in relation to epistemology in Chapter 2.

The point here is the political ambiguity of the idea of the Kingdom of God within, an idea increasingly taken up by George Fox during the Protectorate and standard among Quakers after the Restoration. As Rosemary Moore has shown in detail:

> In the course of a few years, the Quaker movement changed from being one of the most radical of the sects that were looking for the coming of the Kingdom of God on earth, and became an introverted body, primarily concerned with its own internal life.
>
> (Moore 2000: 214)

Just as the early Christian church gradually relinquished the expectation that the crucified Jesus was about to return in glory and overturn the Roman imperial system, and had to find a way of survival in the hostile political climate, so also early Quakers looked to the survival of their communities, and developed an organizational structure that would enable them to endure.

But if the Kingdom of God is within – within the individual, or, as Quakers held, within the community – how should they situate themselves in relation to the wider world? In particular, what does the peace testimony come to? It is one thing to renounce violence if one is confident that Christ will soon appear and do all the violence himself. But what if Christ does not come? There are several possibilities, all of them taken up variously within Christian spirituality generally and also among Quakers. Moreover, all of them have implications for beauty.

One possibility is to turn away from political and social engagement and be concerned exclusively with one's own spiritual welfare. There is plenty of this in Christian spirituality, especially as it draws upon a Neoplatonist background. As I have argued elsewhere, Plotinus' mysticism, encapsulated in his longing for 'the flight of the Alone to the Alone', should be read within its context of the deterioration of political stability, and as an escape from the grim and turbulent realities of his time (Jantzen 2004: 356–57). The path inwards, which was also the path of contemplation of Beauty, was a way of shaking off the material and political, finding inner peace and fulfilment. In the Christian appropriation of Neoplatonism its contours were significantly altered, but one thing that was retained and emphasized was the superiority of the contemplative over the active life, often in an allegorized reading of the Gospel story of Mary and Martha, first taken up by Origen (McGinn 1991: 126) and continued in Augustine, Gregory and many others. When William of St Thierry wrote his *Golden Epistle* to Carthusians (given to contemplation) in the twelfth century, this superiority was taken as obvious.

> You have undertaken the loftiest of professions. It surpasses the heavens, it is on a level with the angels ... It is not for you to concern yourselves feebly with the ordinary commandments ... It is for others to serve God, it is for you to cling to him; it is for others to believe in God, know him, love him and revere him; it is for you to taste him, understand him, be acquainted with him, enjoy him ...
>
> (William of St Thierry 1980: 14; I. v. 15–16

Although within its cultural and literary context this need not in fact be read as a recommendation for Christians to disengage from political and social responsibility, it is easy to see how it could be taken that way. Contemplate divine beauty; seek the purity of your own soul and the beatific vision, and let the rest of the world go to hell. It is a stance that must be confronted by anyone who wishes, as I do, to set beauty and contemplation at the centre of a politically engaged spirituality: are they in fact compatible, or does a spirituality of beauty pull in the opposite direction from political engagement?

With the growing acceptance that Jesus was not about to replace Charles II on the English throne, and the urgent need to consolidate the movement to preserve it through persecution, it is not surprising that Quakers in the late seventeenth and the eighteenth centuries turned increasingly inward. After the Toleration Act of 1689, which marked the end of religious persecution of Dissenters, Quakers no longer looked for a revolution or thought of the Kingdom of God in political terms. The advice issued by the Quaker Yearly Meeting of 1689 shows the shift in policy:

> Walk wisely and circumspectly towards all men, in the peaceable spirit of Christ Jesus, giving no offence or occasions to those in outward government, nor way to any controversies, heats or distractions of this world, about the kingdoms thereof. But pray for the good of all; and submit all to that Divine power and wisdom which rules over the kingdoms of men. That, as the Lord's hidden ones, that are always quiet in the land, and as those prudent ones and wise in heart, who know when and where to keep silent, you may all approve your hearts to God; keeping out of all airy

discourses and words, that may anyways become snares, or hurtful to Truth or Friends, as being sensible that any personal occasion of reproach causes a reflection upon the body.

(quoted in Braithwaite 1961: 160)

It is a world away from the apocalyptic political expectations of Quakers in the 1650s. Instead of being in the vanguard of the 'Lamb's War', ready to welcome Christ to his throne, Quakers were now 'the quiet in the land'. The peace testimony became a policy of being peaceable, not stirring up trouble.

Whereas, in medieval spirituality, inwardness and contemplation were usually predicated of the individual, the inward turning of Quakers was specifically communal. Quakers sought to set themselves apart from 'the world'. They adopted strict codes of behaviour and authoritarian church government. Their dress was a uniform 'Quaker grey'; they did not permit intermarriage with non-Quakers or participation in 'worldly' activities, including in this not only drinking alcohol and gambling but all sorts of arts, sports, and even music lessons for their children (Punshon 1984: 130–32). Anyone who transgressed these boundaries was 'disowned', rejected by the Society of Friends, as it was now called. Quakers were expected to be upright and sincere, plain spoken in all their dealings, and scrupulously honest in business and financial affairs: in fact their reputation for honesty earned them the trust of the wider public, so that in time Quakers became leading bankers, establishing such financial institutions as Lloyds and Barclays and other major businesses.

It is thus possible to argue that Quaker emphasis on uprightness, truthfulness and simplicity actually had a considerable impact on English society in the eighteenth century; but it would be much more difficult to make the case that this was its intention. Here again there are parallels with medieval spirituality and its evaluation of contemplation and action. These two were defined, at least since Augustine, as love of God and love of neighbour respectively (*not*, note, as political activity); and he had been explicit that 'we are always compelled by the gospel command to abandon the delights of contemplation when the demands of active love intercede' (McGinn 1991: 257). But this active love of neighbour was frequently articulated not in its own terms or because of the intrinsic value of the neighbour, but rather as a means of loving God. Thus, for example, Gregory the Great, explaining why the Holy Spirit was given according to the Bible, said:

On earth he was given that we may love our neighbour, from heaven that we may love God. But why first on earth and only afterward from heaven? ... Let us love our neighbour, brethren, let us love the one who is near us, so that we can attain the love of him who is above us.

(quoted in McGinn 1994: 54)

Not only is this not political in intention, it is not even ethical for its own sake. The intention of charity is to purify one's own soul and make it more receptive to the love of God, more able to contemplate. Any positive social effects are incidental. The Kingdom of God – in Augustine's terms the City of God – is not of this world. Even with the qualifications and nuances that should be added to this reading, it is a very long way from the idea that the Kingdom of God is about to be established on earth.

Within eighteenth-century Quakerism, however, as also within medieval spirituality, there were those who continued a more radical social stance and refused to look only inward. One such was John Woolman, a New Jersey Quaker in the Quietist mode, who moved beyond the expectations of his time and his Quaker network to become an early campaigner against slavery and for respectful and just treatment of the native peoples of North America. In both the USA and in England, where Woolman travelled in the ministry, his work against the slave trade combined with his personal simplicity of life to make a deep impact. This was neither a Quaker who cared only for the purity of his own soul or that of the Quaker community, nor one who expected an apocalyptic revolution. Rather, in Woolman's understanding, the peace testimony meant doing what he could to change the world, in particular, to change the way Black and native peoples were treated. The understanding that there is 'that of God in everyone' does not apply to white people only. John Woolman was effective not only in the specific concerns of race relations. He also influenced the Quaker movement in its deeper attitudes, prompting it to look beyond itself, and see spirituality in broader terms than personal or communal piety and moral rectitude.

Another famous Quaker who broadened the understanding of spirituality and its relation to the peace testimony for the whole society was Elizabeth Fry. As a young woman she had been what was known as a 'gay Friend', that is, one who did not observe Quaker traditions of plain grey clothing: there is a story of her sitting in Meeting wearing purple boots with scarlet laces. She took her spirituality very seriously, however. The crucial work of her life was in Newgate Prison, where she worked for better conditions for prisoners, more just correctional policy, and better oversight and care for those who were released after serving their sentences. She also visited women on convict ships bound for Australia, supplying them with sewing equipment as a basis for livelihood. She became a 'plain Quaker' and gave up her purple boots; but it is the prison reform (which later became the Howard League) for which she is honoured. Elizabeth Fry, like John Woolman and others, looked for ways of changing the world to bring it into the Kingdom of God, not by political revolution initiated by Jesus returning with heavenly armies, but by patient hard work for social justice, especially for those most outcast and despised. There was thus tension in the Quaker movement between inward-looking spirituality and active living out of the peace testimony. As John Punshon sums it up:

> Friends remained active in this kind of voluntary social work throughout
> the Nineteenth Century ... The anti-slavery agitation promoted an interest
> in Africa, and this in turn led to schemes for settlement and colonisation
> by emancipated slaves, the development of mission work and the opening
> of schools. Friends were active individually in all these fields though the
> undertow of quietism prevented a wholehearted corporate involvement.
>
> (Punshon 1984: 170)

The ambiguities regarding the relation of spirituality to the peace testimony
are still not resolved. At a corporate level Quakers have deepened commitment
to action for peace and social justice through the twentieth century and to the
present. Many Friends were imprisoned for their refusal to fight in the World
Wars, until conscientious objection was introduced, and Quakers established
the Friends Ambulance Service as an alternative to fighting. Quakers founded
relief organizations like Oxfam, and worked in many countries for reconciliation between groups in conflict and for succour for those caught up in violence
or traumatized by it. From Northern Ireland to South Africa and from
Palestine to Bosnia, Quakers have been actively working to promote peace and
healing, in the meanwhile protesting in the UK and USA against the
arms trade, international debt and wars, including recent aggression against
Afghanistan and Iraq.

It would not be accurate to imply that there is ambiguity about this corporate social involvement among Quakers: rather, it is fair to say that contemporary Friends see such engagement as crucial to the self-identity of
Quakers. Where the ambiguity lies, however, is in the relation of this social
engagement with spirituality. How is the work for justice to be understood? Is
it in some way related to the Kingdom of God – whatever that might mean?
Or is it simply decent human behaviour, without any particular reference to
God or religion? Is there a *theology* of active non-violence? Does it matter?
Quakers would certainly insist that active social engagement is, out of comparison, more important than having a fully worked-out theology about it, let
alone a theology understood as a set of religious truth claims. Still, I suggest
that for many Quakers and others it may be helpful to see how this active
engagement is of a piece with spirituality; and I shall show how this is true if
we give beauty (rather than justified true beliefs) a central place in thinking
and in living.

If there have been ambiguities in relation to beauty and spirituality and in
relation to (non-)violence and spirituality, both among Quakers and in the
wider traditions of Christendom, the same is true about gender. It can be
argued, both for the early church and for early Quakerism, that there was
equality of gender at least as an ideal, and to a large extent in practice. For the
early church, Elisabeth Schüssler Fiorenza (1983, 1993) has argued that women
were prominent in the circle around Jesus and as leaders in the movement
after his death; and Peter Brown (1988) has shown how the early monastic

movement, and early Christendom, more generally, changed sexual expectations and freed women as well as men from the gender roles to which they had been confined, partly by refusing to make reproduction a priority. Among early Quakers, too, women were from the beginning given roles of great prominence, perhaps partly because of the centrality of Margaret Fell in Quakerism's earliest years, and also because, in a time of fierce persecution, much of the weight of maintaining the movement necessarily fell on women's shoulders. Since Quakers had no paid ministry, but in their Meetings 'waited on the Light' and spoke as they felt moved by the Spirit, women as well as men spoke, and took leadership roles.

This gender equality shocked and scandalized many in the seventeenth century. To answer their objections, Margaret Fell wrote a pamphlet, 'Women's Speaking Justified', which became a manifesto for gender equality. Her method was ingenious. She took up the same grounds as her opponents, who tried to show from the Bible that women were the weaker sex, that women were the first to sin, that women should be subordinate to men and should keep silence in church. Point by point she shows that in the Bible itself, women have positions of respect and dignity, that women were among Jesus's disciples and were co-workers with Paul (who did not object to their speaking in church if they were *holy* women), that if sin entered the world by a woman so also did the one who saves from sin, and so on. She turns the tables on her opponents: what if it had been left to men to announce the news of Jesus's resurrection?

> Mark this, you that despise and oppose the message of the Lord God that he sends by women ... if [women's] hearts had not been so united and knit unto him in love that they could not depart as the men did, but sat watching, waiting and weeping about the sepulchre until the time of his resurrection, and so were ready to carry his message, as is manifested, how else should his disciples have known, who were not there?
>
> (Fell 1992: 67)

It is a brilliantly written argument and, together with her example, has rightly made Margaret Fell a foremother not only of Quakerism in general but of Quaker feminists in particular.

With such clear insistence on gender equality, one might have thought that there was no room for ambiguity. Early Quaker men, starting with George Fox and James Naylor, seem to have been in full agreement: not only did they concur with women's right to minister but they encouraged women in travel and missionary activity, often accepting considerable inconvenience and even hardship to do so (Trevett 1991). Indeed a group of influential Quaker men (including George Fox) were willing to let Margaret Fell write a document explaining Quakerism to King Charles in 1660, putting their names to it as co-signatories but in no way disguising her authorship (Fell 1992: 43–55). It is hard to imagine any other religious group of the time taking such a matter-of-fact egalitarian stance.

In spite of all this, the clarity was quickly lost. At the same time as Quakers became more inward looking, they increasingly accepted the standards of respectability current in the world around them, at least in terms of gender relations. In some respects they did remain more radical: women could minister in Meeting, could travel as ministers or missionaries, and could take an active part in the business of the society. Special women's meetings were set up to ensure this; and they were often the context for effective activity.[2] However, many men (and also some women) were threatened by the 'usurpation' of power by women, and insisted that women should remain in their 'natural' sphere of activity: reproduction, caring for home and children, looking after the sick and the poor. A distinction was made between the spiritual and the temporal; and as William Laddington, an influential Quaker of the time, put it, 'So Male and Female are all one in Christ, that is in Spirituals, but Man the Head in Temporals' (quoted in Quaker Women's Group 1986: 14). Just what counted as temporal or as the natural sphere of women was of course open to definition.

To some extent the ambiguity can be traced back to Margaret Fell herself. For all that she insisted on the right of women to minister, she still seemed to accept the common assumption that women are the weaker sex: it was just that God had chosen the weak things of this world and empowered them to carry his message. It was a stance strikingly similar to the 'modesty formula' frequently used by medieval women spiritual writers: God chose a woman to bear his Son, women to bear his messages, the humblest and lowest to be his servants (see Jantzen 1995: 170). Though such a stance provided a strong argument for holy women to speak or minister when they felt God's bidding to do so, it was not an argument for gender equality more generally, nor did Fell ever pretend that it was. Indeed she seems to have accepted without question the principle that wives should be subordinate to their husbands, even though in practice she obviously took a strong role both in her first marriage to Thomas Fell and later in her second marriage to George Fox.

As Quakers became more conservative, so the sexism of the wider society became more prominent, until even the notion of women's spiritual equality was ambiguous, and their right to speak in Meetings for Worship open to challenge. In 1701, one Meeting recorded the following minute:

> This meeting finding that it is a hurt to Truth for women Friends to take up too much time, as some do, in our public meetings, when several public and serviceable men Friends are present and are by them prevented in their serving, it is therefore advised that the women Friends should be tenderly cautioned against taking up too much time in our mixed public meetings.
>
> (Quaker Women's Group 1986: 16)

How much is too much? Why are not men Friends similarly cautioned? The masculinist bias is palpable, even though couched in language which does not actually forbid women to speak or deny their (spiritual) equality.

It was not until the rise of the feminist movement in the twentieth century that Quaker women and men once again properly confronted questions of gender. Nevertheless, when at last they did do so, they were able to reach back and reclaim the radical stance of early Friends, reinterpreting it in the context of late modernity. Although it was not without a struggle, Quakers won through to an acceptance of gender equality (without the distinction between spiritual and temporal) far more thorough going than most other non-conformist denominations (except the Unitarians) and far in advance of the established church, where sexism is still deep seated.

In fact, sexism (like racism and homophobia) is seen by Quakers as a social injustice closely related to violence: it is of itself an attitude that easily results in violence against women, and it fosters attitudes of disrespect for others and a sense of superiority which underlies aggression and warfare. For contemporary Quakers, therefore, gender equality and the peace testimony are all of a piece. In a violent world, peace begins at home, not by enforcing a hierarchy but by cherishing and nurturing 'that of God in everyone'. The openings to a renewed understanding of gender equality are thus inseparable from issues of spirituality and peace; and as I shall go on to argue, they are also closely linked to beauty. It is to the question of beauty that I now turn.

Chapter 2

Beauty denied

This returns us to the question of why it is that beauty has to such a large extent been denied a place in the Christendom of modernity. Is it so unimportant that it is simply ignored? Is it a threat to be repressed? How does the denial of beauty intersect with the escalation of violence, and with issues of gender? How can spirituality, in particular the spirituality of Quakerism, address these questions?

The theologian Edward Farley (2001) gives a short sketch of three basic reasons for the denial of beauty of Christendom. Insightful as is his contribution, he does not connect his insights on the denial of beauty with either gender or violence. In this chapter I shall begin to make these connections, and also indicate how the issues raised interlock with basic principles of Quaker spirituality. In addition I shall suggest a fourth reason for the denial of beauty, namely the fixation upon belief which has come to characterize Christendom. These four reasons, together with their interconnection with gender and violence, will set the agenda for the chapters that follow, in which I shall try to bring them into dialogue with the ambiguities and openings of Quaker thought informed by the broader currents of Christian spirituality.

Beauty displaced

The first of the anti-aesthetic tendencies that Edward Farley discusses is the insistence in Christendom on radical monotheism. This monotheism replaced archaic nature religions, which had conceptualized the divine as immanent powers within nature: the gods and goddesses of rivers, trees, sun and moon, thunder, and so on. If all these things in nature are divine, or at least manifest divine presence, then the beauties of nature are openings to the sacred. As Farley says:

> For most faiths (religions), the world's very coming into being, in meadow and glade, in animal life and starry sky, is itself a manifestation of immanent divine powers. To be related to the world's particulars is also to be related to the divine powers at work in them ... Beautification is not

the only work of the gods, but it is one part of their work as the world is infused with fertility, order, symmetry, differentiation and power.

(Farley 2001: 9)

As Farley points out, the peoples who thought of the natural world as imbued with divinity produced artefacts of striking beauty, artefacts which later crusaders for monotheism all too often perceived as idols. For with the advent of monotheism, there was a rejection of all identification of divinity with the world or the things of nature, a need to eradicate all such immanent deities as false gods, and with that need 'a deep suspicion of their work of beautification' (10). 'If the gods and goddesses make nature shimmer with beauty, then to eradicate them affects people's relation to nature' (10).

It is true, of course, that in Jewish and Christian belief the one God in whose name all these divinities must be ousted is a Creator, and can therefore be seen as the fount and origin of the beauty of the world. The theme of God as Creator is prominent in biblical writings, beginning with the very first chapter of Genesis, and with it metaphors of living beauty. The earth is the garden of the Lord; his people flourish as trees planted by rivers of water; those who abide in Christ the true vine bring forth abundant fruit: all these organic metaphors offer a model of thought, even within monotheism, which celebrates life and fecundity, as the life of the divine flows through all that God has made. Already in the biblical writings, however, and much more emphatically in the theology of Christendom, these organic metaphors are replaced with metaphors of the covenant and the courtroom. God makes a covenant with his people, ratified in blood, whereby they are obligated to keep his laws. God is judge, though he can also provide substitutionary satisfaction for those who fail to keep the divine commands.

This forensic model, which lies for example at the basis of interpretations of Jesus as Saviour, whose death is an atonement for sins, has little space for the celebration of beauty. The emphasis rather is on the moral relationship of Israel and the church to God through adherence to the Torah or through faith in Jesus as Christ. It is rarely asked why the forensic model should be given priority over the organic, why one set of metaphors should be allowed to exclude the other set. Indeed, especially in the Christian theologies of modernity, the metaphors that make up the forensic model – atonement, justification, righteousness – are hardly recognized as metaphors, but are taken as literal description of a divine 'plan of salvation'. Neither the beauty of the earth nor of human bodies, not even the radiant glory of God, is central to this 'plan'. How this forensic model should draw people to a vibrant, living spirituality, based on delight in God and all that God has made, rather than on guilt and shame and fear of divine punishment, is hardly addressed.

Although Farley does not discuss it, the relationship to gender of this displacement of beauty in the monotheistic revolution is easy to see. In the first place, we can see in the Bible and other ancient writings that the One God of monotheism is insistently male. He is the King, the Lord of Hosts, the Father, and there is no Queen of Heaven or Mother God at his side. There are plenty of indications in the biblical writings that the gods, and especially the goddesses, worshipped by the surrounding nations (and sometimes by the Israelites) were a threat and an abomination. There are just enough indications of feminine or maternal imagery for the divine in the Bible to make it possible for medieval writers like Anselm of Canterbury or Julian of Norwich to write movingly of the motherhood of God, but these are very much the exception. For by far the most part, the One God of monotheism is – though without body – resolutely male, 'a relatively genderless male deity', as an Anglican bishop has observed.

Moreover, it is the teaching of monotheistic Christendom that humankind is made in the image of this (male) God. In the pages of the Bible both male and female are created in the *imago Dei*, but it is the woman who succumbs to temptation and who lures her husband into sin; the woman, also, whose punishment is to bring forth children in pain, to be mired in reproduction, the body, the material. The association of the female with sin, the body and the physical world, and the male with the rational, spiritual and god-like is by no means uniform in biblical or Christian writings, but it is nevertheless pervasive. It is a theme that has dominated the construction of gender throughout Christendom, and it could never have begun as long as goddesses as well as gods permeated the natural world. This is not in itself an argument against monotheism, of course; but it does show one of its consequences. As beauty is displaced from the world by emptying the world of divinity, the only divine horizon for humanity is implicitly masculine; the woman, along with the goddess, is associated with evil. I have already given some hints of how these gender constructions were subverted, both in medieval spirituality and in Quakerism, and I shall develop these more fully in Chapters 5 to 7.

There are many levels at which all this connects with violence. In the first place, if monotheism is to be rigidly enforced, then the gods and goddesses – and the people who worship them – must be exterminated; or so, at least, the biblical texts portray it. The people of the monotheistic covenant are not encouraged to live peaceably with others, or even to try to persuade or convert them. Rather, they are repeatedly exhorted to show no mercy to the people who worship the gods of nature, but to utterly destroy them; and their well-being as a nation, seen as God's blessing upon them, varies in accordance with their obedience to this command of their 'jealous' God. To what extent any of the biblical accounts are historically accurate is open to scholarly dispute; but in terms of their effects on the consciousness of Christendom that scarcely matters. What has sedimented into western consciousness is that monotheism is the true religion, and that it is to be rigorously enforced. All else is idolatry. If violence is involved in the enforcement of true religion, that is only to be expected.

The violence in the name of the one God against all false gods and their worshippers is usually represented as deliberate action by God's people, undertaken for worthy moral and religious motives. But of course it can also be seen as the result of fear and anger, the deep sense of threat engendered by the idea of gods and goddesses in competition with the God of Israel. Out of such anxiety, violence easily erupts. And as we have learned from the work of psychoanalysts, if something is a source of dread, then so will be anything that reminds one of that dread. If the thought of gods and goddesses is threatening, then the beauty that evokes the thought of divinity in nature will generate anxiety; and all the tactics of the fearful mind will be brought to bear against all that represents such divinity, tactics including eradication, control, domination, reinterpretation and pretending that it is not there. All of these can easily be traced in western attitudes to the beauty of nature. In Christian theology, for example, nothing earns as immediate a reaction of contempt and dismissive hostility as the suggestion of pantheism: the merest whiff of it is sufficient to contaminate a theory. As Farley says: 'If the gods of the mountains, waters and fertility are idols, even demons as Paul says, the many taboos are replaced with one great taboo – a terror of idolatry so powerful that it empties all the particulars and regions of the world of their mysterious sacral dimension' (Farley 2001: 9). When the sense of threat reaches such a pitch, violence is inevitable. Idols, idolaters, must be utterly destroyed.

The denial of beauty in the name of monotheism, and its consequences for gender and violence, raises fundamental questions. It would be possible, on the one hand, to ask whether monotheism itself need be understood in a manner that leaves so little space for beauty. My observations regarding forensic and organic models of thought point, for example, to one way in which, by giving prominence to a theme flourishing in biblical writings that is often ignored, life and beauty play a much more significant role.

However, I wish also to ask the more fundamental question: what is the relationship between the world and the divine? Is monotheism the most helpful way to conceptualize it? Or is nature itself alive with divine life? – and if so, how can this be understood? Many people feel that they encounter God in nature, or that it is in some sense spiritually uplifting: I suggest that it is immensely important to acknowledge this and to explore its implications. Yet it is also true that earthquakes and droughts, tsunamis and hurricanes cause much destruction and loss of life; and these events are no less a part of nature than are rainbows and bluebells. If the relation between divinity and nature is much closer than is usually granted in the theologies of modernity, how are these disasters to be understood, and how do we respond to them? I shall draw upon the thinking of medieval spiritual writers as well as Quaker thought and practice at an angle to conventional theologies of Christendom to try to articulate a spirituality in which beauty is no longer denied.

Beauty despised

Edward Farley points out a second strand of Christian thinking, inter-connected with radical monotheism, that has little place for beauty. This is the moral and aesthetic asceticism sometimes connected with the label 'Puritan-ism', though reaching back much further than Puritanism as a historical phe-nomenon of rigorous Protestantism. The central feature of this asceticism is its hostility to the body and its pleasures, which are seen as no more than 'the lust of the flesh and the lust of the eyes'. Beauty is indubitably a pleasure of the senses. As such, it is linked to sensuality in many forms; and if sensuality is threatening, then so also is beauty. In Farley's words:

> Here is that strand of the Christian movement that is deeply suspicious of the very thing in which beauty finds its initial mediation – the body and the senses, the whole pleasurable interaction with the world that con-stitutes life itself. To attribute the genesis of human evil to the body, the senses, physical needs and organically originated desires suppresses both the body's graceful beauty and the beauty of the body's environment.
>
> (Farley 2001: 11)

Historically, we can trace Christendom's suspicion of the body and its pleasures to its fascination with Platonism, in which the mind or soul is trapped in the prison-house of the body and every bodily need or pleasure is a distraction from the pursuit of True Reality. In Plato's thinking, this dualism of body and mind was combined with[1] an intense appreciation of beauty, cast in non-material terms as Beauty Itself, the 'open sea of Beauty', to gaze on which is a person's highest good. In Christendom too, the Beatific Vision awaits the blessed: the vision of God at once most beautiful and conferring ultimate beatitude. In theory, there-fore, beauty is not despised but exalted. In practice, however, this exaltation of beauty is removed from this world, deferred to a future life (as I shall discuss further below), and utterly spiritualized. The body – whether the body that is beautiful or the body that perceives beauty through the physical senses – is despised in comparison with the soul or mind. Thus the beauty of nature, the mountains and valleys, the play of light on a river, the song of the skylark and the scent of the wild rose are all as nothing, of no importance in comparison with spiritual virtues and far too easily a snare. This attitude of despising the beauty of the world, at best sloughing it off as of little importance and at worst seeing it as a threat, has dogged Christendom from its beginnings. I shall discuss later how Augustine, for all his acute aesthetic sensibility, struggled with it through much of his life. It was an obvious factor in the iconoclast controversy, when large sections of the church decried all visual representation of divine things, and featured prominently in the sometimes severe asceticism of monastic life and teaching, before percolating into the Puritan attitudes of early modernity, attitudes in which Quakers shared in large measure in respect to beauty and sensibility.

Along with the idea that the appreciation of beauty is a snare because it feeds the senses and gives pleasure to the body, there is a further aspect to treating beauty with disdain. This is the attitude that this life is given us as a sphere of service: service to God and service to others. It is not for self-indulgence, for seeking merely our own pleasures. This being the case, there is little room for beauty or its appreciation. In this view, it is not so much that beauty is thought of as bad or evil, unless it is a distraction from the life of service. There is just no time for it. A life wholly devoted to serving God, under this notion of service, can see beauty as little better than frippery. Again, this disdain of beauty, not so much by active denunciation but simply by ignoring it as unimportant in comparison with morality defined by active service, has been part of one strand of Christendom since its inception and in its Jewish roots, where the life of covenant is the life of active mercy and the Good Samaritan is the model of appropriate behaviour. His duty was to care for the man who had been assaulted by bandits, not to admire the scenery along the way. In many branches of activist and progressive theology, from liberation theology to feminist and Black theology, we can see how the preoccupation with moral issues of justice, sexism and racism has simply left no room for even thinking about beauty. Again, Quakerism, with its large emphasis on humanitarian concern and social action, shares in this dismissal of beauty.

I shall argue later that such dismissal of beauty greatly impoverishes these theologies and hinders spirituality, and that (as medieval spiritual writers knew well) the active life must be balanced by the contemplative if it is not to run into disaster. Here, however, I wish to point out how this second aspect of displacement of beauty in Christendom is as deeply implicated in (sometimes contradictory) gender constructions as is the first. Both strands of moral asceticism reflect and reinforce structures of femininity and masculinity in Christendom, and with them, I shall argue, structures of violence. These are of course not separate from the structures already discussed in relation to radical monotheism and the extermination of idolaters and unbelievers, but rather, interact with them in destructive escalation.

It hardly needs labouring, that the suspicion of beauty because of its sensory appeal and the pleasure to which it gives rise is linked especially to the threat to men of women's attractiveness. Once again we find that women are constructed in terms of the body, sexuality and reproduction. Their beauty is a trap for men, who are more rational and godlike: 'godlike' here standing for passionlessness and detachment from the body and its desires. The trouble is that women arouse men sexually; their beauty attracts and disturbs men. (The converse may be true as well, of course, but Christian thinkers – almost uniformly male – concentrated monodirectionally on what troubled themselves.) The attractiveness of women is similar – indeed is an aspect of – the attractiveness of all kinds of beauty. Beauty lures and seduces desire. And if all desire is suspect, with sexual desire most suspect of all, then women will be seen as the epitome of the threat inherent in all beauty. It is no coincidence that the earth itself is feminized. 'Mother Earth' is material and physical, and her beauty too arouses the senses and seduces men from their single-minded devotion to God the Spirit, whose truth is known to the mind, not seen with the eyes of flesh.

On the activist side of this strand of moral asceticism the gender construction takes a new twist. If true Christianity is the life of active service, this can be construed as a 'muscular' Christianity, a religion of manliness. In this construction the female is seen as passive, while masculinity is active. This linkage of gender with passivity/activity goes back at least as far as Aristotle, of course, and is not always linked with moral asceticism. Nevertheless, it is easy to see how the idea that an active life in the service of God can unite with a construction of manliness such that men are the ones who do the 'real' work of God while women are, at best, their helpers. Such ideas of active service are often expressed in military terms: Christians are 'soldiers of the cross' who 'fight the good fight'. But since, in wars, women stay at home while men go off to battle, 'Christian' is here once again implicitly male. The active soldier of Christ is too busy fighting evil or poverty or racism to have time for beauty: indeed beauty – often reduced to mere prettiness – can be thought of as the domain of women. Active men have more urgent things to do.

This attitude is partly subverted and partly reinforced in Quakerism. It is subverted to the extent that both women and men are engaged in active work for social justice. Although in the eighteenth and nineteenth centuries Quakers fell into patterns of respectability which adopted the gender constructions of the wider society, they always retained the ideal of women as spiritually equal to men and therefore eligible for active ministry, and this ideal was instantiated by outstanding women like Deborah Derby, Lucretia Mott and Elizabeth Fry. But if Quakerism did not always adopt the active–passive gender distinction, it nevertheless reinforced the attitude that active workers for God and humanity have more important things to do than take up time and energy attending to beauty.

It is, I believe, one of the unfortunate consequences of not taking beauty theologically seriously that Christian feminists, including Quakers, can find themselves assuming what is in effect a masculinist position in the effort to 'fight' sexism and other forms of injustice. Feminists seek to challenge and subvert gender stereotypes, rather than allow masculinist structures and norms to dictate how they can think and act. Yet, insofar as we adopt a moral asceticism that has little time for beauty as we struggle 'manfully' against sexism, we may be in danger of adopting masculinist roles ourselves, rather than deconstructing them. This is not to say that women should remain passive! Rather, what I shall be developing in the chapters that follow is the suggestion that deeper consideration of beauty undercuts this whole series of dichotomies – active/passive, masculine/feminine, work/contemplation – and provides resources for the work against injustice which enhance pleasure and delight rather than belittle it.

The ease with which the moral asceticism that finds no time for beauty adopts the language of battle is an early indication of the interconnection with violence. Again, this connection can take varying forms, some of them in tension with one another. In the first place, and closely related to the need to exterminate idolaters that is associated with radical monotheism, is the violence against the threatening body. If the body and its senses and pleasures are suspect or actually evil, then the body must be disciplined and all desires brought under control. The literature of monasticism and piety is full of accounts of the 'mortification' of the flesh: literally, putting the flesh to death. Fasting, sleep deprivation, self-flagellation and many other forms of discipline are used to try to eradicate the desires and delights of the body: so also are strict standards of dress and deportment. Holiness is associated with ascetic extremes. There are of course many spiritual writers who advocate moderation and who reject the idea that violence towards one's body increases godliness; but even the prevalence of such advice is an indication of its necessity. The annals of Quakerism are full of records of 'disownment' of Friends who did not conform to the Quaker standard of plain dress.

One of the forms that violence against the body can take is sacrifice: the rhetoric of self-sacrifice, based on an interpretation of Jesus's death as the sacrifice of the 'Lamb of God', is pervasive in the literature of moral asceticism. The follower of Christ will gladly sacrifice all the things that would give them pleasure in order to increase in godliness: their desires, their autonomy, the esteem of society, even life itself, to say nothing of material possessions or bodily goods. In such a scenario, it is hardly even necessary to say that beauty and its enjoyment will be sacrificed: it is so obviously connected to 'selfish' pleasure of the bodily senses that it is incompatible with sanctity. Moreover, the gender associations are again obvious. Since it is the body and its pleasures which are linked conceptually with the female, it is these – and actual females – who bear the brunt of this 'sacrificial' violence. While there are many accounts of men who have heroically sacrificed their desires or their lives for God, it is often women who are expected – and expect themselves – to sacrifice their desires and their lives for men.

The violence implicit in the rejection of beauty and delight that despises the body and sensory pleasures can also be turned outwards. Rather than discipline and punish one's own body for its susceptibility to pleasure, the blame for this susceptibility can be laid elsewhere, on that which arouses pleasure. Here is once again part of the interpretation of male violence against women: rape, domestic violence, and all the cultural and religious forms of ensuring women's subordination. Women attract men: therefore if attraction is threatening or blameworthy it is women's fault, and women must be dealt with accordingly. But if women are suspect, then so will be everything that reminds men of their repressed desire and fear. Also, every enemy will be constructed on the model of this original enemy: everything that is to be fought and subordinated is feminized. All this is obvious in the long list of violence of war, conquest and colonization, where the object of conquest is seen in female terms: Columbus' perception of the Caribbean Islands as breasts with nipples; English occupation of North America as 'virgin territory'; nature itself described by early modern thinkers like Bacon as a woman who will yield up her secrets to wooing or to force. The warrior hero signifies active, rational masculinity; that which he seeks to master is cast as body, woman and all that is a reminder of its threat.

There is nothing new in this; feminist writers have long been pointing out the gender constructions and sexualized fantasies that have been embedded in violence and conquest throughout western history. What is hardly ever noticed, however, is that all this is deeply related to the moral asceticism that despises beauty. If beauty is disdained as unimportant or derided as a threat and a snare, then 'the body's graceful beauty and the beauty of the body's environment' will have to be drastically dealt with. Putting that the other way around: if we hope to find a remedy for the violence endemic in western civilization, not just for this or that conflict but for its roots, then there is no better place to look than to beauty and aesthetic sensibility. As I shall argue in detail later, openness to beauty's generosity resolves fear and threat, accepts and values the body and its flourishing, and therefore enables response to the other with empathy and interest in place of defensiveness and violence. For theologians to ignore beauty is to ignore the means of transformation. Beauty is essential for a spirituality of social justice.

Beauty deferred

Edward Farley points to a third strand of the displacement of beauty in Christendom, closely related to the two already mentioned. This is the idea that this world is irretrievably fallen and sinful. The best that can be hoped is that we (whoever 'we' are!) can be saved out of it, rescued for heaven. The world in its sinful state is inevitably ugly and cannot but descend ever further into ugliness; however the heaven which awaits the saved is a place of beauty and delight, pleasure forevermore. 'Satan rules the non-beautiful present age: the beautiful new Jerusalem comes in the future' (Farley 2001: 12).

> An apocalyptic type of faith may so despair of the unsavoury present that it places all good things – God, the kingdom of God, salvation, heaven, moral purity and the just society – in the future.
>
> (Farley 2001: 11)

Historically, there have been many forms of such apocalyptic expectation, going back to the time of the Hebrew prophets during the oppression of Israel in the Greco-Persian period, extending into the apocalyptic writing of the New Testament 'Revelations' when Christians were persecuted by Rome, and emerging periodically in the Middle Ages and in the Radical Reformation, as in the followers of Thomas Münster, as well as in seventeenth-century Quakerism. It is alive and well in the burgeoning branches of evangelical and fundamentalist Christianity in North America and elsewhere that look for a Second Coming of Christ, in which true believers will suddenly be taken up into heaven, and the earth consigned to the Armageddon conflict between Christ and Satan and their respective hosts. If this is what is about to happen, then there is no point getting involved in the earth and its beauty. It is in any case sinful and ugly in large measure; and such beauty as there is will probably be destroyed anyway. But no matter: beauty and perfect bliss await us in heaven. It is this sort of thinking that can lie behind a refusal to engage with environmental or ecological concerns on the conservation of resources. If the world as we know it is going to end before much longer, then there is no point in sacrificing present wealth and prosperity to try to save the earth for future generations. There won't be any.

Not all strands of Christendom subscribe to such blatant futurism, and not all who do would see engagement with the earth and its resources as pointless. Nevertheless the idea of heaven as the place of beauty and bliss is widespread in Christendom, as also is the idea that this earth is the place of sin from which we must be saved. Moreover, these ideas are often combined with the strand of moral asceticism which seeks freedom from the material realm: the earth, the body and all sensory pleasures are the chains from which death will release us to the salvation of heaven. It also of course assumes radical monotheism, and a sharp separation of the divine from the material. Within such a constellation of ideas, beauty has no place.

Conjoined with these ideas, there is often the view of salvation that sees it as a quasi-legal transaction: the forensic model discussed earlier. Human sin must be paid for to a God of justice whose righteousness forbids him to ignore or forgive sin without requiring the penalty to be paid. Christ offers himself as the price for sin: he is the recompense, the redeemer who pays the debt to God so that sinners can be justified. The metaphors are already present in New Testament writings, and become so prominent in Christian theology that their metaphorical status is often forgotten and they are taken as literal truth. In such a mode of thought, as Farley points out:

> Potentially beautiful things, the splendour (*doxa*) of God and the new life of redemption, are overwhelmed by metaphors of the courtroom, the judge, the saved and the unsaved, and the legal imputation of righteousness. In these juridical schemes beauty is simply absent as part of the human being's relation to God, nature, or other human beings. It is apocalyptically postponed as an element of future salvation.
>
> (Farley 2001: 12)

Later in this book I shall discuss further the issue of metaphor and the ways in which the choice of metaphor shapes thought. In Chapter 9 I will examine the thought of Augustine and his ambivalence towards beauty. As I have argued in my book *Becoming Divine*, if the metaphor of flourishing were given prominence instead of or alongside the metaphor of salvation, the living and organic alongside the legal, it would quickly correct the current distortion in which beauty is absent from theological consideration.

Enormously important as is Farley's analysis of the strands of thinking in Christendom which serve to displace beauty, he once again omits consideration of this lack in the construction of gender and violence. In the strand of apocalyptic thinking which defers beauty to a future heaven, it is at first hard to see how this deferral impacts upon gender construction, since surely the sinfulness of this world and the beatitude of heaven are shared by men and women alike. But things are more complicated than that. As already discussed, the earth, the body and the sensory have traditionally been linked with women; so also has sinfulness. Men sin too, to be sure; but it is women who put temptation in men's way. It is therefore not at all surprising that a theology which emphasizes the sinfulness of this world and defers beauty to heaven would be particularly suspicious of any supposed appearances of beauty in this world as a trap from the devil himself to distract men from single-minded pursuit of their heavenly goal. The beauty of women, and especially any attempts by women to beautify themselves, comes in for special censure. A famous early example is Tertullian's denunciation of Christian women for what he considered inappropriate attention to clothes, jewellery and hairstyle.

> And do you not know that you are (each) an Eve? The sentence of God on this sex of yours lives in this age: the guilt must necessarily live too. *You* are the devil's gateway: *you* are the unsealer of that (forbidden) tree: *you* are the first deserter of the divine law: *you* are she who persuaded him whom the devil was not valiant to attack. *You* destroyed so easily God's image, man. On account of *your* desert – that is, death – even the Son of God had to die. And do you think about adorning yourself ... ?
>
> (MacHaffie 1992: 27)

Any such adornment, any pleasure a woman might take in the beauty of her body or its enhancement, would be wholly inconsistent with the abasement woman ought to feel at her sinfulness and would only exacerbate the situation by tempting men further. Women must be submissive and humble, ruled by the men of their family and the church, if they are to have any hope of the true beauty of heaven. All else is false: a delusion of the devil; idolatry. Whatever the relation of the sexes in heaven (and that is debated in Christendom), on this sinful earth sexual equality cannot be an appropriate goal. We have already seen how even Quakers thought men should be the head of the 'temporal'.

Neither, on this view, is it at all realistic to hope for a cessation of violence, as long as this sinful earth lasts. Indeed on many an apocalyptic view, including some in the Bible itself, violence will increase until it finally erupts into the last battle of all, the Battle of Armageddon, when earthly armies will be joined by heavenly ones. What will be important on that fateful day is being on the right side, God's side, against the hosts of evil. That, in fact, is what is important all along. History itself can be read as a struggle between good and evil, if often a very complicated one. Many an army has gone to war not just praying for divine aid but actually believing that it was fighting God's battles. Even today, the west, especially the USA, involves itself in wars in which the veneer of secularism over such apocalyptic attitudes is only very thin. It goes to war to promote freedom and democracy; and whatever the difficulty (so goes the rhetoric) it will prevail: not because it is strongest or most brutal but because it is 'right'; read: 'it is on God's side'.

When this set of ideas is coupled, as it regularly is, with the radical mono-theism that sees the religion of the other as idolatrous or heretical, and the moral asceticism in which life is constructed as a struggle against evil, the recipe for unending violence in God's name is complete. The resulting ugliness and brutality is only to be expected. Violence is ugly. But beauty awaits those who fight for God and hope for heaven.

There have been many ways, historically, in which spirituality has engaged with politics in Christendom. The constellation of ideas of beauty, gender and violence takes a different shape if it is expected that God is about to come to earth and set up his throne and his kingdom in Jerusalem or in London, as was held by the first Christians and the early Quakers respectively, than if that expectation is deferred. When the church becomes the dominant political force, as it did from the conversion of Constantine onwards, art and beauty are used as tokens of power, often deeply implicated in war and violence. When, on the other hand, a religious group sees itself as a 'holy remnant', a small band preserving purity in an evil world, as did eighteenth-century Qua-kers, then the attitudes to beauty, gender and violence are conceived not as tokens of power but as indicators of holiness. If, as yet another possibility, divine life and justice is not a matter of some future heaven brought about by divine intervention but is something to work for here on earth, then the beauty and flourishing of the earth and its peoples press upon us with urgent concern and delight. Beauty can never be separated from politics. Neither can spiri-tuality. If we are to move forward in a spirituality in which aesthetic sensi-bility has a significant place, then it is imperative that its implicit politics not be left unexamined. I shall deal with this in more detail in the final section.

Beauty and belief

The three strands of the displacement of beauty in Christian thinking as articulated by Farley, together with my indications of their correlations with gender constructions and violence, go a long way to show why beauty has not been high on the agenda of theology in modernity. There is a small scattering of books on beauty and theological aesthetics,[2] but for the most part beauty has been displaced by attention to truth and truth claims. Theology in modernity has focused largely on what can legitimately – truthfully – be said about God, Christ, the Incarnation, and the other dogmas of the church and creed; it has hardly been noticed that we might also ask how the beauty of the divine in all its manifestations in the world can be discerned and how we might learn to appreciate it. Neither has that appreciation (or its lack) been connected with gender constructions and with the violence of the world. It is conventional to ascertain a person's religious stance by what they believe and the part beliefs play in their lives, or sometimes by their moral attitudes and behaviour, but not by what they find beautiful or the emphasis they place on beauty in their daily round. The focus on truth, doctrine and belief rather than beauty is so completely taken for granted that society is divided, religiously, between 'believers' and 'unbelievers': what, if anything, they find beautiful and how they respond to it does not enter the equation.

Beliefs are of course indispensable. To be a person is to have beliefs: beliefs about the world and other people and oneself, about what is important and how to live. These may be well articulated or left implicit; they may be justified by evidence, taken for granted, or even false or misguided. In that everyday sense of beliefs, it would of course be impossible to be religious (or even irreligious) without having some beliefs or other about it, even if that amounted to nothing more than believing that it is better (or worse) to live by certain conventions than not, for whatever reasons.

That is a very different matter, however, from defining religion in terms of beliefs: seeing religion as consisting of a set of claims to which one gives assent. To some extent such definition has been characteristic of Christendom since its early centuries, when it set itself apart from its Jewish roots and its Hellenistic and Roman context and Christians argued among themselves about such things as the nature of Christ and the doctrine of the Trinity. These arguments resulted in the formation of creeds – from *credo*: 'I believe' – which served to separate 'believers' from 'heretics'. The interplay of piety with power politics in all of this has often been studied. Yet along with the efforts to articulate beliefs (and appropriate morality) there was in the early church and through the Middle Ages a persistent recognition of the importance of beauty (Eco 1986; Bredin and Santoro-Brienza 2000). Spiritual writers like Hildegard of Bingen, Bonaventure and Thomas Aquinas appealed to beauty, often drawing on their heritage from Augustine and Pseudo-Dionysius. Their spirituality cannot be understood without taking as central the role of beauty and the way in which its attractiveness inspires desire and joy.

All of this changed drastically with the Reformation and its aftermath. Luther's 'breakthrough' to faith in Christ was represented, by him and even more by his successors, as a contrast between 'faith' and 'works'. Faith came to be construed more and more in terms of beliefs (rather than, say, trust), while 'works' included everything else, especially ritual, and with it, its aesthetic sensibility. Calvin's insistence on original sin and the depravity of humankind put a further obstacle in the path of any spirituality of beauty. In the Calvinistic tradition, it is only by divine revelation that God can be known, and that revelation comes through the Bible, the Word – and words – of God. By the preaching of the Word, God is proclaimed, whether in a Methodist revival or the tomes of Karl Barth. Salvation comes by faith in that Word. Even the divine act of creation is regularly represented in Christian theology as a *verbal* event, divine fiat rather than divine making, let alone the overflowing of divine beauty. The incarnate Christ, similarly, is the *Word* made flesh. In all the vast libraries of theological books written to interpret the incarnation, the theme of beauty is rarely considered, whereas the theme of word, belief and truth is all-pervasive.

In philosophy a parallel development was taking place with the 'epistemological turn', which was given its impetus by Descartes. The quest for certainty, for clear and distinct ideas, for justified true beliefs has been the hallmark of philosophy in modernity. Nowhere is this more prominent than in Anglo-American analytic philosophy of religion, which has dominated the field since the mid-twentieth century. Out of comparison more attention is given to proofs of the existence of God, the coherence of theism, and the evidence for religious claims than to a consideration of beauty and its significance for religion: indeed there are those who would assert that the former constitutes philosophy of religion while the latter has nothing to do with it.

What I am arguing in this book is that this is not good enough. Beauty has an importance out of all comparison with the slight attention it receives in western theology and philosophy. The one-sided emphasis on truth and ethics has generated a distorted theology and an impoverished religious life, and is connected with oppressive gender constructions and with ongoing, escalating violence in the name of God or his self-appointed, thinly secularized representatives.

It is easy to see how the exaltation of beliefs is related to masculinism. Throughout western Christendom, and reaching back into ancient Greek philosophy, rationality has been conceptually linked with men; and bodies, reproduction and the senses with women. If rationality and religion are constituted in terms of justified true beliefs, then they are paradigmatically in the domain of men. Beauty is to do with the senses and the body, hence with the feminine. Men retain control of beliefs by ensuring that educational opportunities are regulated by men for men, so men in Christendom have been able to use rationality as a technology of mastery. From this, and interacting with the insistence on monotheism and the extermination of idolaters and heretics, it is only a short step to violence, as we have seen.

To gain a sense of the radical deficiency of all this, for spirituality and even for basic human decency, consider the following. Suppose we were to encounter a person who said in all sincerity, 'I'm a very busy person, so I have little time for truth, especially during the working week: I do try to make some time for truth at home and at weekends and on my annual holiday ... '. We would regard such a person as seriously unbalanced and certainly not to be trusted, theologically or otherwise. Yet if we substitute 'beauty' for 'truth' in the above locution, it would not seem a very strange or unusual thing to say. Should it? What are we doing to theology, to ourselves, to the world, by treating beauty as an optional extra? Turning the question around: how would our theology, the world and we ourselves be enriched if we opened ourselves to the wonder and delight of beauty?

What sort of spirituality does beauty enable?

In the spirituality of Christendom, and also in Quaker practice, there is an alternative to the one-sided emphasis on the Word, doctrines and beliefs that characterizes much of the theology of modernity. At least since the time of Origen in the third century, and taken up by Augustine and Bernard of Clairvaux, there has been an emphasis on inwardness, on discerning the divine and responding to the divine spirit not by a system of beliefs (though as already acknowledged, beliefs of one sort or another must always be present) but by entering into oneself. God could be found 'in the centre of the soul', as Teresa of Avila put it, echoing a long line of mystical writers. There are, it was held, spiritual senses that parallel the physical: the inner ear that hears the divine voice; the spiritual vision that gives insight into God and the working of the divine spirit. Early Quakers tended to express this in terms of the 'inner Light', where the soul that waited upon God in silence would receive illumination and empowerment for the work it was called upon to do. Quakers quite explicitly set this ideal of attentiveness to the inner Light over and against a system of doctrines and beliefs (which they called 'notions') and even against scripture, important though the Bible was for them.

The constellation of ideas around inwardness or inner Light is, I suggest, rich for the renewal of spirituality. There are, to be sure, many problems with it that will need to be addressed. But there are also significant openings. In the first place, it encourages a spirituality that is not focused exclusively on doctrines and beliefs, but on the life of the spirit within. This immediately offers possibilities of alternative gender constructions, not based on narrowly defined rationality as a technology of mastery. Second, the issues involved with the inner Light – issues of recognition, contemplation, subjectivity and the possibility of mistake or of evil – are very close to issues involved in aesthetic sensibility. How we recognize and respond to the divine in our hearts is much more like how we recognize and respond to the beauty of a sunrise or the flash of a kingfisher than it is like accumulating evidence for the justification of a set of doctrines. I shall try to show, in fact, that beauty and spirituality are very closely linked. Third, and related to the above, an emphasis on inner Light, linked as I shall show to beauty and flourishing, is one that deepens empathy and compassion and leads away from violence. By encouraging recognition of the divine in everyone, the beauty of the earth and of its peoples, it offers resources for peace.

Because this understanding of the inner Light is basic, I shall begin in the next chapters by examining it more closely, showing how it relates to beauty, and addressing some of the problems associated with it. In the final chapters, I shall discuss the implications of this for our understanding of the divine, including the questions of monotheism, creation and its beauty and disaster, and the relation of God and the world. This will include discussions on the issues of beauty and the body, with special attention to desire, and will offer suggestions as to how a spirituality of beauty offers alternatives to violence and resources for peace.

Part Two

Beauty, Quakers and the inner Light

Chapter 3

Beauty and spirituality

And I have felt
A presence that disturbs me with the joy
Of elevated thoughts ...
Therefore am I still
A lover of the meadows and the woods,
And mountains; and of all that we behold
From this green earth ...

(Wordsworth 'Tintern Abbey', 1984: 134)

To Wordsworth the connection between beauty and spirituality is obvious. All nature is aglow with the disturbing joyful presence of the divine. The question is not whether woods and mountains, clouds and daffodils reveal this presence, but whether we recognize it, preoccupied as we are with 'getting and spending'. The Romantic poets lift up their voices against the desecration of the earth by narrow commercial interests that shrivel the spirit and make us oblivious to beauty. Beauty is not an optional extra for those with time on their hands. It is essential for the human spirit. It is what sets us apart from calculating machines and makes us sing.

Many today who value the spiritual would agree. In the beauty of nature, in music and painting and poetry, the spirit is refreshed. Here, if anywhere, the divine can be encountered. To value the spiritual is not necessarily to believe in God or a set of religious doctrines, let alone to belong to an institutional church. Neither is it to believe that there is a soul or spirit separate from our bodies that lives on after our bodies die. It is, however, to believe that there is more to be said about us than can be said in strictly physical terms. Love is more than chemistry; thought and creativity and joy is more than an arrangement of neurons and brain cells. When the medical and physical has been fully defined, the inwardness remains; and it is this which makes us human rather than mere animate mechanisms. Similarly, when the physical laws of the universe have been specified, when gravity and atomic energy and tectonic plates are understood, the beauty of nature remains. Just as music cannot be reduced to the performance of a set of notes, or painting to blobs of colour on a canvas, so the beauty of a rainbow cannot be reduced to the laws of physics. Important as these laws are, there is more to be said.

What more? The answer to this will become clearer as the book proceeds. For now, it is enough to note how closely beauty and spirituality are connected. They are dependent on the physical: without the laws of optics there would be no rainbow; without our visual apparatus we could not appreciate its beauty. But they cannot be defined in strictly physical terms. Whatever precisely we might mean by beauty and by the spiritual, and even if we have no very articulate representation of either, beauty and spirituality are inseparable. 'My heart leaps up when I behold a rainbow in the sky.'

The chapters that follow develop the interconnections between beauty and spirituality in more detail, but it is worth noting some of them at the outset. First, beauty feeds and re-creates the spirit. Beauty produces refreshment and energy; it is life giving and life enhancing. Often it does so by generating joy and peace, a sense of well-being and harmony. Beauty can, to be sure, be confused with mere prettiness, and spirituality can degenerate into superficiality or self-indulgence that takes no heed of the ills and violence of the world. Both can be exploited by narrow commercial interests: thousands of mugs printed with Wordsworth's daffodils; millions of 'Mind, Body and Spirit' self-help books. Yet I propose that it is from beauty and spirituality that both the motivation and the resources can be drawn to deepen such shallow preoccupations and to face and challenge the ugliness and ills and violence which distort the world. It is from this source that our desires can be strengthened for the flourishing of the earth and its peoples, and the empathy and sensitivity be fostered that make for kindness, mutuality and respect rather than destruction.

My intention, therefore, is to develop a spirituality of beauty. I call it a 'spirituality' rather than a 'theology' of beauty because there is every reason to suppose that it will not take the form of conventional theologies of modernity, premised as they almost invariably are upon the primacy of beliefs. I am not presupposing a Christian creed or a monotheistic idea of the divine. More importantly, since I am looking for resources for peace and justice rather than violence, a system of theological beliefs will not do, since a system of beliefs lends itself naturally to a forensic model interrelated with a masculinist drive for mastery. This means that social activism is all too easily driven by guilt or a sense of debt or a need to prove something. By contrast, beauty inspires joyful sharing and creativity, as I shall show. Moreover, beauty and a spirituality of beauty is something that invites engagement: if it is to be understood, one must enter into it not only with the mind, important though that is, but with the whole of oneself. A world of escalating violence and destruction is in sore need of a spirituality of beauty.

What shape would such a spirituality of beauty take? As I have already indicated, there are no theologies of beauty in modernity which can serve as a model. What is needed is an account that is intellectually credible and morally and politically engaged, sensitive to issues of gender, justice and violence, and of high aesthetic sensibility. Nothing exists that combines these requirements. However, there are theologies and philosophies that have developed one or more aspects. In what follows, I shall draw heavily on aesthetic theory, feminist thought and, for reasons already discussed, Quaker thought and practice and the history of Christian spirituality. The appropriateness and usefulness of such disparate resources will become clear as I proceed; but the result will be something new, much more than the sum of these parts and different in intention from theological systems whose aim is simply to develop a coherent set of doctrines. Although I shall of course seek intellectual adequacy, my aim is as much to provide resources for a politically engaged spirituality as it is to produce a set of ideas. Thus, while I shall consider such issues as what we might mean by the divine, and how this relates to what it is to be human – issues which are part of conventional theological systems – I am not worried by the fact that the conclusions I shall draw are far from conventional, or that there are many topics standard in systematic theology which I do not address at all. A spirituality of beauty that can speak to the violence of the world invites creativity and imagination.

It must begin, however, as any theology must begin, by establishing its starting point. A theology whose primary category is truth will at this point have a variety of possibilities. Evangelical theology appeals to the Bible as its source of knowledge and guarantor of validity. Barthians appeal to the Word of God: not identical with the Bible but very closely related. Roman Catholics add Christian tradition and the teachings of the church. Liberal theologians (Protestant or Catholic) make a stronger appeal to reason and rationality, looking particularly at what sort of evidence is available to warrant beliefs, whether drawn from scripture, tradition or experience. All these approaches aim at truth, and assume that truth is most important.

But what if beauty were given the central place? What is the starting point for a spirituality of beauty, and what are the guiding questions that will frame its development? In this case, I suggest that the first issue that must be addressed is that of recognition. How do we recognize beauty? What enables us to recognize spiritual claims? How can the claims of a spirituality of beauty be received, measured and validated? I am not interested in developing a checklist, or a system of doctrines under another name. But it is crucially important that we be able to discriminate between that which is shallow and self-indulgent on the one hand, and on the other that which nourishes the human spirit and provides resources for creative political and social engagement. When the project is framed like this it is obvious that truth questions are not far away. However, I suggest that in the current religious and political climate, in which truth questions are routinely given dominance, it is important to privilege beauty, and hence to begin with questions of recognition.

How do we recognize beauty? It might seem obvious. We just do. We see the stars, we hear birdsong, all nature is filled with beauty: how could we not recognize it? There is a living immediacy in our encounters with beauty; and if we do not recognize it no amount of argument or persuasion will help. I believe that there is quite a lot in this response, as I shall argue later. But it is obvious that there are also problems, not least the concerns about self-indulgence and shallow perception already mentioned. How can depth and discernment and discrimination be fostered? How can sheer subjectivity be met: after all, might not the whole appeal to beauty be summarily dismissed with the observation that beauty is in the eye of the beholder? Surely this is enough to see off the whole idea of a spirituality of beauty before we begin.

Now, what is striking is that it is precisely questions of recognition, discrimination and discernment which also preoccupy the central writers in the tradition of Christian spirituality as well as in the Society of Friends. Here also we find appeals to direct intuition or illumination, unmediated apprehension, and personal subjective experience. Here also we find that there were many in the churches and outside of them who dismissed such appeals to direct illumination or encounter as heresy, self-delusion or 'enthusiasm': a term of contempt for those who claimed direct dealings with God.

Even more insistent than these attacks from the dubious or contemptuous were the anxieties from within. In medieval Christian spirituality there was ceaseless concern that what seemed to the devout to be encounters with the divine were really deceptions of the devil. Early Quakers maintained constant vigilance against self-delusion or 'running into notions'. In both cases, while there was dependence on the inner Light, and recognition of it (rather than scripture, tradition or reason) was the source and starting point, there was much emphasis on how to discriminate the genuine from the deceptive, strategies of testing and discernment. Basic to all this was the assumption that recognition and discernment were not automatic. Training was essential. The whole personality must be formed to be receptive to the divine light and to recognize its reality in oneself and others while not being led astray by delusion or too easily contented with the self-indulgent.

These, obviously, are just the same sorts of questions as arise for a spirituality of beauty. It will therefore be good to begin with a more detailed study of inwardness in Christian spirituality and in Quaker thought and practice. What did they mean by inwardness or the inner Light? What is involved in recognition, and how is it fostered? How is delusion avoided? What can be done about those who claim illumination to justify their own dominance, whether of gender or social or political hierarchy? How can encounter with the inner Light nourish the spirit and deepen its resources to challenge violence? In short, what does it contribute to a spirituality of beauty?

In the following chapters I shall try to develop and address these questions. I shall discuss Quaker ideas of the inner Light, showing how their thought developed as well as their strategies of recognition. We shall see that for them, the inner Light provided resources for political engagement and social concern; but that until very recently it was hardly connected with beauty, which was viewed with Puritanical suspicion. (In a later chapter I shall show that this was not the case in medieval Christian spirituality, that beauty played a much more central role in their account of illumination, the ultimate goal of which was the beatific vision.) This, however, was so strongly connected with an idea of God beyond anything to do with this earth, and ultimately with the life after death when that God will be seen face to face, that spirituality was in tension with political engagement. This will lead me, in the final chapters, to a more direct discussion of recognition and discernment in a spirituality of beauty, a well-spring of energy for creative intervention for justice and peace.

Chapter 4

Quakers and the inner Light

Take heed, dear Friends, to the promptings of love and truth in your hearts. Trust them as the leadings of God whose Light shows us our darkness and brings us to new life.

(British Yearly Meeting 1995: 1.02.1)

These are the first words of the quaintly named 'Advices and Queries', a booklet of distilled insight of Quakers through the centuries and still taken seriously by Friends as wise counsel. Quakers have, since their inception, placed much emphasis on the inner Light, wisdom and love that arises not from some external source, not the Bible or the church or Christian tradition, valuable as these may be, but out of 'the promptings of love and truth in your hearts'. Because these are personally experienced, rather than imposed from without, they cannot be easily dismissed or shrugged off without damage to one's integrity: recognition of the inner Light and acceptance of its promptings thus makes for whole-hearted engagement with its leadings. Thus Quakers place great stress on silent listening, on discernment of the promptings of the inner Light; and they place at least as much stress on being obedient to what they thus come to understand. The promptings of love and truth are not fundamentally sets of doctrines or beliefs but clarification of attitude and action: answers not to the perplexities of systematic theology but rather to the questions: 'What should I/we do about a particular situation now? How are we to live?' It is the combination of attention and obedience to the inner Light that is at the heart of Quaker work for peace and justice, rejection of violence and war, opposition to slavery in any form, and affirmation of racial and gender equality long before these causes were more widely established.

In such a broad sketch, it is not difficult to see the connections in the constellation of ideas. However it is also easy to raise questions which serve as an invitation to go deeper. What exactly is the inner Light? How is it to be recognized? What is its relation to reason, or emotion, or conscience? In what sense, if at all, is it from God or divine, and how does it connect with Christian (or other) religious traditions? How can counterfeits or deceptions be discerned and avoided? What is the relationship between the individual and the group in recognition of the inner Light? Above all, what is the connection between the illumination of the Light and obedience to it? How, precisely, does this offer resources that provide alternatives to violence? All these questions are internal to Quaker thought and practice, and are obviously crucial to a spirituality of beauty.

There is, in the nature of the case, no definitive Quaker creed or systematic theology from which answers to these questions could be sought. Rather, it is in the continuing faith and practice of Friends that we can find clearer indications of what is involved in the inner Light. Neither is it at all surprising that there have been changes and development of understanding. I shall therefore begin historically, with George Fox and some of the early Friends, before addressing issues more thematically.

George Fox and the inner Light

England in the seventeenth century was in religious and political turmoil. There were many, of conflicting persuasions, who were all too confident of what should be done and where the truth lay: Royalists who stood by Charles I, Parliamentarians who opposed and eventually executed him, Catholics, Latitudinarians and Puritans, and a great variety of sects, each of them sure that they were right and all others were wrong. But there were also many people who were more thoughtful, perplexed by all these conflicting 'certainties' and looking for constructive ways forward for themselves as individuals and for their country. There were many variations among these people, but collectively they were labelled 'Seekers' (Gwyn 2000).

George Fox was one of these. In his *Journal* he describes the confusion he felt as a young man, and his attempts to get clarification. He went to priests for help, to Baptists and other Dissenters, to those educated in the universities, but always he remained unsatisfied. Not only did their words fail to convince him, but all too often their lives did not measure up to their teaching, and left Fox disillusioned: 'none among them could speak to my condition'. Finally, after a long period of struggle in which he felt very much alone, he began to realize that no one outside him could show him the way, but that he must rely on divine Light within himself.

> And when all my hopes in them [i.e. priests and preachers] and in all men were gone, so that I had nothing outwardly to help me, nor could I tell what to do, then, Oh then, I heard a voice which said, 'There is one, even Christ Jesus, that can speak to thy condition', and when I heard it my heart did leap for joy.
>
> (Fox 1952: 9)

It was from this point that Fox was able to move forward, relying on no one else to help him.

> My desires after the Lord grew stronger, and zeal in the pure knowledge of God and of Christ alone, without the help of any man, book, or writing ... And then the Lord did gently lead me along, and did let me see his love, which was endless and eternal, and surpasseth all the knowledge that men have in the natural state, or can get by history or books ... Christ it was who had enlightened me, that gave me his Light to believe in, and gave me hope, which is himself, revealed himself in me, and gave me his spirit and gave me his grace, which I found sufficient in the deeps and in weakness.
>
> (Fox 1952: 9–10)

Apart from Fox's disillusionment with priests and ministers of religion, his words might initially be taken as conventionally Christian. In some respects this is true. Fox and the early Quakers shared with nearly everyone else in seventeenth-century England assumptions about God and the Bible as in some sense revealing God; and Fox used the language of Christendom to express himself. Yet the more closely we look, the less conventional his teaching appears. Certainly those who heard Fox were in no doubt that it was different, whether those who were convinced or those in the churches who felt so threatened by the Quaker movement that they attacked Quakers in every way they could, from sticks and stones and beatings to imprison-ment for long periods in such dire conditions that many died or were per-manently weakened.

What, then, was distinctive about Fox's teaching? In the first place, his rejection of the authority of priests and ministers of religion had enormous religious and political consequences. It meant that the traditions of the church, including its systems of theology and its creeds, were all open to question, and of themselves fundamentally unhelpful. Because they seemed to provide people with answers for their deepest concerns, they were actually harmful, since they would provide spurious satisfaction and thereby distract people from attending to the inner Light. Politically, too, there was fallout. The churches and their priests were maintained by a compulsory tax or 'tithe'. This, Fox and the Quakers refused to pay. Why should they support an institution which did harm to people? Much of the initial persecution of Quakers focused on their withholding of tithes and rejection of the authority of priests, bishops and presbyters together with their 'steeplehouses'. For Quakers, however, this stance was not simply one of disrespect, though it is easy to see why it was often taken as such. Rather, it was based on principle. The creeds and doc-trines and systems of belief and ritual promised people a way to God and eternal life, but that promise was deceptive. God can be encountered, eternal life can be gained, only by engagement with the Light within. It could be argued that creeds and rituals could be means toward such engagement, but Fox and early Friends did not find it so. In their experience these things gave false assurance. It was by waiting in silence, individually and, above all, in a group, that they encountered the Light. It will soon become clearer why this was so.

To some extent this stance could be seen as a radical but logical consequence of the Reformation. Luther too, after all, had challenged the authority of pope and church and ecclesiastical tradition. But Luther, Calvin and their followers had done so on the basis of *sola scriptura*: the Bible alone, not the tradition of the church, showed the way to God, and every person could read the Bible for themselves. Fox's attitude to the Bible was quite different. Although he had great respect for it, it is not the scriptures that show the Light, but rather the other way around: only by the Light can the scriptures be properly understood. As Fox describes his own experience:

> This I saw in the pure openings of the Light without the help of any man, neither did I then know where to find it in the Scriptures, though afterwards, searching the Scriptures, I found it. For I saw in that Light and Spirit which was before Scripture was given forth, which led the holy men of God to give them forth, that all must come to that Spirit, if they would know God, or Christ, or the Scriptures aright, which they that gave them forth were led and taught by.
>
> (Fox 1952: 33)

Fox never doubted the historical and literal accuracy of the Bible. In that sense he, like his contemporaries, believed that the Bible is 'true'. Yet Fox meant much more than this by truth. For Fox, truth is *lived*, not merely believed. Truth, ultimately, is reality itself, not simply words or beliefs that correspond to a state of affairs. In technical terms, it is an ontological quality, and only in a secondary sense is it a property of propositions or beliefs. Reality, Truth, is God, in Fox's terms; the life of the divine. Living in the truth, doing the truth, is living with integrity in that divine life. What this comes to and why it is so will become clearer as we proceed. What is important at this point is that, according to Fox, it is the inner Light that leads to Truth, to divine Reality, not the words of scripture, accurate though they may be. Over and over, Fox warned early Friends, 'Heed not words without life' (Ambler 2001: 74).

For Fox, even Christ himself must be understood in terms of the inner Light. In one sense it is apparent that Fox identifies Christ with Jesus of Nazareth, and sees Jesus, thus, as the one especially filled with the divine life, the living Light who is within, not simply a historical figure. Thus Fox writes in an early letter:

> Keep within. And when they shall say, 'Lo here', or 'Lo there is Christ', go not forth. For Christ is within you ... The Word of God is within

you and you are the temples of God ... God has said he will dwell in you and walk in you. Then what need you go to the idols' temples without you?

(Jones 1989: 14)

External things like churches or creeds or even the words of scripture become the equivalent of 'idol's temples' if they usurp the place of the inner Light.

He that feeleth the light that Christ hath enlightened him withal, he feeleth Christ in his mind, which is the power of the cross of Christ, and shall not need to have a cross of wood or stone to put him in the mind of Christ or his cross, which is the power of God.

(Fox 1952: 205)

Although Fox uses standard Christian terminology, it is evident that the meanings of such basic concepts as Christ, the cross and even God have shifted, and are qualified by his understanding of the inner Light.

What, then, is this Light? It is obvious from what has already been said that the Light is identified with Christ, or the divine spirit, and that it is not external but within. In a sense it is self-defeating to say more. The whole point is that it is not a matter of words or doctrines or theories. In some respects it is analogous to psychotherapy: it is possible to give an account of it, but anyone who thinks that such an account is a substitute for the experience has completely missed the point. Fox himself often refused to give people explicit accounts, let alone doctrines or a set of beliefs, even though that was what preachers of other sects did and it was expected of him too. Rather, he insisted: 'Your teacher is within you; look not forth' (Fox 1952: 143). He went, for example, to Ulverston and instead of telling his audience what they should think, he exhorted them to look within.

I was moved of the Lord to come into your public place to speak among you to the directing of your minds to God, being sent of the Lord that you might find your teacher; that your minds might be stayed alone upon God, and you might not gad abroad without you for a teacher: for the Lord God alone will teach his people ...

(Ibid.)

It might be thought a high-risk strategy. If people turned to the inner Light, there could be no guarantees that what they came to would be the same as what Fox held to be true. And yet it was only in this way that what they came to would be truly their own, not imposed upon them. It would be known 'experimentally', as Friends were fond of putting it: known in their own lived experience. Again, the parallel with psychotherapy is clear: only that which a client arrives at for herself, through her own inner exploration, will ultimately be helpful. The therapist can facilitate the exploration, but an imposition of her own views would in the long run be counterproductive.

The difference from psychotherapy is that Fox explicitly identifies the inner Light with the divine spirit. In other respects the analogy can be sustained. As in psychotherapy, the inner Light both enables people to see what has gone wrong in their lives and illumines the path to a better way, not in a sudden burst but by patiently attending to it and moving step by step, in accordance with what is recognized. Each of those aspects is important.

Thus, first, the inner Light, when attended to, activates and illuminates the conscience and gives an accurate sense of where things are not right.

> As the light opens and exercises thy conscience, it will ... let thee see invisible things, which are clearly seen by that which is invisible in thee ... That which is invisible is the light within thee, which he who is invisible has given thee a measure of. That will let thee see thy heart.
>
> (Ambler 2001: 28)

The conscience can be distorted, made dull or made hypersensitive, shaped or misshaped by early upbringing, society and our own previous choices. Fox knew this just as well as Freud did. So the inner Light is not the conscience itself, but rather that which, by patient exploration, will illuminate the conscience, correct its distortions and recognize the motivations for our actions: it 'will let thee see thy heart'.

The Light is gentle, but it is unsparing and can be painful as the seeker takes responsibility for their actions:

> Mind the pure light of God in you, which shows you your sin and evil; and how you have spent your time; and shows you how your minds go forth.
>
> If ye love the light it will let you see all your evil thoughts, words and actions, which be wrought out of God, and turn you from them; and coming into the light your works will be wrought in God, and your words will be from him, and so good.
>
> (Ambler 2001: 32)

This, after all, is the point: to empower a better, more constructive way of life, not simply to feel guilt or remorse but to be freed of it and enabled to live creatively. What Fox meant by 'sin and evil' or by 'works wrought in God' is yet to be explored: it will emerge in later chapters that this has more to do with violence and hatred (including self-hatred) on the one hand, and creativity and flourishing for oneself and all people on the other, than with conventional lists of 'sins' and good deeds.

Fox recognizes that it can be very painful to sustain honest attention to the Light, and very tempting to project its illumination onto other people rather than owning it oneself. He speaks of those who read in the Bible about people who did evil: Cain, Esau, Judas and others.

> And these said that it was they, they, they that were the lead people; putting it off from themselves; but when some of these came, with the light and spirit of Truth, to see into themselves, then they came to say, 'I, I, I, it is I myself that have been the Ishmael and the Esau', etc.
>
> (Fox 1952: 30)

Finding fault with others, or turning away from the Light oneself, may feel like the easier option, but in the end it is not the way that leads to inner freedom.

> In the light that shows you all this, stand, neither go to the right hand nor to the left; here patience is exercised, here is thy will subjected ... For the first step to peace is to stand still in the light (which discovers things contrary to it) for power and strength to stand against that nature which the light discovers: for here grace grows, here is God alone glorified and exalted, and the unknown truth, unknown to the world, made manifest.
>
> (Ambler 2001: 34)

What we have here is not the expectation of a sudden, overwhelming mystical experience, but rather a slow process of patient discernment, in which these things that have gone wrong are not projected onto others but acknowledged, and a way is found to move on.

Although this process requires recognition of wrong-doing, its purpose is not to intensify feelings of guilt or inadequacy but to set people free from such burdens. As I shall discuss in more detail in the following chapters, Quakers differed from those in the Calvinist traditions who emphasized sin and guilt and total human depravity. Sin and guilt there certainly is; but Fox also insisted that there is 'that of God' in everyone: that all people are created by divine goodness, and that goodness, though dirtied and clouded, is never completely effaced. Indeed it is because of it that we are able to respond to the Light, repent of wrong, and find a better way. By attending to the inner Light, darkness is dispelled and the good is raised up and nourished. Thus Fox writes,

> Keep your habitations, that ye may every one feel your spring in the light which comes from the Lord, and feel your nourishment and refreshment; which waters the plants and causeth them to grow up in the Lord, from whom the pure, living springs come.
>
> (Ambler 2001: 46)

The central model for Fox is the organic model of life and growth, for which such favourite terminology as 'light', 'seed', 'springs of life' and 'nourishment' has obvious relevance. Even though it uses much standard Christian vocabulary, it is a thought world removed from the forensic model of sin, guilt, debt and depravity for which payment must be made to a God of judgement: we shall see further aspects of this contrast in later chapters. Openness to the Light enables growth and flourishing.

> For those with the light ... loving it and walking in it and waiting in it, power is given and strength; and being obedient to it and faithful in a little you will grow up to be rulers over much.
>
> (Ambler 2001: 90)

Again there are clear parallels with psychotherapy. The truth which is revealed by waiting in the Light is not primarily a truth to be believed or given a tick in a checklist of assertions. It is to be lived. It is a practice, a whole way of life, not a doctrine: the question is not so much one of *knowing* the truth but of *doing* the truth, living step by step in accordance with what the Light reveals.

> Every one is to be in it, and to walk in the truth, and in the spirit, and to come to the truth in their own particulars ... And so none can worship the God of truth, but who come to the truth in their own hearts.
>
> (Ambler 2001: 16)

Complete integrity is required, not as an external imposition but because without honestly living by what one already knows one will never be able to gain any further insight. Self-deception, or refusal to live in the Light one already has, forecloses the possibility of progress.

> When once you deny the Truth then you are given over to believe lies ... Oh, therefore, tremble before the Lord ye hypocrites, and mind the light of God in you, which shows you the deceit of your hearts, and obey that. Disobeying your teacher is your condemnation.
>
> (Fox 1952: 135)

Again, this is not a condemnation or punishment handed out by an angry God demanding payment for sin. Rather, it is the natural consequence of refusal to live by what we know, deliberate self-blinding.

It is impossible to be completely honest before the Light if one is simultaneously harbouring practices of deceit towards others. Thus 'doing the truth' is not only a private or personal matter, but extends to all practical relations. Fox wrote to merchants and all involved in financial transactions:

> Be plain, righteous and holy ... Loathe deceit ... hard-heartedness, wronging, cozening, cheating or unjust dealing. But live and reign in the

righteous Life and Power of God ... doing the Truth to all, without respect to persons, high or low whatsoever, young or old, rich or poor ... In all your dealings, buyings, sellings, changings and commerce with people, let Truth be the head and practice it ...

(Jones 1989: 154)

It was this principle of scrupulous honesty in business and monetary affairs that, with time, led to Quakers being trusted by the wider populace and contributed to the success of such financial institutions as Barclays Bank and Lloyds of London, both initially Quaker enterprises. It was also this which was at the basis of Quakers' refusal to take oaths, as though their word might be less than honest when they had not sworn. Many were imprisoned for this refusal (indeed not tendering an oath of loyalty to the king was often a pretext for persecution), but they remained firm in their conviction that they must live in the truth at *all* times and that swearing of oaths tacitly cheapened that principle. This was not a matter of adherence to a set of moral rules that included prohibitions against lying, swearing or cheating. Rather, it was the logical consequence of valuing the inner Light, which will reveal truth – the truth that is to be *done* – only insofar as we live truthfully, faithful to what we already know.

Accordingly, those who are faithful to the Light within are illumined by it not so that they know more truths or have a longer list of correct beliefs but so that they are the Light of the world. Having integrity themselves, and having no stake in dishonest practices, they are more able to assess what is going on without delusion. As Fox was fond of saying, 'In the light walk, and ye will shine' (Ambler 2001: 82). It is not that Quakers are inherently wiser or better people than anyone else. Rather, because their first concern is to attend to the Light within and obey its promptings, they are out of step with any sort of pretence and have no investment in corruption of any kind, whether at the level of the individual or the political system. Neither are the forms of pomposity to be regarded. A person is of value in themselves, not because of their clothes or customary forms of address or ceremony. Thus Quakers held to principles of plain speaking and respect for everyone equally: no bowing and scraping to the upper classes or even the king, and no belittling of the poor. These attitudes and practices foster the freedom to have real insight into what is going on around them without being preoccupied with their own honour or status. Fox wrote:

And so, live in the Truth, by which you may see over that which stains, corrupts, cankers, loads and burdens the creation. By which Power of God and Truth you may answer the Spirit of God in all.

(Jones 1989: 169)

And again,

> This light which is of God lets thee see all the works of the world, and draws thee out of the worships of the world, and keeps thee in the fear of God.
>
> (Ambler 2001: 102)

If Friends are able to see into pride, corruption and evil doings, the point is not to adopt a self-righteous vantage point but to do their best to improve matters.

> In the meantime, while ye are ... taking notice of others' cruelty, tyranny and persecution, turn your eyes upon yourselves, and see what ye are doing at home. To the light of Christ Jesus in all your consciences I speak, which cannot lie, nor err, nor bear false witness; but doth bear witness for God, and cries for equity, justice and righteousness to be executed.
>
> (Ambler 2001: 80)

It is from this source, therefore, that the peace testimony ultimately flows, not simply a refusal to commit violence but an engagement with equity and justice. I shall leave fuller discussion of the peace testimony to Chapter 5, but point out here that it is not an incidental precept but follows directly from the teaching of the inner Light, a Light which illuminates only as it is practised. It is not for nothing that Fox exhorts most solemnly:

> I do charge you all in the presence of the living God to dwell in what you speak and profess. None to profess what he does not dwell in and none to profess what he is not; a sayer and not a doer ... Wherefore to you I speak, Friends, that dwell in the light and love it, that to the light in all consciences of them that hate it ... you may be manifest ...
>
> (Jones 1989: 33)

Hypocrisy is not simply one in a list of possible moral failings. A hypocrite turns away from the Light within and thereby chooses darkness. One who does not obey the Light cannot expect to see further.

In this, Quaker teaching of the inner Light is again remarkably similar to psychotherapy, as I have observed several times. There is no progress without honest, patient attention and obedience to the Light already understood. Quakers used much more overtly Christian terminology than does modern psychotherapy, and although they stood at an angle to traditional Christendom they took the Bible, God and Christ very seriously. But though their terminology was different, their method was much the same.

There is, however, a glaring difference. There is no therapist. Friends gathered in silent meetings to attend to the inner Light, each one for themself, but also for the gathered meeting. Anyone, male or female, rich or poor, young or old could speak to the meeting if they felt prompted to do so, but the value of the meeting did not depend on such ministry. Nevertheless, the group was of immense support to its members; and regular meeting was crucial to early Friends, much as consistent sessions are necessary for effective therapy. In a sense, the group *is* the therapist in Quaker thinking.

> Mind the light, that all may be refreshed one in another, and all in one. And the God of power and love keep all Friends in power, in love, that there be no surmisings, but pure refreshings in the unlimited love of God, which makes one another known in the conscience, to read one another's hearts: being comprehended into this love, it is inseparable, and all are here one.
>
> (Ambler 2001: 58)

Friends were encouraged to open their hearts to one another and to be generous in their love, encouragement and support of each other as they sought, individually and collectively, to attend to the Light. It was also in the group that the leadings and promptings felt by an individual would be sounded out, tested, weighed for error, and given approbation and support – including practical and financial support – if the group could unite with it. I shall return to the question of error in Chapter 6.

The collective nature of attending to the Light reveals a further difference from modern psychotherapeutic practice. The latter is private, personal and individual, though of course a person who has come to inner freedom and resolution may have a public impact. But in early Quaker teaching, attending to the Light was more than a matter of finding an individual way forward. Though it was certainly that, it was also for the meeting – or even the Quaker movement – as a whole. There was group commitment to social and political action prompted by the Light within, which directed Friends to a 'concern'. In the years following the restoration of the monarchy there were periods of intense persecution, and a central shared concern was how to conduct themselves in the face of it and how to help Friends who were imprisoned or otherwise suffering. In 1683 Fox wrote to a small group of Quakers in the American colony of Carolina, encouraging them to use their liberty well, and contrasting it with the situation in England at the time.

> For we are here under great persecution, between thirteen and fourteen hundred in prison; an account of which has lately been delivered to the King. Besides the great spoil and havoc which is made of Friends' goods by informers; and besides the great spoil upon the two-thirds of our estates, and upon the twenty pound a month acts, and for not going to the steeple house; and besides many more are imprisoned and praemunired for not swearing allegiance, both men, women, widows and maids; and many are fined and cast into prison, as rioters, for meeting to worship God; and

we are kept out of our meetings in streets and highways in many places of
the land, and beaten and abused; therefore prize the liberty, both natural
and spiritual, that you enjoy.

(Jones 1989: 419)

In later years, when they were no longer being persecuted, Quakers felt prompted to concerns that looked outward from themselves: slavery and racial justice,
economic equity, mental health, education, wars and empire, and more recently
issues of nuclear war, militarism, ecology and international debt. Typically a
particular prompting would lead an individual or small group to raise a concern
with a local meeting, and if it was shared or 'owned' it would be passed on to
regional or national meetings where a course of appropriate action would be set
in motion. Although human fallibility and frailty naturally comes into play, the
intention is that ultimately all action is grounded and guided by the inner Light,
discerned by the individual and the group in ever widening circles. I shall say
more about specific instances later.

I have already acknowledged that early Friends, Fox among them, did not
place great emphasis on beauty. In this they were similar to their Puritan
context. However, this lack of emphasis must be qualified in ways that point
to a richer evaluation. The Light within not only illuminates one's own inner
life but also enables a new appreciation of the beauty of creation. Fox writes
of his own experience of moving into the Light:

Now was I come up in spirit through the flaming sword into the paradise
of God. All things were new, and all the creation gave another smell to me
than before, beyond what words can utter … The creation was opened to
me, and it was showed me how all things had their names given them
according to their nature and virtue … And the Lord showed me that such
as were faithful to him in the power and light of Christ, should come up
into that state in which Adam was before he fell, in which the admirable
works of the creation, and the virtues thereof, may be known, through the
openings of that divine Word of wisdom and power by which they
were made.

(Fox 1952: 27)

This appreciation was related not only to beauty but also to utility: the experience caused Fox to consider briefly whether he ought to 'practice physic'. He
realized, however, that those who found inner freedom by attending to the Light
within were thereby given the delight of the beauty of the earth.

He that believes in the light sees the joy, the comfort, the paradise, the
garden of God, the garden of pleasure. He sees how they walk under
curtains, how God has garnished the heavens and clothed the earth with
grass and trees and herbs, how all the creatures stand in their places,

keeping their unity. He sees the sun and moon in their courses, and the stars keeping the law of the covenant of God ...

(Ambler 2001: 100)

The admiration was focused on order and harmony, key elements in early ideas of beauty; but the response was not one of cool assessment but of joy and delight in the 'garden of pleasure' that is the world of nature. It is an opening to a more explicit development of spirituality than is usually found in the writings of early Quakers.

Chapter 5

Choose life!
Early Quaker women[1]

Early Quakers, wanting a mark that would distinguish them from worldly ostentation, adopted a plain style of clothing that came to be known as 'Quaker grey'. Not all of them approved of this, however. Opposition came even from Margaret Fell, often seen as the Mother of Quakerism, who had lived all her life in south Lakeland, with its vibrant colours of hills, sky and sea. She wrote with some acidity against the grey uniform:

> we must look at no colours, nor make anything that is changeable colours as the hills are, nor sell them, nor wear them: but we must all be in one dress and one colour: this is a silly poor Gospel. It is more fit for us, to be covered with God's Eternal Spirit, and clothed with his Eternal Light, which leads us and guides us into righteousness. Now I have set before you life and death, and desire you to choose life, and God and his truth.
>
> (Fell 1995: 20.21)

History went against Margaret Fell. Quaker grey was adopted; and although for many it indicated the plainness and simplicity which characterized all of life, it also symbolized an inward turning, away from the radical religion and politics of the early years of the Society of Friends and toward a preoccupation with details of dress and the keeping of rules (cf. Punshon 1984; Mack 1992).

Discussion of Quaker simplicity and its outward expression must wait another occasion. What I wish to do here is to note the stark terms in which Margaret Fell presented the choice. Was she not being unnecessarily extreme in her rhetoric? – after all, one would hardly think that the decision whether or not to wear grey was a matter of life and death. Yet that is how she put it. To her way of thinking, drab uniformity was a betrayal of the Gospel itself, a refusal of the light and life and flourishing in which she had taken her life's stand.

The seventeenth century in England was a period much preoccupied with death and violence, a preoccupation which has significantly shaped modernity (see Dollimore 1998). This chapter is a case study of some of the ways in which early Quakers, particularly Margaret Fell and other early Quaker women, stood at an angle to this preoccupation with death and offered a creative alternative.

It is a truism to say that early Quakers were at odds in significant respects with the social expectations and norms of seventeenth-century England as it stood on the cusp of modernity; and they suffered much for it. It is also obvious that some of the things for which they were feared or ridiculed had as much to do with perceived intervention in the social symbolic as with material things: the refusal of hat honour, for example, or the adoption of plain speech or indeed Quaker grey. These characteristics, which were given enormous importance both by Quakers themselves and by their detractors, were not things that had physical or economic impact on society in the same way that refusal of tithes or refusal of military service might have: if a Quaker did not pay a tithe, somebody would have less money as a result; but if a Quaker refused hat honour, the effect was on a purely symbolic level. Though early Quakers did not put it in these terms, of course, it is clear that they were quite deliberately disrupting the social symbolic of early modernity and offering an alternative to it. If, as I would hold, the social symbolic of the seventeenth century set the pattern for the development of western culture in modernity, especially in relation to death and violence, then it is worthwhile investigating the Quaker women's writings to see what alternative can be offered.

I have chosen to focus on early Quaker *women* for several reasons. First, although they wrote a good deal, and their writings are increasingly accessible, they have been much less studied than their male counterparts, and some redressing of the balance is in order. Second, because of the radical reconsideration of gender and equality among early Friends, Quaker women took on quite different gender roles from that which was common in society at large. They were thus already differently situated; and thus in a position where they had to rethink aspects of the taken-for-granted symbolic. It is to be expected, then, that this situation gave them a particularly sharp focus on the norms and conventions of gendered society, and in some respects clear differentiation from it. However, I would not wish to be understood as saying that Quaker men were not also at an angle to the prevailing symbolic: clearly they were, and usually in ways similar to women. The detail of that must await another study, as also must consideration of the parallels and contrasts between Quaker and non-Quaker women like Margaret Cavendish, Mary Astell or Aphra Benn.

Quaker women were of course part of seventeenth-century society even while standing against it in some respects. It should therefore not be surprising that the symbolic which we find operating in their writings is often ambiguous. They were part of the life and thought of their time, and it is no wonder that they shared its patterns and assumptions. What is surprising is that they challenged them as often and as radically as they did. I shall therefore investigate four related aspects of early Quaker women's writings to see how they stood with and against the preoccupation with death and violence of early modernity.

Quaker women's claim of authority

Early Quaker women like Margaret Fell, Dorothy White, Sarah Blackbarrow, Katharine Evans and Sarah Chevers used a self-consciously prophetic and apocalyptic rhetoric of the time as vigorously as did any male writers. The authority of their voice is striking: they never apologize for their gender or for claiming the right to preach and write, whether to those in power or to common humanity. Margaret Fell, in her 'Letter to King Charles' in 1666, written from her imprisonment in Lancaster Castle to admonish him to release Quakers from persecution and prison, reminds the king that

> every Mortal Man hath but a Moment in this Life, either to Serve, Fear, and Honour the Lord, and therein to receive Mercy from him; or else to Transgress, Sin, Disobey, and Dishonour him, and so receive the Judgment of Eternal Misery.
>
> (Garmen *et al.* 1996: 45)

These were strong words for a woman to address to a king. Just as strong, and at much greater length, were the words of Katherine Evans when she and Sarah Chevers were imprisoned in Malta en route to Alexandria on a missionary journey, and in Malta were interrogated by the Inquisition. Katherine Evans went on what today would be called a hunger strike and, at the end of it, having eaten her first food in twelve days, writes:

> in the midst of our extremity the Lord sent his holy Angels to comfort us ... and in the time of our great trial, the Sun and Earth did mourn visibly three dayes, and the horror of death and pains of Hell was upon me: the Sun was darkened, the Moon was turned into Blood, and the Stars did fall from heaven and there was great tribulation ten dayes, such as never was from the beginning of the world; and then did I see the Son of man coming in the Clouds, with power and great glory, triumphing over his enemies; the Heavens were on fire, and the Elements did melt with fervent heat, and the Trumpet sounded out of Sion, and an Allarum was struck up in Jerusalem, and all the Enemies of God were called to the great day of the Battle of the Lord.
>
> (Garmen *et al.* 1996: 180)

And so on and on. Nor does there seem ever to be a moment of self-doubt or questioning. Katherine Evans is entirely clear that her enemies are to be identified with Babylon, the Devil and the Pope, while she and her companion are of God. She is unsure of whether they will get out of prison alive, or escape the Inquisition; but she is never unsure that she is in the right. Although her certainties strike me as arrogance, I cannot but be amazed at the self-confidence of this (extra)ordinary woman in 1662, separated from her companion by the prison warders, alone in a cell in very unpleasant conditions, interrogated for months on end by delegates of the Inquisition who promised her only torture and imprisonment until she died.

Along with the authority claimed by these and other early Quaker women in their apocalyptic utterances and throughout their writings, their immersion in scripture is also striking. Virtually every phrase of the above quotation is from the Bible, lifted and strung together to convey Katherine Evans's message. This saturation in biblical language, reminiscent of medieval monastic writers like Bernard of Clairvaux (Bernard of Clairvaux, 1977–80), is characteristic of many Quaker women. It is used to great effect, for instance, in Margaret Fell's *True Testimony from the People of God*, as well as in her defence of women's ministry, *Women's Speaking Justified, Proved and Allowed by the Scriptures*; we find it also in Dorothy White's apocalyptic *Trumpet of the Lord of Hosts*, and in Elizabeth Bathurst's much more sober doctrinal treatise, *Truth's Vindication*, and indeed in most Quaker women's writings of the time. Sometimes the interweaving of Biblical phrases is so dense that the woman's own voice gets lost: when Susannah Blandford writes that she cried to God out of the deep because her brethren were involved with a golden calf, but God told her to be still and wait for the Wind to separate the Wheat from the Chaff, it is not exactly obvious what incident she might have been referring to in the medley of Biblical allusions (Garmen *et al.* 1996: 300). I shall come back later to the relationship between their use of the Bible and the way these women understood the inner Light. For the present, I wish simply to note that the thoroughness with which they knew and were able to marshal the scriptures in their writings shows a level of literacy and education well above the average for the mid-seventeenth century, and indicates both the importance attached by Quakers to women's education and immersion in scriptures and also probably something about their class background (see Mack 1992 and Graham *et al.* 1989). This does not by itself account for their courage and competence to claim the authority to speak and write publicly; there were, after all, many Puritan women of the rising middle class who were well educated but who did not take such things upon themselves (Hannay 1985). But once the breakthrough to women's ministry had been made by early Friends, the women had the skills to carry out that ministry with great effect.

This world and the next: apocalyptic writing and Quaker women

Quaker women in the seventeenth century believed that they lived in momentous times. They were right: the seventeenth century was, after all, the century of the civil war, regicide, the rise of parliament and the restoration of the monarchy. The political turmoil was paralleled by social and economic upheaval: the rise of modern science and medicine, the beginnings of colonialism, the fur trade and the slave trade, the growth of competitive individualism. It was 'a world turned upside down' (Hill 1972). Perhaps it is only to be expected that in such turbulent times people with intense religious sensibilities would think in terms of the end of the world: certainly there is a strong apocalyptic tone to many of the Puritan writers, as well as to the many separatist sects that flourished during the civil war and its aftermath. Puritans made much of Calvinistic doctrines of election and predestination (Haller 1938: 85), looking forward to eternal salvation in a heavenly place after bodily death. A devout Puritan was a 'stranger and pilgrim in this world' whose citizenship was in a heavenly city (Barbour 1964: 3).[2] Puritans thundered against the cities of this world, which they identified with the whoring Babylon of the apocalypse; the king and popery were manifestations of the Antichrist.[3] At first sight such attitudes seem to have all the classic characteristics of obsession with death and life after death.

When we look more closely, however, that impression turns out to be a distortion, at least of the period before and during the civil war. The New Jerusalem to which these Puritans and sectarians looked forward was not a heavenly city in the sky after death, but a heavenly city built upon earth, a Jerusalem built 'in England's green and pleasant land', as Blake was to put it several centuries later. John Eliot, a missionary to native North Americans and by no means a firebrand in his time, wrote that 'Christ is the only right Heir of the Crown of England ... and he is now come to take possession of his Kingdom, making England first in that blessed work of setting up the Kingdom of the Lord Jesus' (quoted in Barbour 1964: 29). As Hugh Barbour points out in his study of the period, it was the widespread expectation of Christ coming to be King that prevented Cromwell from taking the throne of England for himself.[4]

Along with the hope that the world itself would be transformed into the New Jerusalem went an appreciation of the world, an emphasis on science and exploration, whether of the stars, the seas, or the plants and animals of the earth. Christopher Hill has shown how scientific exploration, invention and navigation aligned themselves with the Puritan and Parliamentarian groupings of pre-revolutionary England (see Hill 1965). Richard Baxter, the great Puritan preacher, exclaimed:

> All the world are our servants, that we may be the servants of God ...
> How many thousand plants and flowers and fruits and birds and beasts do attend us! The sea, with its inhabitants, the air, the wind, the frost and snow, the heat and fire, the clouds and rain, all wait upon us while we do our work.
>
> (Quoted in Barbour 1964: 8–9.)[5]

The idea of the Puritan as one who hates this world would find very little support in the first half of the seventeenth century. Their apocalypticism, rather, is a denunciation of the corruption and degradation of the world by those who do not honour its Creator and King, and a concerted effort to reclaim the world as the Kingdom of God.

All this changed with the collapse of the Protectorate and the restoration of the monarchy in 1660. Charles II, not Jesus Christ, was on the English throne. The often frivolous and dissipated court found ways to punish and marginalize the Parliamentarians and Puritans, and to indulge in the sorts of pleasures typified by Restoration comedy – anathema to the Puritans. For those who had expected the New Jerusalem, disillusionment set in. Although many continued to look for the Kingdom of God, they increasingly looked more toward heaven and the world to come beyond the grave, and tacitly gave up the expectation that God's Kingdom was about to arrive on earth. Puritan and radical writings increasingly condemned this world and all its works, showed disgust with the material body and its sexuality, and looked forward to death as a release from this evil state to the heavenly kingdom in the life beyond.

It is within this changing and complex political context that early Quaker writing must be understood (see Gwyn 1995). George Fox's *Journal* recounts his calling, in his early life, to preach to people, 'forewarning them of the great and terrible day of the Lord which would come upon them all': it is set in a context of denunciation of hat honour, 'popish' ceremonies and rituals, social customs of music, games and public festivities, and an exhortation to school-masters and mistresses to teach children the 'new covenant of light'.[6] It is to this extent consistent with the apocalyptic writings of the early Puritans who looked for the establishment of the Kingdom of God on this earth rather than for another world beyond death. The same is true of other male Quaker apocalyptic writings, such as Edward Burrough's *The Great Mistery of the Great Whore Unfold* (1659). None of this should be taken to imply that the early Quakers (any more than the early Puritans) did not believe in life after death, final judgement, heaven and hell. They did, of course. The point, rather, is that they saw the task of their lives as bringing about social and religious change in *this* world, rather than merely preparing themselves for the next.

Although Quaker women of the second half of the seventeenth century adopt an apocalyptic rhetoric, sometimes stridently, I find in their writings a stance that is at an angle to the death-obsessed apocalypticism prevalent in these times of disillusionment at the restoration of the monarchy and the failure of Christ's Kingdom to arrive on earth. Esther Biddle, writing in 1662 – two years after the restoration of the monarchy – addresses her apocalyptic writing to issues of justice and integrity in *this* political situation, not in some other world beyond the grave. She entitles her tract, 'The Trumpet of the Lord Sounded forth unto these Three Nations' – that is, England, Scotland and Ireland – and specifies 'especially unto Thee, Oh England, who art looked upon as the Seat of Justice, from whence righteous Laws should proceed' (Garmen *et al.* 1996: 129). Her exhortation to the king and his court, as well as to the bishops and priests of the established church, is an exhortation to repentance and justice, for this world, not for some other. Though she does not fail to warn them that 'the Fire is kindled, and the Furnace is even hot, in which your works and worship, Faith and Religion must be tryed' (131–32) these are not the fires of hell but the fires of purification. Only if their deeds are not just will they eventually be 'Banished from the presence of the King of Heaven for evermore ... and you shall be a stink to Ages to come' (134).

Much more overt in her emphasis on life rather than death is Dorothy White, writing in the same year (1662), a tract with a rather similar title, 'A Trumpet of the Lord of Hosts, Blown unto the City of London and unto the Inhabitants Thereof ... '. Her pronouncements of judgement on the injustices of London are vehement, yet she keeps breaking into the theme of Life, that 'true Light which leadeth to Eternal Life' (139). When, toward the end of her tract, she addresses fellow Quakers, she pleads with them, 'O little Love, overcome, overcome all your hearts, that Life may fill your vessels ... ' (140). And in a second section of 'A Trumpet' she says of the 'Glorious Day of the Lord God':

> So all must be gathered into the Fold, all must know an entering into the Rest, all must know a gathering into the Life, and into the Power, which maketh all things new.
>
> (142)

This emphasis on Life and its potential for newness and creative change, both of the individual and of the social order, is on a different plane from the focus on death and doom found in much apocalyptic writing of the later seventeenth century.

It is this clear sounding of the note of life, newness and creativity that comes out most clearly in Margaret Fell's *A True Testimony from the People of God*, presented to King Charles II on his accession to the throne in 1660. The language, particularly of the preamble 'Epistle to the Reader', is the language of the biblical book of Revelations: 'The day of the Lord is come', Margaret Fell declares; the nations have drunk 'the cup of abomination and fornication', and now 'the day is come that Babylon is come up in remembrance with the Lord. The day of her judgments is come. The vials are pouring upon the seat and head of the beast' (Fell 1992: 15). Up to this point in her text, Fell's writing is standard apocalyptic fare, not much different in kind from that thundered out by many a Puritan divine in the seventeenth century. The pronouncements of judgement were taken to extremes, even by the standards of the time, by sects like the Fifth Monarchy Men (see McGregor and Reay 1984), and attracted the wrath of the authorities. Because Quakers also were perceived as radical, a good deal of the ensuing persecution fell upon them as well (see Gwyn 1986).

Yet in this text of Margaret Fell's, we can discern a difference from other sects. Rather than simply pronounce judgement and doom, Margaret Fell continues: 'The darkness is expelling. The light is arising out of obscurity and shining secretly in the hearts of people where God's appearance and manifestation are, where he writes his law, and puts his spirit in the inward parts ... ' (Fell 1992: 15). Rather than look only toward catastrophe and punishment, Fell's emphasis is on the new possibilities emerging among Friends, and is an account of what those new possibilities are and why they should now be coming to the fore. If the king and society will not take heed to this 'current of life' which is now on offer (30), then they should beware, because 'the Lord is arisen in his mighty power, with his fan in his hand. He is separating the chaff from the wheat, is gathering the wheat into his garner, and will burn up the chaff with unquenchable fire' (16). Yet for all the sharpness of the warning in the 'Epistle', the central message of *True Testimony*, to which it forms a prologue, is a discussion of the way in which God's Spirit comes, not through outward things like the letter of the scripture or the authority of the church, but through the inner life and teaching of the Spirit, available to all, including the king, if he will but heed the living spirit of God. I shall come back to this point.

It is a central feature of the preoccupation with death in the west that it denigrates *this* world and looks for some other, better world not contaminated by this world's faults. In apocalyptic writing of the Restoration period this is regularly expressed as damnation and destruction of this present evil world and the salvation out of it of a special remnant who are taken away to a heavenly kingdom. In some ways these characteristics also appear in Fell's *True Testimony*: she warns of judgement, as we have seen, and she writes in advocacy of a remnant, the true people of God. But there is also a great difference. Margaret Fell's *True Testimony* vibrates with references to life: life not in some heaven or other world, but life here, now, welling up in hearts alive to the fountain of life.

Thus the reason for the 'apostacy and darkness' which had come over the world was that 'false apostles' had 'turned aside from the life and power' and were thus unable to discern the inner voice of the Spirit (Fell 1992: 20). This Spirit Margaret Fell again and again describes as the 'Spirit of life' or 'the Spirit of life and power' or the 'Spirit of life and truth that nourishes the soul and leads into all truth', 'the Spirit of the living God', the 'Spirit that gives life', as contrasted with the letter that kills (23; 32; 33). All these phrases are of course quotations or near quotations of biblical sources, and it might be thought that their use would be unremarkable in religious writing. Up to a point that is true; but I suggest that the ways in which Margaret Fell uses the trope of life go well beyond standard usage of the time. Her message is that this life is creative, it offers new possibilities, of which the emergence of the Quakers is evidence and promise. Far from emphasizing death and some other, better world, Margaret Fell emphasizes the new life and new possibilities for justice and truth that are springing up in this world, offering hope and flourishing. It is the denial of this life, the 'endeavour to limit the Spirit of the living God' (38), which has caused the ungodliness and death dealing of the age, says Fell, and it is by returning to the life of God and finding in oneself that welling up of divine life which is the remedy, because it brings the possibility of radically new insight and action. There is, here, a challenge to the ways of thinking of early modernity, the contours of a different approach.

The Lamb's war and the symbolic of violence

This challenge emerges more strongly when we see how early Quaker women confronted issues of warfare and violence that were a significant part of the symbolic of death and that took particular forms in the late seventeenth century. There was of course plenty of actual war and violence and death in that turbulent period: the civil war, the beheading of Charles I, and the war with the Dutch took up much of the century, to say nothing of Cromwell's forcible occupation of Ireland and the violent 'pacification' of dissenters nearer home. England was also busy exporting violence, as Canada was opened up for the fur trade, and colonialism and the slave trade of the Atlantic triangle got into full swing. Not much attention has been paid to the fact that north Lancashire and Westmorland, which was crucial as a cradle of Quakerism, was also at that time crucial to navigation and slavery: Ulverston was a significant port and a centre of ship building, and Spark Bridge nearby had a large slave market where men and women newly brought from Africa were sold at auction for the West Indies plantations. Swarthmoor Hall (one of the historic centres of the birth of Quakerism in 1652) was only a few miles away, within easy walking distance. The warfare and violence of the age were so deeply ingrained that major thinkers took it for granted. Thomas Hobbes, in 1651, assumed that in a 'state of nature' there would be 'a war of all against all' (Hobbes 1968). That much could be taken without argument; the question was only how to deal with it. Other philosophers and political thinkers shared the premise and differed from Hobbes only in terms of what to do about it.[7]

Against all this, early Quakers took a stand. George Fox sought not only not to do violence but 'to live in the virtue of that life and power that took away the occasion of all wars' (Fox 1952: 65), refused to enlist in the army (67; cf. 197–98), and warned against 'doing violence to any man' (157) though much was done to him. In spite of their frequent and violent imprisonments, beatings and other sufferings at the hands of church and state, Friends were committed to pacifism, both in the negative sense of not reciprocating violence and in the positive sense of working for that which makes for peace. In 1659 George Fox wrote to Quakers:

> All Friends everywhere, take heed to keep out of the powers of the earth that run into wars and fightings, which make not for peace but go from that ... Keep in peace, and the love and power of God, and unity and love to one another ... and so know a kingdom which hath no end, and fight for that with spiritual weapons, which take away the occasion of the

carnal; and there gather men to war, as many as you can, and set up as many as you will with these weapons.

(358; cf. 357; 398–404)

It was a radical stance in a world filled with violence.

George Fox was of course not alone in emphasizing spiritual warfare, nor was he the first. For Puritan thinkers, too, 'the main business of Christian wayfaring was war', the war of the spirit against the flesh and the world. William Haller, in his classic work on the period, asserts that the supreme image which, for that purpose, they sought to impress upon the minds of the people was that of 'the soldier enlisted under the banner of Christ' (Haller 1938: 150). Thus, as Haller goes on to observe, the symbolism of the Christian year, of nativity and even of atonement gave way to the symbolic of conflict between Christ and Satan: at the Fall in the garden of Eden, in Jesus's temptations in the wilderness, and in the Armageddon to come. This agonistic symbolic was reinforced in countless sermons, pamphlets and books (152). The preoccupation of the age with death and violence was thus internalized. The civil war was fought not only between Royalists and Parliamentarians: according to Puritan thinking, a civil war was perpetually fought within every Christian soul. The outer reality and the inward symbolic of death and violence reflected and reinforced one another.

A crucial difference of this from the early Quakers, as already observed, was that the Quakers renounced the outward expression of this violence: the warfare was to be exclusively spiritual. Yet I suggest that this was not the only difference. In their turning inward, the early Quakers also changed the shape of the symbolic, much mitigating its violence and its preoccupation with death. James Naylor called it 'the Lamb's War'; it was a gentle name for the inner struggle, and found much favour with early Friends.

> The Lamb ... hath called us to make War in righteousness for his name's sake, against Hell and death, and all the powers of darkness ... And they that follow the Lamb shall overcome, and get the victory over the Beast, and over the Dragon, and over the gates of Hell.
>
> (Burrough, quoted in Barbour 1964: 40)[8]

And it was overtly seen as a struggle for life, rather than an obsession with death.

> The Lamb's War you must know before you can witness his kingdom ... The Lamb wars ... in whomsoever he appears, and calls them to joyn with him herein ... with all their Might ... that he may form a new Man, a new Heart, new Thoughts, and a new Obedience ... and there is his Kingdom.
>
> (Naylor quoted in Barbour 1964: 40–41)

That this would have social consequences was not in doubt. This was not, in the seventeenth century, a turn away from the world, much less a romanticizing of it: the numbers of Friends in prison and enduring persecution would eliminate any such tendency. It was, however, a rejection of the world's methods of violence and warfare, an effort for a new symbolic and a new society.

In the lives and writings of women Quakers, the emphasis on life and newness receives further emphasis and the symbolic of violence – even the internal warfare stressed by Quaker men – is less pronounced. It does not disappear altogether: especially in the apocalyptic writings, images of battle and destruction are prominent. Nevertheless many of the women do not write in terms of warfare, and when they do, the emphasis falls differently. Sarah Blackbarrow, writing in 1658 (only six years after Quakers emerged as a coherent body, and while Cromwell was still alive) pleads with her readers who reject her message, that in them 'the pure spirit of the Lord which is light and life' is ignored, 'and the begotten of the Father of life eternall, strangled ... ' (Garmen *et al.* 1996: 51). Although she tries to persuade her readers, her imagery is less that of conflict or violence than a mixture of seeking, illumination and integrity. She speaks of the inner witness of God, 'which is faithful and true, and will not lye', and says, 'as you obey it you will come to see and know it, to be the beginning of the creation of God in you again ... ' (51). This newness of life was the aim, not simply the vanquishing of sin or Satan.

In 1660 Margaret Fell wrote an account of Quaker principles and practice to the newly crowned King Charles II and his parliament, which she called *We are the People of God called Quakers*. She asked for toleration and justice, freedom from the persecution to which they had been subjected. This declaration was signed also by thirteen prominent Quaker men, including George Fox. (That they were willing to have a woman represent them to the King, and to put their names to what a woman wrote, says much both about gender relations among early Friends and about Margaret Fell's personal stature and competence.) An important part of her reasoning with the King consisted of a presentation of the Quaker peace testimony, as it has come to be called; and in this the imagery of warfare, even internal warfare, is subdued. It is not completely absent: she speaks (quoting scripture) of 'weapons ... not carnal but spiritual', and she is honest about the internal conflict involved. But she states the Quaker position forthrightly, almost flatly:

> We are a people that follow after those things that make for peace, love and unity. It is our desire that others' feet may walk in the same. [We] do deny and bear our testimony against all strife, wars, and contentions that come from the lusts that war in the members, that war against the soul, which we wait for, and watch for in all people. [We] love and desire the good of all. For no other cause but love to the souls of all people have our sufferings been.
>
> (Fell 1992: 54)

It is this 'waiting for the soul', watching for the seeds of life in all people, that characterizes the writings of early Quaker women much more strongly than do metaphors of violence and war, even the gentler 'Lamb's War' of Quaker men. And these seeds of life and newness were not merely spiritual, leading to heaven beyond the grave; they were, rather, simplicity, integrity, plain speech and efforts for social justice that early Friends paid for with persecution, imprisonment and violence.

Women, along with men, did not shrink from the logic of this peace testimony whose aim was life and goodness rather than death and violence. If they were intent on trying to remove the occasion for war, this could best be done by opening channels of communication with those who might have resorted to violence, and trying to eliminate causes of oppression and inequality. Thus we find early Friends undertaking journeys which even by today's standards would be daunting, and by the standards of the time were nothing short of heroic. Among the earliest to 'travel in the ministry', as it came to be called, were Katherine Evans and Sarah Chevers, who, after various journeys in Scotland and England where they were imprisoned and publicly stripped and beaten, went together in 1658 en route to Alexandria: not the sort of destination that would be immediately obvious, but part of the concerted Quaker effort to publish the news of life as they understood it. I have already mentioned their suffering when they fell into the hands of the Inquisition when their ship put in at Malta. Other Quakers went to Holland, Germany and other parts of the continent of Europe, while still others went to the New World, as did Fox himself. Quakers' efforts to work for peace and understanding took them into situations where they themselves experienced violence, often from the same groups of Puritans who gave them trouble at home.[9]

Clearly illustrative of the efforts of women to work creatively for better understanding and a refusal to collude with oppression was the journey of Joan Vokins to New England and several Caribbean islands. George Fox with some companions had been there ten years before, and had met with both Blacks and whites (Fox 1952: 594–611). In the meantime, however, a law had been passed prohibiting Blacks in Quaker meetings in British colonies,[10] and when George Fox was asked about what the Quaker response should be, he encouraged 'civil disobedience' (Fox 1952: 717). By the time Joan Vokins went, she experienced difficulty even getting to the islands; but by various means she managed to get from one to another, often against the advice and wishes of those on whose ships she took passage, and sometimes in peril of her life. Against considerable odds, Vokins got to Barbados, and says of her time there,

> most Days I had two or three Meetings of a Day, both among the Blacks, and also among the White People: And the power of the Lord Jesus was mightily manifested, so that my Soul was, often melted therewith, even in the Meetings of the Negro's or Blacks, as well as among Friends.
>
> (Garmen *et al.* 1996: 270)

The troubling distinction between 'Blacks' and 'Friends' – the implicit assumption is that Friends are white – shows something to be desired in Vokins' attitudes. Nevertheless, this is light years ahead of her time: while others were capturing and enslaving Black Africans and selling them to the Caribbean market, Vokins goes to Meetings with them, 'her Soul ... often melted therewith'. It is an enactment of the peace testimony, at great personal cost; and it stands in direct contrast to the violent exploitation and death as enacted in British imperialist policy in the late seventeenth century.

'Come home to within': locating the divine

Nobody doubts that early Quakers, especially early Quaker women, had different principles and practices from their contemporaries in seventeenth-century England. What I am arguing is that not only is this the case, but that at the deeper level of the social symbolic, their perspective was fundamentally different. Whereas society was mired ever more deeply in an obsession with death and violence which became the symbolic of later modernity, Quaker women were much more concerned with choosing life, developing life and peace. I do not wish to overstate the difference between Quaker men and women in this regard: Quaker men were as deeply committed to the peace testimony as were the women, and suffered as much for it. My impression is that women were just a little farther out on the same limb as the men in the development of a symbolic of life as against the symbolic of violence and death.

But if it is the case that the Quaker symbolic was at an angle to that of the late seventeenth century, the question that cries out for an answer is how this came to be so. What was at the root of the difference? What enabled Quakers to focus on justice in this world while others called for its destruction and thought that a better world could be found only beyond the grave? What gave them the insight and courage to develop a peace testimony in a world as full of violence as theirs?

One answer may be that because war is a gendered activity, women, who did not go to fight, were able to see and deplore the violence and carnage all around them. This would be true of non-Quaker women too, of course; but because of the greater gender equality among Quakers than in the rest of society, Quaker women's voices were heard more strongly and with greater respect, and therefore had greater influence on the collective testimonies of Friends. There is probably something in this, but it can hardly be the whole story, not least because their peace testimony seems to me to *flow out of* a symbolic of life rather than to precede or cause it.

I suggest, rather, that the key to the difference of symbolic is a difference in the Quaker location of the divine, a difference which became more acute with the passage of time. Whereas the rest of society – for all their religious differences – held to a concept of God sharply other than the world (a concept which in its extreme forms came to be known as Deism), Quakers believed that the divine was *within* human persons, a life and light and seed and fountain – they mixed their metaphors happily – in everyone. To show something of what they meant by this and how I think it grounded their symbolic, I will once again turn to the writings of women, though I would emphasize that men, too, held to and developed the teaching of God within.

Every Quaker knows Margaret Fell's account of her convincement. She reports that, as she sat with her children in Ulverston parish church, George Fox challenged the priest and congregation with the words, 'You will say, Christ saith this, and the Apostles say this; but what canst thou say? Art thou a child of Light, and hast walked in the Light, and what thou speakest, is it inwardly from God?' And Margaret Fell continues:

> This opened me so, that it cut me to the Heart; and then I saw clearly, we were all wrong ... And I cried in my Spirit to the Lord, We are all Thieves, we are all Thieves; we have taken the Scriptures in Words, and know nothing of them in ourselves.
>
> (Garmen *et al.* 1996: 235)

In some ways this recognition of the importance of internalizing the Gospel would hardly have been disputed by any Christian group: the Puritans after all emphasized personal faith and commitment; and the standard teaching of the established church, in word and sacrament, would concur with the need for personal, inward appropriation. Yet Margaret Fell seems to have meant something well beyond this standard teaching (which by all accounts of her early life she was already taking very seriously). Whatever exactly she meant at the time of her convincement, her subsequent thought led her to an understanding of God within that put her and those with her into a quite different symbolic frame.

By the time Margaret Fell wrote her *True Testimony* in 1660, the question of locating the divine was one that she found necessary to confront head on. Her central message is that Quakers base their teaching and practice and authority directly on 'the Spirit of life and truth that nourishes the soul and leads into all truth' (Fell 1992: 23). Whereas others insisted on the authority of the Bible and the teachings of the church, Margaret Fell writes (citing Jesus's saying to the woman of Samaria):

> Now I do ask all the teachers and professors of Christendom, where this Spirit is, that God is to be worshipped in, if it be not in man? ... Where this worship of God in the Spirit is performed, if it be not in man? Where God's throne is, where the Ancient of Days does sit? Where the scepter of Christ is swayed, which is a righteous scepter? Where the King is, that shall reign and prosper, whose name is called, The Lord our Righteousness?

(25)

It is only by the life of God *within*, locating the divine not in some far off heaven but sitting as King in the human heart, that it is possible to discern truth and righteousness. As Margaret Fell says in her *Declaration*: 'No people can retain God in their knowledge, and worship him as God, but first they must come to that of God in them' (53).

This insistence on the divine within was already crucial in the earliest Quaker writing. In 1650, several years before Margaret Fell's convincement, a woman named Sarah Jones, who identified herself as 'a poor widow of Bristol', wrote an epistle called 'This is Light's appearance in the Truth to all the precious dear Lambs of the Life', that is, to the earliest clusters of Friends in Bristol and beyond. Even at this very early date, her central message to her 'dear Lambs' is that they should 'sink down into that eternal word, and rest there, and not in any manifestations … sink down into that measure of life that ye have received, and go not out with your in-looking at what is contrary to you … ' (Garmen *et al.* 1996: 35). The Word, the Spirit of God, she insists, 'is in thy heart', and only harm can come to one who turns from this and 'goes a gadding and hunting after the manifestations that proceeds from the word in others' vessels' (36). As Dorothy White was to put it twelve years later, the Spirit is within; it is 'your choicest treasure'; and therefore 'let every man come home to within, and search his own house, that he may find that precious Pearl which hath been lost, even that true Light which leadeth unto Eternal Life' because it is this which 'brings up the soul of man out of death' (139). The linkages of the divine within rather than beyond, the emphasis on life, and the contrast with death are already firmly in place.

The question which the early Quakers would be bound to have to face, and sooner rather than later, was the relationship between the inner Light of the divine within and the authority of the Bible. I have already discussed Friends' saturation in scripture: it is obvious that they treasured and internalized it, learned it by heart so that their very thoughts were shaped by biblical phrases. Nevertheless, early Quakers held that it was only by the inner Light that one could recognize the truth of scripture, a truth which was as much a question of obedience and action as of belief: ''tis not Inky Character can make a Saint', said Elizabeth Bathurst in 1679 (Garmen *et al.* 1996: 341). It was this same Elizabeth Bathurst who developed a careful theological account of the Quaker understanding of Scripture, *Truth Vindicated*, which was as well reasoned and important in its time as Barclay's *Apology*, with which it was roughly contemporaneous.

Before her convincement Bathurst had struggled with the accusation that Quakers 'deny the Scriptures', the sacraments, and the sacrifice of Christ, together with the resurrection of the body and other standard Christian teachings. Bathurst completely rejects the idea that Quakers deny the scriptures. Yet she appeals to many instances in the Bible itself, which prove, as she says, 'by Scripture road' that while the Bible is to be believed and obeyed, it can only be understood by the Spirit within. She points out that the Bible itself never claims to be the Word of God, that Word who 'was with God and was God'; it claims only to 'bear witness of Him'. The words of the Bible are 'the Lord's words', but not *the* Word. 'So here it may be seen', she says, 'there is good reason to distinguish between written Words, the Writing or Letter, and the living Word, which is a quickening Spirit' (351). It is a fine distinction; here as elsewhere, Bathurst shows herself to be a careful scholar and an acute logician. She argues that, in view of the distinction, it is the Spirit of God who is the Rule of Faith and Guide of Life for Quakers, but 'yet doth not this detract from the Scriptures; or the respect in which they are held'. Quakers, she says, 'own' the scriptures.

> But they dare not ascribe them that Glory which is due to God, nor exalt them above his Son Christ Jesus, nor prefer them in his Spirit's stead; neither yet is it any Derogation from the Scriptures, to exalt Christ and his Spirit more than they.
>
> (352)

Long before it was usual to do so, Bathurst appealed as well to two further facts: first, that through corruptions of translation and transmission the Bible as we have it is not in any case infallible; and second, that the vast majority of humankind have lived and died without the scriptures, but it cannot be the case that there was 'no other means appointed for their Salvation' (352). This was radical theology for the late seventeenth century, though she did not take the further radical step of asking whether there might be any case of the inner Light and the scriptures not agreeing, and which should take priority in case of such conflict.

With the sacraments, Bathurst dealt rather more sharply. The baptism that is necessary for salvation is 'inward and spiritual', a baptism of the Holy Ghost, not a water baptism. Indeed, she asks, since the Bible says that Christ's followers are to be baptized 'with the Holy Ghost and with fire', why don't literalists set themselves alight before being sprinkled with water? (363–64) She is scathing about transubstantiation; more sympathetic to the Lord's Supper as an act of remembrance, though once again she warns that this substitutes the outward for the inner divine reality. Her conclusion strongly emphasizes the choice between a symbolic of death and the potential for new life which she placed before her late seventeenth-century readers:

> If any shall be offended at what I have written to vindicate the laying aside of this outward Sign, where the thing signified is inwardly come; if they will dwell upon the Figure of the Death of Christ without, and care not to come to know and witness his Resurrection and Life in themselves, I'll leave them where they are.
>
> (369)

But Bathurst's message, like that of the other early Quaker women, is clear: Choose Life!

Life and death at the cusp of modernity

It would be misleading to give the impression that Life was the only trope used by early Quakers, or even the most frequent: Light, for example, is hugely important in their writings. Nevertheless, it has been my suggestion that early Quakers' emphasis on Life, especially the divine life within, is at an angle to the developing symbolic of death and violence of early modernity. God was not far off, in another world to which the soul might escape after death, as was held in acute form in Deist writings and which had resonances also in Puritan thought. The divine, rather, was near at hand, 'that of God in everyone', not just as a divine spark, but as the Light that illumined scripture and every aspect of 'the outward'.

It was consonant with this location of the divine within, I believe, that Quakers reconsidered many of the attitudes and actions common in the seventeenth century, starting with gender relations and working through to their peace testimony and their eventual opposition to exploitation and slavery. If they aimed to 'answer that of God in everyone' it could not be by violence. Yet while this stance led to the appreciation of individuals, it would not be merely as atoms of competition in an increasingly market-driven world, but as fundamentally sharing in the divine. Moreover, while a Quaker stance would make for delight in and appreciation of the physical world, and thus for an enthusiasm for scientific investigation and discovery, this enthusiasm would not be on the basis of a removal of God from the world, as in the increasing secularism of the time. Rather, they sought to discern and cooperate with the divine Life. Hence their approach left room for ecological concern rather than exploitation and domination of the physical world.

The seventeenth century in England was by any standards a turning point for the west. It is my contention that modernity takes its shape from the choices that were made then: choices to construe the divine as other-worldly, to rank people and the earth into hierarchies of domination and exploitation, to pursue competitive individualism, violence and war, and to invest in an increasingly market-driven economy that gradually destroys the earth and its peoples. Modernity chose a love affair with death.

Early Quakers offered a different symbolic: if it had been chosen, modernity would have been incalculably different. We cannot now go back and make the choices otherwise: we must deal with the violent history of the intervening centuries and the symbolic which is our habitus. But rediscovering the contours of an alternative symbolic at the cusp of modernity may give us resources for thinking and living otherwise, working to subvert from within our life-world of death and violence. As Margaret Fell wrote in 1653 to Friends who were paying with their lives for their witness to the divine life within:

> So Life and Death is set before you; and if you be obedient to the Light, which never changeth, it will lead you out of death, and out of the fall from under the Curse, into the Covenant of Life ... and so wait for the living Food, to come from the living God.
>
> (Garmen *et al.* 1996: 455)

Chapter 6

Fanny Henshaw and the question of self-deception

The obvious question that arises regarding this strong doctrine of the inner Light is the question of its validity. Is it indeed the 'promptings of love and truth', or might there be a strong element of deception involved? How could we know? How can we be sure that the light is accurately recognized and discerned, either in our own case or in the claims that others make? The question was bound to exercise early Friends, partly out of their own concern and partly because of the accusations of enemies.

It was of course not a new anxiety, though in the seventeenth century its form changed in an interesting way. In medieval spirituality the worry would have been demonic intervention: the devil could appear as the proverbial 'angel of light' and deceive even those who most wanted to discern the voice of God. Seventeenth-century religious sensibilities, including those of Friends, did not dismiss this concern, but with the rise of Protestant emphasis on the Bible and with the rise of science, the mood was shifting to a more secular notion of deception: what evidence was there – and where should evidence be sought – to bear out any claim to inner Light? Could individual assertion be sufficient? Rather than (or along with) anxieties about demons, there grew anxieties about truth and beliefs, and how they might be justified. From the perspective of the twenty-first century, we might be preoccupied with issues of self-deception and lies. In the seventeenth century the term of opprobrium was 'enthusiasm'. It was all part of the epistemological shift of early modernity.

That story has often been told. My concern is not to repeat it, but to point out the extent to which this same shift is a part of the displacement of beauty, and its close involvement in what could count as spirituality. From a medieval sense of the immediacy of beauty, grounded in the beauty of nature created by God, there grew the suspicion of 'beauty is in the eye of the beholder': the worry that beauty is, after all, no more than subjective, and that the subjective is somehow not to be trusted. Recognition and discernment, indispensable for a spirituality of beauty, is thrown into question. Indeed, I would suggest that contrary to what is often thought, we could see the epistemological shift of early modernity, not as the work of overbearing confidence and rationality, but rather as a crisis of confidence, a deep self-doubt which cannot anymore rely on its own capabilities of discernment and recognition but must have external validation. The implications for a spirituality of beauty are part of what I shall be exploring in the rest of this section. My aim, however, is not primarily critical. Rather, I wish to show how early Friends tried to deal with the anxieties to which concerns about deception opened them. In so doing, I shall reconsider what is involved in recognition. Ultimately, it is all we have. The question, I shall argue, is not whether it is fundamental, but rather how it can be trained and strengthened, how we can overcome our fear and learn to trust in the inner Light, for a deepening spirituality of beauty that can confront and heal the violence and brokenness of the world.

Again, it is useful to start small, with a historical case study. There were many instances, in the lives of early Friends, where they were challenged regarding their claims to the inner Light. I have chosen the story of William Law and Fanny Henshaw: a spiritual writer of influence and power in the land, and a young woman whom he tried and failed to persuade against following her own discernment. Although Law (and Henshaw too) appealed to reason and objectivity, the story is stuffed with technologies of gendered power: but in the end they did not prevail.

In the year 1734, Fanny Henshaw was 20 years of age, living in a privileged household in Cheshire in the north of England. With her younger sister, she was under the guardianship of her uncle and aunt, their parents having died when she was a small child. It was a deeply religious, Protestant household, reasonably affluent; and the two young women had returned to it after a boarding-school education which had given them not only the singing and dancing abilities of genteel women, but also good training in reading, writing, literature and more, and a grounding in the Bible and the practice of the Church of England: Fanny could never be dismissed as a pretty but illiterate young thing!

Yet that, in effect, was the way in which William Law attempted to deal with her claims to the inner Light. In a memoir which Fanny wrote later in her life, she describes her experience. When she was about 20, her sister became seriously ill; and the thoughts of both young women, devout as they were, turned to the question of death and what they must do to prepare for it. To Fanny, who had previously observed Quakers with respect and admiration, an inner answer came to her question.

> A query arising in me what this could import and what this change must be, I presently had an answer uttered to my breast with great weight and solemnity to this effect, 'the change is this: thou must with others bear the cross in the closest way, and become a Quaker!'
>
> (Hobhouse 1927: 83)

For Fanny this seemed bad news: she knew that her guardians would disapprove, and she had no wish to offend them. She realized that becoming a

Friend would lead her into unknown and costly paths. For about a year and a half she struggled against it with such intensity that it affected her health and mental balance. In the end, however, she could not deny what was happening within her without violation of her integrity. As she put it, having come to her resolution:

> But though I should incur the disesteem of the whole world by obedience to the discovery of the truth, God forbid I should conceal it any longer from any, for should I lie against the light, my wound would be incurable.
>
> (Hobhouse 1927: 91)

It is as clear a case as we could find of the principle that the inner Light is not a matter of beliefs or information but a way of life centred in obedience. There is no progress to a further stage until the step in question has been taken; and refusal to do so is a violation of one's very soul.

Her guardians, predictably, did not see it like that. To try to dissuade her, they enlisted the help of a friend of their family, one John Byrom, who took an avuncular interest in Fanny. Byrom was an eminent man, a doctor, a teacher and poet, inventor of shorthand. He was well connected, having as pupils such eminent young men as John and Charles Wesley and Horace Walpole. He was devout, and had a great admiration for William Law, a noted theologian and spiritual writer, and for a considerable time tutor in the household of Edward Gibbon. Byrom sent letters to Law, which he had Fanny write, so she could explain her situation and receive his written replies.

In Law's responses emerge the standard responses of modernity to the inner Light, showing the deep scepticism that was arising regarding the ability of human recognition. First, Law told Fanny that her sense of the inner Light was completely unreliable. It was, he said, explicable purely in terms of psycho-physical causes, including the trauma of her sister's illness: there was no need to appeal to God. With breath-taking self-confidence in his own insight, he wrote to her:

> You know how much I am a stranger to you, but as soon as I read your paper, I knew a great deal more of you than you had there related, and was fully convinced that I could send you a much deeper and fuller account of yourself than I have had from you ... These tempers are the greatest part of your disorder ... Your case is of a mixt nature, and your disorder is both in mind and body ...
>
> (Hobhouse 1927: 32)

Having thus medicalized her anxieties, Law proceeded to accuse her of spiritual pride. In her letter, Fanny had referred to the writings of the apostle Paul.

But let me tell you, that you are here seemingly reproached with that, which really flatters you, and must in all likelihood kindle the most dangerous pride in you. For how can you look at St Paul in that extraordinary time as an example for you, unless you think yourself to be what he was at that time, *a chosen vessel of God*?

(Hobhouse 1927: 49)

It was ridiculous for her even to think in such terms.

When Paul had been summoned by God, Law argued, it was in order to establish the church, with its doctrines and sacraments. The Quakers, by contrast, rejected outward sacraments and stood lightly in relation to traditional doctrines. This challenge to the authority of the church Law could not tolerate.

The Church with all its holy offices, orders, institutions, and services is the true refuge, relief, and sanctuary for distressed souls; everything is there ready, prepared, and appointed by God to help the soul that feels the necessity of renouncing the world and living wholly unto God.

(Hobhouse 1927: 33)

Anything else is sheer hubris. If Fanny turns from the Church of England to the Quakers, rejecting its sacraments and institutions, Law says, she is in effect rejecting salvation.

No greater mark of the new birth's arising in us, than a reverential love and esteem of these institutions, and an earnest longing and desire to partake of them … That new birth which either proceeds from or brings forth a contempt and renunciation of these divine institutions, is only being born again of our selves, by the will of the flesh, and by the will of man.

(Hobhouse 1927: 38)

What she must do is accept scripture and the Church of England as authoritative, give up all pretensions to direct recognition of the inner Light, and above all not join with the Quakers.

The final straw for Law, it seems, is that Fanny was interested in hearing a Quaker woman preach. This was simply beyond the pale: he throws at her all the scriptural passages forbidding such a thing, taking no notice whatever of the ways in which Quakers and others had already shown that even if one were to take them at face value, these passages were of particular rather than general application. Law's gendered outrage is palpable.

In the time of this greatest liberty of speaking in the publick assemblies [that is, in the early Christian Church], the Holy Spirit in the greatest solemnity of words excludes women from it, as a thing unlawfull, shamefull, and against the very order of nature ...

(Hobhouse 1927: 72)

It is hard not to feel that at bottom, it was a question of power and gender. Quite apart from any real argument regarding self-deception, Law could not bear the idea that a young woman should have as much access to the inner Light, as much ability to recognize it, and as much need to obey it, as he himself who was taken as an authoritative and towering spiritual master.

Law was unsuccessful. When Fanny Henshaw had to decide between integrity and obedience to authority, she chose integrity. She became a Quaker and led a productive and influential life travelling in the ministry and doing much in working for the poor and for social justice. William Law drops out of the picture of her life: what she made of him we do not know. Neither is there any further reference to her in his writings. But maybe she had a far bigger influence than she knew.

In later life Law himself came to recognize the importance of the inner Light: that recognition and discernment of that light within the self, and obedience to it, is fundamental to spirituality. No external authority, whether scripture, church, or rational argument (important as all these are) can take its place. As he put it repeatedly in his late and influential book, *The Spirit of Prayer*:

> For this turning to the Light and the Spirit of God within thee, is thy only true turning to God, there is no other way of finding him, but in that place where he dwelleth in thee. For though God be everywhere present, yet he is only present to thee in the deepest, and most central part of thy soul ... Awake then, thou that sleepest, and Christ, who from all eternity has been espoused to thy soul, shall give thee light. Begin to search and dig in thine own field for this Pearl of Eternity, that lies hidden in it ...
>
> (Law 1969: 44)

A Quaker could not have put it better. It is customary to attribute Law's change in attitude to his study of German mystical writers, especially Jakob Boehme. Without wanting to deny their importance for him, however, it is hard not to think, especially in view of his much more conciliatory comments about Quakers in his later life, that his dealings with Fanny Henshaw continued to affect him. It would not be the first time that an influential man drew his best thoughts from a woman without ever acknowledging her impact upon him.

Enthusiasm

The case of Fanny Henshaw reveals the importance of discernment and recognition of the inner Light for spirituality. I suggest, however, that it reveals much more. What I want to argue is that the inner Light as the grounding of knowledge – both epistemology and ethics – stands as an alternative to the paradigm of knowledge of modernity; and that it is the latter which has acted to displace life and beauty, and which underlies the violent structures of thought and behaviour of our time. If these structures are to be overcome, a spirituality of beauty centred on recognition is the way forward.

These are large claims; and to substantiate them I begin by returning to the questions of self-deception and the justification of beliefs. William Law was not the only one, after all, who was sceptical of the inner Light. In the seventeenth and eighteenth centuries there were many who wrote against 'enthusiasts'. 'Enthusiasm' literally means 'God within' – *en theos* – directly illuminating the mind and conscience. The term, however, was not usually used by Quakers of themselves: it was more often used as a term of scorn by their enemies, who scoffed at them for pretending – or so their detractors said – to be possessed by God. Influential men wrote diatribes against 'enthusiasts': the overcharged rhetoric of such attacks shows, if nothing else, the level of threat felt by them at the very idea that God could directly illuminate the mind. Henry More, the Cambridge Platonist, wrote *Enthusiasmus Triumphatus* (1662), a veritable invective against supposed 'enthusiasts' (whom he mostly equated not with Quakers but with papism – an indication of the awareness that the idea of the inner Light was also a feature of medieval spirituality). Jonathan Swift satirized 'enthusiasm' as only he could do; and there were dozens of lesser figures who wrote tracts and diatribes (Locke 1959: II.19.432, n1). Perhaps most influential of all, however, was John Locke, whose theory of knowledge became central to the development of modernity and did much, I shall argue, to displace beauty and inculcate an epistemology and ethics of violence.

In John Locke's chapter on 'Enthusiasm', set in the context of his *Essay Concerning Human Understanding* (1959), we can see the contrast taking shape, and the technologies of mastery emerge which Locke did much to set into place. It is instructive that in this chapter the level of reasoning falls far below his usual standard: it is not hard, observing the invective, to sense the level of threat. One of the ways it is made apparent is that he does not reply to the actual points at issue but, with sweeping generalizations and not a single actual case or argument, he characterizes them as mad or bad. Enthusiasts, he says, depend on 'the ungrounded fancies of a man's own brain'; they are those who 'in all ages' are 'men in whom melancholy has mixed with devotion, or whose conceit of themselves has raised them into an opinion of greater familiarity with God, and a nearer admittance to his favour than is afforded to others', so that they consider themselves recipients of special communication from the divine. Forthwith, without any rational examination, they act upon such impulses: 'whatsoever odd action they find in themselves a strong inclination to do, that impulse is concluded to be a call or direction from heaven, and must be obeyed'. It arises, however, 'from the conceits of a warmed and overweening brain' and could simply be dismissed were it not for the fact that such enthusiasts have large followings and can cause major social and political turbulence (Locke 1959: II.19.8–11). These, indeed, are precisely the kinds of comments which we have seen William Law make to Fanny Henshaw: he might have been lifting his objections to her directly from the philosopher.

But who exactly did Locke have in mind in his diatribe against enthusiasts? Locke never names them, nor studies any actual texts nor analyses any particular claims. He just sweeps them up into a generalized heap of noxious opinion built upon 'laziness, ignorance and vanity' who build on nothing but 'internal light', which Locke dismisses as 'ungrounded persuasion of their own minds': again, mad or bad (Locke 1959: II.19.11). 'Enthusiasts', clearly, are cast in Locke's thinking as the 'other' against whom the system of rationality which he is working to develop must be constructed, the danger which must be expelled in order for its purity to be maintained. Read in this way, the teaching of the inner Light, and the spirituality in which it is centred, is far more than a peculiarity of a small religious group, or even an admirable but idiosyncratic way of life. Rather, it is that which must be eradicated if the epistemology of modernity, with its emphasis on justified true beliefs and its characterization of life in terms of calculation of profit and loss is to be established. And once it is established, beauty will become peripheral to modernity; and a spirituality of beauty that could disrupt violence and bring newness into the world will be displaced.

It is not often noted how thoroughly such a Lockean epistemology eliminates beauty, let alone a spirituality of beauty, from consideration. Yet I suggest that this is one of the most significant negative effects of the empirical rationality that he promoted and that became characteristic of modernity. Locke's system has no room for life, for growth or the organic: all essential to a spirituality of beauty. The simple ideas themselves, the atoms out of which all our knowledge is built up, are lifeless. They have been dissected, resolved to the point where they are dead, inert. And the procedure of rebuilding them into complex doctrines or theories is also lifeless: it is a mathematical or mechanical procedure which could and eventually would be done more accurately and efficiently by computers, which Locke would surely have loved if he could have envisaged them. Lifelessness, indeed necrophilia, is at the very basis of Locke's epistemology.

Chapter 7

Before the rooster crows

In this chapter I will compare the gendered epistemology of John Locke and Margaret Fell as representatives of a choice between life and death in early modernity. Locke's epistemology, based on ideals of putative neutrality and objectivity and disturbed by 'enthusiasts', became the model of knowledge in modernity. I show, however, that it is premised on death. Not only does it take objects (rendered lifeless by the removal of God from the world) as a paradigm for knowledge, but it also renders the process of knowledge itself as based on calculation rather than sympathy. I also show that in the writings of 'enthusiasts', in particular the Quaker Margaret Fell, a life-giving and life-affirming knowledge was affirmed. Unfortunately, this was heavily repressed by Locke and his fellows both in terms of gender and in terms of its (related) understanding of the divine, so that modernity was structured upon a gesture of death.

My primary aim in this chapter, however, is not just diagnostic. Rather, I wish to help effect a shift in western consciousness and practice, disrupting the symbolic of death and beginning to open out a new imaginary in which knowledge and reality are otherwise constituted. I propose to start the process by reconsidering the deathly configuration of Lockean epistemology, in particular by asking deconstructive questions: who does it leave out? What does it repress? It is noteworthy that Locke, usually urbane and unruffled, was, as I described earlier, completely discomposed by those he called 'enthusiasts', against whom he launched the sort of poorly reasoned diatribe that he would not have countenanced for one minute in any other context. 'Enthusiasts' were the only group capable of generating for Locke even more anxiety than 'superstitious nurses' or 'the authority of old women' (whom he also greatly disliked) (Locke 1693 [1989]: I.3.22), and when the two groups were conjoined, as they were in the authoritative old Quaker woman Margaret Fell, he became, by his own standards, quite irrational. Now, I suggest that anyone who could so unsettle Locke's well-oiled 'punctual self', as Charles Taylor has aptly described him (Taylor 1989: 159), deserves our respectful attention! Locke won, of course: he was in a position of power, such that he and those like him could define what should count as a respectable rhetorical space (Code 1995: 7) and banish 'enthusiasts' as Others. I suggest, however, that these Others, silenced in western philosophy's account of its own knowing, not only destabilize its structures but also open the way for a different approach to epistemology in which gender, particularity and flourishing can be taken seriously.

Moreover, since the Lockean programme effectively established the secularism of epistemology, a reconsideration of that programme also reintroduces the question of religion. It is my belief that the secularism of the Lockean project is as patriarchal and necrophilic[1] as the religion it replaced; moreover that in this construction of secularism religion itself was also fundamentally altered so that in modernity the forms of secularism and religion are reciprocally constituted. They deserve each other as surely as an ill-assorted couple in a relationship of co-dependence. Now, I have no wish to reinstate western Christendom in a business-as-usual approach, even if that were possible: it is far too deeply mired in death-dealing over many centuries. However I do want to argue that in this respect secularism is no better. Feminists who have been quick to reject the former have too often assumed the latter as the taken-for-granted alternative. I suggest that this is too easy; that in fact secularism (here in terms of Locke's epistemology) re-inscribes many of the worst aspects of traditional Christendom. By probing it, therefore, in the light of its repressed Other(s) we find that we are also probing issues of the construction of religion in modernity; and by imagining an alternative epistemology centred on life rather than death we are engaging in a radical shift of the symbolic which moves us beyond secularism and religion. Or so I shall try to show.

Of knowing men and prattling parrots

The beginning of Locke's epistemology appears innocent enough. Like many another philosopher, Locke starts with a metaphor, in his case the famous *tabula rasa*.

> Let us then suppose the mind to be, as we say, white paper, void of all characters, without any ideas: – How comes it to be furnished? Whence comes it by that vast store which the busy and boundless fancy of man has painted on it with almost endless variety? Whence has it all the *materials* of reason and knowledge?
>
> (Locke 1959: II.1.2)

Locke's answer will be, 'in one word, from experience', and I shall come to this in a moment. But it is worth pausing briefly on the metaphor itself. It is, first, intended literally: not, of course, that we have sheets of paper in our heads, but that we have no innate ideas, that the mind at birth really is empty. Only gradually, through experience, is it filled up and thereby given the materials with which to think.

> Follow a child from its birth, and observe the alterations that time makes, and you shall find, as the mind by the senses comes more and more to be furnished with ideas, it comes to be more and more awake, thinks more, the more it has matter to think on.
>
> (Locke 1959: II.1.2)

Although Locke's urbane and sociable self-presentation gives a very different impression from that of Descartes' solitary self sitting in front of his stove, Locke's founding metaphor is just as individualistic. Locke's 'white paper' is a paper not essentially interconnected with other people or 'imprinted' by anyone. The child's blank mind is developed not in emotional connection with its mother or principal carer, for example, who might as well not exist so far as Locke's theory of knowledge is concerned, but by the acquisition of ideas – of which, more in a moment. This individualism, in which contact with others is accidental or actually pernicious, is deeply ingrained in Locke's account of the self, and coheres well also with his atomistic idea of knowledge, as we shall see. Locke's 'white paper' defines the knower in terms of essential isola- tion (and knowledge, as we shall see, in strictly intellectual terms); yet it is presented without argument, in Locke, as nothing more than a metaphor. It is a metaphor, however, which has proved foundational for the epistemology of modernity (Laslett 1960: 97–105) and contrasts sharply with the metaphor favoured by Margaret Fell, as we shall see.

Now, the metaphor of the white paper could be taken in more than one way. It could be thought of as profoundly egalitarian, for example. If the mind is originally blank, and only subsequently 'printed upon' by experience, then at least in the original state the minds of all are equal. Taken in this way, from this metaphor it would follow that the minds of a woman and a man, a black person and a white, a master and a slave are made different only by the experiences they have undergone, not by anything inherent in them; and it would then fall to anyone who wanted to retain social hierarchies (as Locke did) to justify them in the light of such original equality of mind. To the extent that all minds are equally 'white paper' it must be the structures of society which generate experience that also generate inequality, and they must there- fore be evaluated in that light. It is this interpretation that lies, for instance, behind Peter Laslett's understanding of Locke's epistemological radicalism.

Locke himself, however, went in a different direction. Although he accepted the consequence that all children are potentially equal, what he looked for was the very opposite of social conditioning. He did not particularly want children to be taught the principles of their culture, since these would very possibly amount to nothing more than the unreflective attitudes of those nearest the children and thus most able to influence them. 'Doctrines, that have been derived from no better original, than the Superstition of a Nurse, or the Authority of an old Woman', he feared, would then 'grow up to the dignity of Principles in Religion or Morality' (Locke [1693] 1989: I.3.22).

He continues: 'For such, who are careful (as they call it) to principle Children well instil into the unwary, and as yet, unprejudiced Understanding, (for white Paper receives any Characters) those Doctrines they would have them retain and profess' (I.3.22). What Locke wants instead is to protect children from the imposition on their vulnerable minds of all such ill principles, and to instil in them instead the method of right reason. Locke wanted children to grow up to become 'knowing men', not 'prattling parrots'. His method of right reason, which is needed to become a 'knowing man', Locke looked on as being the means of mastery, first of all of one's own self, especially one's feelings and passions, and consequently also of the wider world: this also is constitutive of manliness (Schouls 1992: 191, 204–17). Such reasoning, in Locke's opinion, would actually enable a person to be free of social structures or conditioning, rise above it to the plane of reason and autonomy. Lorraine Code has shown how such an approach to knowledge, which takes right reason built on sense perception as paradigmatic, consistently bypasses other forms of knowing, particularly those of infancy and childhood in which we learn when to give or withhold trust. Yet without such learning, we would never have learned *how* to know (Code 1995: 46).

Although he differed from Descartes in significant ways, Locke openly acknowledged that Descartes had a huge impact on his thinking. Perhaps most important was the method of resolution and composition, the means by which Descartes sought to achieve certainty.[2] Briefly, in the Cartesian method, ideas are to be 'resolved' or broken down into their simplest components, components about which no doubt is possible. They are then to be built up by sequences of logical deductions, 'composed' into more complex thoughts whose certainty can be relied upon if the composition has followed strictly rational procedures (Descartes 1969: *Discourse*, Precept 3). Now, as is well known, Locke differed from Descartes in holding that the origin of all our ideas is experience, in which sense experience is crucial. But sense experience is always already complex: the objects that affect us are, in Locke's scheme, possessed of primary qualities which occur not singly but in combination: 'solidity, extension, figure, motion or rest, and number' (Locke [1693] 1989: I.3.22); moreover, these give rise to the secondary qualities of colour, taste, smell and the rest. It is we ourselves who must – and do – break down these complexities, resolving them even as we perceive them into the simple ideas of sensation. 'Though the Qualities that affect our Senses, are, in themselves, so united and blended, that there is no separation, no distance between them; yet, ''tis plain, the Ideas they produce in the Mind, enter by the Senses simple and unmixed' (I.3.22). These simple ideas, always arriving in combinations, are resolved by us from the complexity in which they are experienced to their simplest components (Schouls 1992: 158–72). These are the basic ingredients of our knowledge, which Locke thinks are shared, at least in the main, by all people if only they will go through the requisite process of resolution.

> I imagine that men who abstract their Thoughts, and do well examine the Ideas of their own Minds, cannot much differ in thinking. ... But if it should happen, that any two thinking Men should really have different Ideas, I do not see how they could discourse or argue with one another.
>
> (Locke: [1689] 1959: II.13.27).

This is obviously true of simple sensory ideas like colour or taste; but that is not usually where major human disputes occur. In what all acknowledge to be matters of taste we readily agree to differ. Rather, it is in the conflict between the large and complex systems of ideas that have been built up out of the simple ones to form doctrines and customs, and those conflicts can be rationally dealt with only by breaking down the ideas once again to their simple components and then ensuring that the process by which they have been built up is logically watertight.

> Tis not easy for the Mind to put off those confused Notions and Prejudices it has imbibed from Custom, Inadvertency, and common Conversation [to say nothing of nurses and old women]: it requires pain and assuidity to examine its Ideas, till it resolves them into those clear and distinct ones, out of which they are compounded; and to see which, amongst its simplest ones, have or have not a necessary connexion and dependence one upon another.
>
> (II.13.27)

Thus, what Locke looks for is a 'chain of reasonings' which proceed from 'very plain and easy beginnings' (IV.12.7), with the simple ideas derived from the senses but abstracted by the process of resolution into the atomic constituents of thought, and then combined in ways that can 'be learned in the Schools of the Mathematicians' into dependable knowledge. All of this is ostensibly possible for rational agents, who are in this respect interchangeable. It is in fact a technology of power for excluding radical difference, and thereby effectively limiting who shall count as 'knowers' to 'men like us': witness Margaret Cavendish's exclusion from the Royal Society (Shapin 1994).

The Strasbourg clock

An illustration Locke used more than once was that of the complicated clock of the cathedral in Strasbourg. Locke says that if we could have a detailed understanding of the ways in which simple ingredients work together to form a complicated thing, our idea of it

> would be as far different from what it is now, as is his who knows all the springs and wheels and other contrivances within of the famous clock of Strasburg, from that which a gazing countryman has of it, who barely sees

the motion of the hand, and hears the clock strike, and observes only some of the outward appearances.

(Locke: [1689] 1959: III.6.3)

Locke's ostensible purpose is to point out the limitations of our knowledge: only God the Maker has real knowledge of why things work together as they do, what the real essences of plants and animals or even minerals might be, 'what makes lead and iron malleable, antimony and stones not' (III.6.9). Our experience can assure us *that* certain simple ideas are constantly conjoined – that there are stable objects in this world – but not *why* this should be so. These deeper reasons are the divine prerogative; nor do we have any need to understand them in order to make scientific or technological progress, to have 'a quiet and prosperous passage' through the world (cited in Woolhouse 1994: 170).

But again, Locke's metaphor is revealing. The things of this world, plants, animals and people as well as minerals and stones, are like the cathedral clock: they move, there is action and apparent life, but behind the scenes what we have is mechanism, matter in motion. Locke followed Descartes in thinking that all matter is mechanical, without any life of its own; and in this he was of course 'clearing the ground', as he himself put it, as an 'under labourer' for Boyle, Huygens, Newton and others of the Royal Society. Nor was Locke the first to use the clock as a guiding metaphor: as Steven Shapin has said, one could write the whole history of the 'Scientific Revolution' by tracing the use of the clock metaphor in the early modern period (Shapin 1996: 32). Boyle himself had referred to the Strasbourg clock as an exact and informative metaphor for the universe: it seemed to show purpose and design, when in fact it was all a 'curious engine' without inner life (34). Somewhat earlier, Johannes Kepler had said that his aim, in investigating the physical causes of the universe, 'is to show that the machine of the universe is not similar to a divine animated being, but similar to a clock' (33).

It is, therefore, consummate irony that Locke actually uses the mechanical nature of the universe as his fundamental argument for the existence of God, who is now construed not as its animating soul or principle, but as the one who created this clockwork universe and set it in motion while remaining sharply distinct from it. He begins by thinking of 'any parcel of matter', perhaps a pebble. Even if it were eternal, he says, 'if there were no other being in the world, must it not eternally remain so, a dead inactive lump?' (Locke 1959: IV.10.10). Matter by itself 'cannot produce in itself so much as motion' and even if it could, matter in motion could never produce thought, any more than the clock in Strasbourg could know that it was time for tea. Divide matter into the smallest possible parts, Locke says, and even suppose it to be in eternal motion: all you will get are small components that 'knock, impel and resist one another, just as the greater do; and that is all they can do'. His argument is, therefore, that there must be a God, omniscient and omnipotent, who is outside this lumpish, lifeless matter, who creates it and sets it in motion, and who also creates thinking beings, some of whom – people – are connected to some of these lumps of matter. In a Lockean epistemology, God (and any knower who by his knowledge is rendered godlike) is thus constituted as the binary other of matter. The God of secular modernity is the precise counterpart of the godless universe: but what a universe, and what a God!

The world and everything in it – at least everything material – is dead, as dead as are the 'springs and wheels and contrivances' of the Strasbourg clock. Locke defines matter as lifeless. This might seem the more surprising because Locke had been trained as a physician; how could a physician reject the idea of organic matter? Yet in the seventeenth century that was not uncommon: the medicine of the time increasingly saw the human body as a machine. One example was Harvey's recent discovery of the circulation of the blood: here, surely, was one instance of an organ of the body analogous to a pump. The contrast against which these medical mechanists were struggling was a view of the human body and things in nature as 'sympathetic' and in organic unity, perhaps as microcosm to macrocosm. This older view, going back to Paracelsus and beyond, was that which often informed local healers and midwives at however rudimentary a level, and was strongly rejected by the emerging medical establishment. Indeed during Locke's time people could still be convicted of witchcraft; and the medical fraternity was neatly caught between its wish to get rid of the local healers on the one hand and its refusal to attribute supernatural powers to them on the other.

Locke was firmly of the mechanist view, and rejected all such ideas of sympathy. Central to the mechanist position, as far as medicine is concerned, was the belief that all bodies are collections or aggregates of atoms in motion, and that these motions bring about any changes in the body and any sensations – colour, taste, smell – that we might have of them, 'that is to say, all causation involving bodies is mechanical causation' (McCann 1994: 57). Now, if this is the case then a whole different view of health and illness, for example, becomes possible. No longer is illness a question of 'humours' being out of balance, perhaps because of not living in proper attunement to the living world; nor could sympathetic medicine be of any avail. Rather, illness was a question of some part of the mechanism not working properly. If physicians wanted to understand what was wrong, they would need to take the machine apart, not ask spiritual or psychological questions. Thomas Willis, whose lectures on medicine Locke attended in 1661–62, wrote that 'In mechanical things when any one would observe the motions of a clock or Engine, he takes the machine itself to pieces to consider the singular artifice, and doth not doubt that he will learn the causes and properties of the Phaenomenon' (cited in Sawday 1995: 31). It was no accident that from this time forward dissection of corpses began to play a very prominent role. The technological body had appeared, mechanical in itself and knowable by mechanical means. No more mystery, now, or sympathy or communion: what was needed was for a physician to know how the springs, cogs and wheels managed to turn together. As Jonathan Sawday puts it in his perceptive account of the changes, 'The modern body had emerged: a body which worked rather than existed' (32). It was a body which of itself was lifeless in a lifeless world: nothing more than matter in motion.

Jonathan Sawday has also shown how this shift to a mechanical conception of the human body was associated with wider historical and political shifts: if the body is a machine, then the image of the king as head of a commonwealth has quite different resonances than if the body is a living, dynamic inter-connection, hierarchically organized. Even more important, if the body – and the whole world of bodies – is a machine, then although God might be needed to construct the machine and set it in motion in the first place, and might occasionally make a slight adjustment to its workings, God was in no sense required to be inside the machine. 'Rather he was a mechanic, an engineer, a watchmaker even, whose presence was no longer required for the continuing operation of the orderly movement of the machine' (29).

Now, I think that it is important to recognize that we have here far more than a banishment of God from the world (though we certainly have that too), but that the banishment is reciprocally connected with a whole new con-ceptualization of the divine. Put another way, it is not the same old God, only now confined to heaven rather than tinkering with things on earth. Rather, what the divine *is* is reconceptualised, just as much as what the earth is. It is this reshaped religion that is the obverse of secular modernity. In Locke's scheme, God is an incorporeal, omnipotent and omniscient being, utterly other than the world and detached from it in a grand cosmic dualism. The fact that this strikes us as the 'traditional' understanding of God is at least in part due, not to its actual constancy throughout western history, but to the success of the Lockean project. Moreover, given such an understanding of God, the worship of God is directed away from the world, having nothing to do with it. The worship of God, religion, has become essentially other-worldly: from this point forward it also therefore becomes ever more apolitical, private and increasingly gendered feminine. It is much concerned, as Locke himself was, with the Great Day of Judgement in which one's personal beliefs and morality will be weighed up, and with questions of life after death; but it is not focused on – indeed views with great suspicion – any encounter with God in this world or through things of nature: since the world is mechanical, such ideas could hardly have a place. They would be labelled 'mystical' or 'enthusiastical.'

Locke was no atheist; he wrote a book on *The Reasonableness of Chris-tianity*, he offered a proof for the existence of God, and toward the end of his life he wrote commentaries on some of the Pauline epistles. I am in agreement with those who say that this religious interest was central to him, not incidental (Schouls 1992: 216f.). What I suggest, however, is that its centrality is a coherent part of his removal of God from the world, forming a secular space – literally the *saeculum*, the age between creation and the Day of

Judgement – which God watched from a heavenly distance but in which God rarely if ever intervened. Locke's critics noted that in *Reasonableness of Christianity* he had little to say about incarnation, and roundly accused him of being a Socinian or Unitarian (Nuovo 1997); and although Locke was far more clever and sophisticated than most of his critics, the charge was generally accurate. The important point here is that for Locke there is no place for the divine in the world: no place that is 'sacramental' in the sense of a meeting point of heaven and earth. The world is lifeless, and God is not a part of it. In this, Locke was an important precursor of Deism, which stressed the total separation of God and the world in a cosmic dualism (Byrne 1989). At one stroke, this renders religion other-worldly and focused on life after death, and this world secular, empty of the divine or of immanent life. The fact that we take so much of this for granted, as also Locke's view of medicine and science, shows how successful he was in developing the secular discourse of western modernity.

Of Velcro and the God-trick

But if matter is lifeless, it does not yet follow that knowledge is necrophilic. In part the mechanical nature of knowledge follows as a consequence of the method of resolution and composition, as I have already explained: knowledge is a matter of building up simple items of information by strict logical procedures into more complex ones. Moreover, the quest for knowledge is itself for knowledge of mechanism, and therefore looks for facts; it is in no sense an effort to enter into things – plants, animals, other people, the earth – with sympathetic understanding (Poovey 1998). Rather, it is detached and neutral, carefully marshalling its facts into arguments by logical processes. In that respect the mechanical lifelessness of matter is paralleled by the mechanical construction of knowledge.

However, there is, I believe, a far more telling aspect to Locke's necrophilic epistemology, and that is to be found in his account of personal identity. Locke, again like Descartes, holds to a strongly dualist view of the human individual, a dualism which in fact precisely mirrors the cosmic dualism he constructs between God and the world. Just as the world is composed of lifeless matter set in motion by a transcendent, incorporeal God, so the human body is a mechanism set in motion and (in some sense) inhabited by an incorporeal soul.

> For should the soul of a prince, carrying with it the consciousness of the prince's past life, enter and inform the body of a cobbler, as soon as deserted by his own soul, everyone sees he would be the same *person* with the prince.
>
> (Locke 1959: II.27.15)

Whether 'everyone' sees this or not is another long chapter in the history of modern philosophy, of course; but the point is that, as far as Locke is concerned, it is memory that constitutes identity and that it is this, rather than bodily continuity, which determines such things as moral accountability.

Now, to be sure, Locke is at pains to assert that personal identity does not reside in substance, whether spiritual or material, but rather in identity of consciousness, in particular memory. Looking toward the Day of Judgement, 'wherein the secrets of all hearts shall be laid open', Locke is confident that whatever sentences shall be pronounced, they 'shall be justified by the consciousness all persons shall have, that they themselves, *in what bodies soever they appear*, or what substances soever that consciousness adheres to, are the same that committed those actions, and deserve that punishment for them' (IV.27.22 and 26).

Locke's idea of consciousness seems like a bit of incorporeal Velcro, attaching itself to this or that substance to which it then 'adheres'. Whether such an idea is actually coherent is highly contestable. What matters for my present purpose, however, is that personal identity or consciousness is not corporeal, nor is it necessarily bound to any body. It can float free, neutral, remaining itself irrespective of context or social situation or history. In principle, it could 'adhere' now to the prince, now to the cobbler, could cross genders and race, could – who knows? – perhaps attach itself to plants or animals or move across vast geographical or temporal distances or even remain temporarily or permanently unattached: this would give a whole new meaning to the idea of becoming unstuck! Locke never considers these latter possibilities, and would presumably bless providence that in fact the soul's Velcro normally stays stuck to a single body; but in his System, that is a matter of contingent fact rather than built into the logic of personal identity (IV.19.5).

What is most striking about Locke's account of personal identity is how very like God it is: not the God of incarnation or sacrament or divine presence in the world, but Locke's God, defined as the detached knower, separate from any particularities of space or time and utterly other than matter. It is in this context that we need to understand the epistemology of modernity, with its emphasis on subject–object distinction and the refusal of connection with others. These aspects of epistemology have been importantly exposed for their patriarchy and philosophical inadequacies by feminist writers, including Lorraine Code and Donna Haraway (Code 1991; Haraway 1991). Yet for all the insightfulness of their critique they do not see the extent to which, in Locke at least (and I would argue that variations on the theme can be found in many modern philosophers) this 'God-trick', as Haraway calls it, is of a piece with a peculiarly modern construction of God and the world which completely severs them from one another, constructing at a stroke a deathly secular modernity and an idea of the self and reason whose true nature is separate from the body and would feel most at home in some variant of Plato's heaven.

Locke's others: enthusiasm's noxious weeds

One can see all this in another way. There was apparently very little that could shake Locke from his studied equilibrium, but a few things did get under his skin. One was any threat to his money or property: apparently he was something of a skinflint (Cranston 1957). Another was women, not least among them Mary Astell, whose well-directed criticisms stung him to protracted reply. A third, most important of all, was 'enthusiasm', against which he wrote a diatribe so unlike his usual careful reasoning, and inserted it into his fourth edition of the *Essay*, that if it shows nothing else, it shows that he was seriously discomposed.

Now, one could make a case for saying that for all her trenchant criticisms of Locke, Mary Astell and her likes could to a considerable extent be accommodated into a Lockean thought system. What Mary Astell or Margaret Cavendish wanted was not to overturn, say, the Royal Society or Locke's programme for education; rather, they wanted a share of it for themselves and for other women. It would be ungenerous to them to label them 'me too' feminists; after all, if they had been able to get what they wanted such liberal feminism might have had a more radical future than even they themselves could have foreseen. Still, to quite an extent Locke could protest that he was actually a champion for women's rights, of parentalism rather than paternalism, of education for little girls as well as little boys: in short, that some of his best friends were women. (They were, too: Locke caused more than one raised eyebrow at the *ménage à trois* at Oates, where he stayed for protracted periods with Damaris Masham and her apparently lacklustre husband.)

But if the women challenging Locke's system could be accommodated as the 'Other of the Same', that could certainly not be said for the groups that really got under Locke's skin, the groups he lumped together as 'enthusiasts'. Here we have the 'Other of the other', groups who didn't just want an equal share in the growing mechanistic value system to which Locke's philosophy gave articulation but who challenged – or even ridiculed – it from top to toe. And Locke felt it. From the essay on 'Enthusiasm', discussed in the previous chapter, we can sense the level to which he felt his system threatened. Locke, indeed, was far from alone in writing hostile tracts against (usually unnamed) 'enthusiasts'. As we noted in the previous chapter, Henry More, the Cambridge Platonist, wrote *Enthusiasmus Triumphatus* (1662), whose overcharged rhetoric makes Locke seem mild by comparison. Jonathan Swift satirized 'enthusiasm' as only he could do; and there were dozens of lesser figures who wrote tracts and diatribes (Locke 1959: II.19.432, n.1). From Damaris Masham, Locke's companion, we get one clue about who she (and maybe Locke himself?) thought these 'enthusiasts' were, when she writes ridiculing Mary Astell's *Serious Proposal* for women's education. She fears that women 'whose Imaginations' in any case 'are stronger than their Reason':

will turn to as wild an Enthusiasm as any that has been yet seen; and which can end in nothing but Monasteries, and Hermitages; with all those sottish and wicked Superstitious which have accompanied them where-ever thay have been in use.

(Cited in Springborg 1997: xv–xvi)

Monasteries and hermitages: how dreadful! The danger of Catholicism was a common theme of Puritan-Whiggish England; and anything 'other', from Native American 'savages' to East Asian 'Hindoos' would be assimilated to what has become known as 'pagano-papism' (Harrison 1990). And now the enemies inside the camp, the 'enthusiasts', might be similarly described.

And yet in actual fact those who were most often known as enthusiasts were from the opposite end of the religious spectrum, the radical dissenting Protestants. They were the Diggers and Ranters and Seekers, the Quakers and Muggletonians, Fifth Monarchy Men and Levellers and a host of other sects who were critical of the religion and politics of the monarchy, Protectorate and Restoration alike, and who sought much more radical reform than was ever on offer from Oliver Cromwell (Hill 1972). They hardly ever used the term 'enthusiast' of themselves: it was more often used as term of scorn by their enemies, who scoffed at them for pretending – so their detractors said – to be possessed by God. Most of these sects were short lived, the Quakers alone surviving until now, and even they in a form so modified that it would hardly be recognized by the early leaders (Braithwaite 1955). It is a measure of the success of the campaign against enthusiasm of which Locke was so pro-minent a member that we hardly now know what the enthusiasts taught or even who they were, although the historical sources are readily enough available.

But should Locke have been so successful? Not because of the quality of his reasoning, certainly. And more importantly, if Locke was a major influence on the necrophilia of modernity, as I have argued, should his success be celebrated or deplored? I suggest that at the cusp of modernity, some at least of the radical groups could see the deathliness that would become the mainstream and struggled to develop an alternative in both thought and practice. Locke and his friends suppressed them by invective and ridicule, and modernity pro-ceeded. But now that we can assess its direction and effects, perhaps we might look again at those who so deeply threatened Locke's spirit of mastery that he would not even name them or engage with their arguments, but only raged against them.

The groups were very different from one another, and this is not the place to survey them: I shall restrict myself to the Quakers. It is not my view that they were always right; and even where I think they were, it does not follow that we could simply adopt their views as though the intervening Lockean centuries had never happened. But if I am right that Lockean epistemology is deathly in content and method, and if, as I shall argue, the Quakers were trying to develop a way to 'choose life' and a related understanding of truth and how to come to it, then feminist epistemology may have much to gain from reconsidering their stance. It is the more attractive because it entailed gender equality; and it went in a different direction to either the religion or secularism of modernity, setting both at an angle. Or so I shall argue, considering the interlocking themes of the method of knowing, the nature of the world, and the construction of religion, all of which were in marked contrast to Locke and all of which he and his allies worked to render not admissible to the rhetorical space of modernity.

We could do worse than go back to Margaret Fell. In her account of her 'convincement' to Quaker thinking (as described on p. 88), she tells of how she sat with her children in their respectable family pew in Ulverston parish church when George Fox, the early leader of the Quakers, came and began to preach. He challenged the priest and congregation with the words, 'You will say, Christ saith this, and the Apostles say this; but what canst thou say? Art thou a child of Light, and hast walked in the Light, and what thou speakest, is it inwardly from God?' And Margaret Fell continues:

> This opened me so, that it cut me to the Heart; and then I saw clearly, we were all wrong ... And I cried in my Spirit to the Lord, We are all Thieves, we are all Thieves; we have taken the Scriptures in Words, and know nothing of them in ourselves.
>
> (Garmen *et al.* 1996: 235)

In some ways her recognition of the importance of internalizing the Gospel would hardly have been disputed by any Christian group of the time. The Puritans, after all, emphasized personal faith and commitment (Nuttall [1946] 1992); and the standard teaching of the established church, in word and sacrament, would concur with the need for personal, inward appropriation. Even John Locke said as much (Locke 1958: 46). Yet Margaret Fell meant something well beyond this standard teaching, which every account of her early life shows that she was already taking very seriously in any case (Young Kunze 1994).

By the time Margaret Fell wrote her *True Testimony* in 1660, the question of the foundation of epistemology was one she found necessary to confront head on, because she, like Locke after her, needed clarity about the basis of her political and religious stance. At the crux of her position is the assertion that Quakers base their knowledge and their practice directly on 'the Spirit of life and truth that nourishes the soul and leads into all truth' (Fell 1992: 23). This Spirit is not some heavenly or incorporeal being external to the human person, but neither is it identifiable with Lockean reason, whether intuition or deduction, or his notion of personal identity. It is, rather, what Fox called the 'Truth in the heart' (Fox 1952: 34). The insistence on its centrality is evident already in the earliest Quaker writing. As Sarah Jones, a Bristol Quaker, put it in 1650, 'sink down into that measure of life that ye have received, and go not out with your inlooking at what is contrary to you ... ' (Garmen *et al.* 1996: 35).The Word, the Spirit of God, she insists, 'is in thy heart', and only harm can come to one who turns from this and 'goes a gadding and hunting after the manifestations that proceeds from the word in others' vessels' (36). Yet although this Spirit is held to be within, often spoken of by Quakers as 'that of God in everyone', which illuminates and leads to truth those who are in obedience to it, it is clearly not the same thing as what Locke meant by reason. It is, rather, precisely 'enthusiasm', the divine within as the light by which truth can be discerned, and which Locke so greatly disliked and feared, describing it as demonic (Locke 1959: IV.19.8).

Now, John Locke certainly believed in revelation; but usually what he meant by that was the Bible. This, he thought, provided 'a surer and shorter way' to know God's laws, especially 'to the apprehensions of the vulgar,' than if it had been left to unassisted natural reason.

> The greatest part of mankind have not leisure for learning and logic, and superfine distinctions of the schools. Where the hand is used to the plough and the spade, the head is seldom elevated to sublime notions, or exercised in mysterious reasonings. 'Tis well if men of that rank (to say nothing of the other sex) can comprehend plain propositions, and a short reasoning about things familiar to their minds, and nearly allied to their daily experience.
>
> (Locke 1958: 76)

Therefore the divine wisdom had given humanity (or at least that portion of it with which Locke concerned himself) the scriptures, to teach us what to believe and do. And yet nothing in the scriptures was contrary to reason, both of those terms being properly understood.

But if Locke would 'say nothing of the other sex', they were busy speaking up for themselves, at least among Quakers, where their right to do so was upheld from the beginning. Their idea of the value of scripture was as much at an angle to Locke's as was their understanding of reason. Early Quaker writing leaves no doubt about the high value that they placed on the Bible. Their writings are saturated in it, reminiscent in this respect of medieval mystical writings like those of Bernard of Clairvaux. It is obvious that they treasured and internalized it, learned it by heart so that their very thoughts were shaped and turned by biblical phrases. Nevertheless, early Quakers held that it was only by the inner Light that one could recognize the truth of scripture, a truth which was as much a question of obedience and action as of belief. ''Tis not Inky Character can make a Saint,' said Elizabeth Bathurst in 1679 (Garmen *et al.* 1996: 341).

Characteristically, however, it was Margaret Fell who put the matter most forthrightly, taking the challenge to those who would oppose her. While conventional Christians insist on the authority of the Bible and the teachings of the church, Fell writes (discussing Jesus's telling the woman of Samaria that 'God is Spirit' and must be worshipped 'in spirit and in truth'):

> Now I do ask all the teachers and professors of Christendom, where this Spirit is, that God is to be worshipped in, if it be not in man [*sic*]? ... Where this worship of God in the Spirit is performed, if it be not in man? Where God's throne is, where the Ancient of Days does sit? Where the sceptre of Christ is swayed, which is a righteous sceptre?
>
> (Fell 1992: 25)

Here is a set of metaphors to place beside Locke's metaphor of the *tabula rasa*. Obviously Margaret Fell does not mean that there are little thrones inside our bodies where God sits holding a sceptre, any more than Locke thought that our heads were stuffed with white paper. But she does mean that there is 'that of God' in everyone, that we are so constituted as to be 'the human form divine', as Blake would later put it. Attentiveness and obedience to this, which is at once divine and the true self, is, for her, the basis of any worthwhile knowledge and the centre of integrity. In comparison, the question of which, if any, of the traditional doctrines one accepts or how one interprets them is of minor importance. Moreover, it is obvious that the concept of the divine as central to one's subjectivity and as the very life of the universe is a very different concept from that of God the universal clockmaker. It is only by the life of God *within*, locating the divine not in some far-off heaven separate from the world, as the Deists following Locke were to do, but sitting on the throne of the human heart, that, according to Margaret Fell, it is possible to discern truth and righteousness: not just about religious doctrine, but about anything else too. As she says in her *Declaration*, 'No people can retain God in their knowledge, and worship him as God, but first they must come to that of God in them' (Fell 1992: 53). The only way to know God, and indeed to know anything at all, is to be, literally, an 'en-thusiast'; one in whom the divine dwells, even if unrecognized.

So here we have accounts of the nature of knowing, the nature of what is known and the nature of religion radically different from what we find in Locke and what has become standard in western modernity. In regard to the nature of knowledge, it is obvious that the mechanistic or calculative method which has middle-sized lifeless objects as paradigmatic is about as far from Quaker thought as one could get. Rather, it is moral knowledge which is central, not in the sense of a code of ethics but in the sense of recognition of what is good, and living by that recognition, cost what it will. For Quakers, the most important attitude is thus integrity, obedience to the inner Light carefully discerned. This is an epistemological attitude as much as an ethical one: indeed the distinction between ethics and epistemology could not be drawn in the way that analytic philosophers do. Moreover, the recognition of what is good is always interactive, both in the sense that its accuracy and trustworthiness is communally tested and also in the sense that the good always concerns one another, never oneself alone. Quakers are fond of stressing that we must 'know one another in the Light', or as Fox put it, 'walk cheerfully over the earth, answering that of God in everyone'. The patterns of speech are quaint; but what they point to is an epistemic responsibility in which lively care for one another is central to a conception of knowledge far removed from lifeless calculation.

Locke, as is obvious, could not accept this idea of an inner Light which gave immediate awareness of God – or anything else. Although he (of course) had to concede the possibility of revelation, he insisted that any alleged revelation must be tested by reason for its authenticity; it must be grounded in evidence beyond itself. What he writes about 'enthusiasts' generally would apply specifically to the Quakers I have been considering:

> For men thus possessed boast of a light whereby they say they are enlightened, and brought to the knowledge of this or that truth ... If they say they know it to be true, because it is a revelation from God, the reason is good: but then it will be demanded how they know it to be a revelation from God. If they say, by the light it brings with it, which shines bright in their minds, and they cannot resist: I beseech them to consider whether this be any more than what we have taken notice of already, viz. that it is a revelation, because they strongly believe it to be true. For all the light they speak of is but a strong, though ungrounded persuasion of their own minds.
>
> (Locke 1959: IV.19.11)

But what, for Locke, would then count to 'ground' such persuasion? On what foundation could it be built? What Locke is looking for here is 'evidence', independent confirmation of the truth of the inner Light (Wolterstorff 1996: 121). Miracles, for example, would be a good start: Locke held that it was miracles or 'visible signs' that provided the evidence for the authenticity of traditional revelation.

> Thus we see the holy men of old, who had revelations from God, had something else besides that internal light of assurance in their own minds ... They ... had *outward signs* to convince them of the Author of those revelations.
>
> (Locke 1959: IV.19.5)

Moses, for instance, had the burning bush; Gideon had an angel and then the miraculous fleece. If the enthusiasts could supply a burning bush or two, Locke seems to imply, that would do very nicely.

But would it? Locke is here on very boggy ground. For one thing, enthusiasts like the Quakers thought they did indeed have plenty of 'visible signs' supporting their claims. Their books are full of miracles, signs and wonders: people healed from diseases or even raised from the dead, miraculous escapes or protection from danger, knowledge of secrets or of the future, and on and on. If this was the game Locke wanted to play, Quakers could play it with a will. In fact, however, although Locke called for evidence such as miracles, he did not pay any attention to the accounts of miracles on offer, writing rather as if such accounts did not exist. For their part, Quakers did not press them. Anyone who did not acknowledge the inner Light would hardly be convinced by alleged miracles. In their view, the things that happened were indeed a witness to the living God among them, but not crude 'outward signs' to be collected as evidence for an intellect bent on calculating possibilities.

And this is the crux of the matter. Locke's epistemology was one of calculation, as we have seen, a 'mechanical' resolving of sense experience to its basic components and building up from that ground an edifice every aspect of which would ideally be founded in evidence and composed by strict rational principles. Quakers, for their part, held that they were in direct and living contact with the divine; that the Light within them was not a matter of calculation but of vibrant contact with the source of life. One can of course probe further and ask what they meant by this, or think that they were wrong; that they were at least sometimes mistaken is inevitable, and that their social behaviour on the basis of it was often infuriating is indubitable. But it is obvious that Locke's arguments would never convince them, because from their perspective such as epistemology has no life in it. Calculators would be better at doing sums. But is doing sums what epistemology is about?

The answer, no doubt, depends on the nature of what is known: if that which we are most interested in knowing is lifeless mechanism, then mathematics is very useful. But central to what I have been presenting is the theme that treating the universe in that way is not inevitable. It was a choice made in the seventeenth century and taken up in secular modernity. Moreover, it was a choice that could have been made differently: there were alternatives on offer. Part of what was at stake in scoffing at enthusiasts was discrediting these alternatives, not so much by argument as by elbowing them out of the available rhetorical space.

Thus, for example, closely related to their teaching on the Light within, and central to their symbolic, is the Quaker location of the divine, a difference from philosophical thought that became acute with Locke and later Deist writings. Whereas these held, as we have seen, that God must be sharply other than this world, which in itself is matter in motion, Quakers believed that the divine life permeates everything. They taught that the divine was within human persons: a Life and Light and Seed and Fountain – they mixed their metaphors happily. But there are indications that some of them at least also thought that the whole world was alive with divine life, could we but see it.

George Fox, for example, tells of an incident early in his adult life when, for the first time, he was clear about the basis of his spiritual existence:

> Now was I come up in spirit through the flaming sword into the paradise of God. All things were new, and all the creation gave another smell unto me than before, beyond what words can utter ... The creation was opened to me.
>
> (Fox 1952: 27)

And it is striking that he thereupon wondered whether he should practise *medicine*: he would have approached it very differently from Harvey and Locke. There are echoes here of an older epistemological tradition of sympathy; perhaps of Paracelsus and Boehme (Jones [1914] 1971). They are hints of a road not taken, a pre-modern idea of a living world and a lively knowledge of us that now strikes us as alien, almost bizarre, so inured are we to the worldview of the Strasbourg clock of Locke and Boyle. And yet perhaps holistic medicine is now raising as serious a challenge to the idea of bodies as mechanism, as the threatening ecological disasters raise questions about the mechanistic idea of the earth. Margaret Fell saw it long ago: 'Must we turn God out of the earth?' she asked. 'Is he not the God of the whole earth?' (cited in Mack 1992: 364).

Lorraine Code suggests that instead of according paradigmatic epistemological status to knowledge of lifeless bits of matter, we might take our knowledge of one another as exemplary for epistemology. Thus far she is challenging the Lockean system in a way that has parallels with what I have been describing. But she then asks how such a model 'could work in situations where the object of knowledge is inanimate' (Code 1995: 49), where rocks and cells don't answer back when the scientist works with them. I wonder, however, whether this problem might be moved forward somewhat by reflecting on the pre-modern conception of the living universe that early Quakers seem to have held, a universe that embodies the divine. When Lorraine Code speaks of rocks and cells as inanimate, in what sense does she mean that term? Literally, of course, it means 'lifeless': we are back with a dead universe. But why should we just accept that idea? From the fact that rocks and cells are in many respects unlike us, it does not follow that they are therefore like the Strasbourg clock: nothing compels us to construct such a binary, or to equate 'inanimate' in Code's sense with 'mechanical' – though I would suggest that in that case 'inanimate' is perhaps not the most useful term. As Code says, an epistemologically instructive aspect of knowing other people 'is that even knowing all the facts about someone does not count as knowing her as the person she is' (52): might the same be true of other animals, plants, maybe even rocks and stars? In other words, if we were interested in them not just for factual knowledge and utilitarian ends but as part of a living world where beauty and goodness had as great a part as truth and helped to define it, how might our knowledge and our ethics be changed? But to answer that question perhaps we would have to pursue it for three hundred years, as the mechanistic alternative has been pursued in modernity.

And what of religion? Locke and the Deists banished God from the world, making him – and it certainly was 'him' – a cosmic clockmaker and final judge, and making the world meanwhile a secular space. In due course the clockmaker was no longer necessary, and God was dumped altogether: and no bad thing, I think, if what we are talking about is Locke's patriarchal oppressor. But again, why should we just swallow Locke's conception of the divine? Especially in the light of the masculinism of western modernity, its violence, and its preoccupation with destruction and death, it is at least worth considering whether we should not rethink not only secularism but religion as well. I have written elsewhere (Jantzen 1998) about an understanding of the divine as horizon of our becoming. Here, I have only time to hint at it, and to note that it is striking how often early Quaker writings speak of life. In the seventeenth century they are addressing themselves to political issues, not philosophical ones, and the context has more in common with Bunyan's rough-edged Puritanism than with Locke's urbane *Reasonableness of Christianity*. Nevertheless, the epistemological implications are apparent. For example, Margaret Fell's *True Testimony*, presented to King Charles II on his accession to the throne in 1660, vibrates with references to life: life not in some heaven or Celestial City such as Bunyan's Pilgrim hoped to find, but life here, now, welling up in people alive to the fountain of life. Far from thinking of this world and our knowledge of it as dead and a question of mastery, Fell emphasizes the new life and new possibilities for justice and truth that are springing up in this world, offering hope and flourishing. It is the denial of this life, the 'endeavour to limit the Spirit of the living God' (Fell 1992: 38,) which has caused the ungodliness and death-dealing of the age, says Fell; and it is by returning to the life of God and finding in oneself that welling up of divine life which is the remedy, because it brings the possibility of radically new insight and action. There is, here, I suggest, a challenge to the necrophilia of early modernity whose epistemological foundations are laid by Locke, and the contours of a different imaginary, which I have elsewhere called an imaginary of natality (Jantzen 1998).

But the repressed returns. At the top of the Strasbourg clock, there is a mechanical rooster. Each day, just before the clock strikes twelve, the rooster emerges and crows three times. Thus, in the mechanization of the world, its divine life is denied.

Part Three

Beauty, desire and engaged spirituality

Chapter 8

In the eye of the beholder?

One of the standard ways of dismissing beauty from serious consideration, in theology and elsewhere, is to assert that 'beauty is in the eye of the beholder'. Beauty, like taste, is subjective: what one person enjoys another might not. As David Hume put this position:

> Beauty is no quality in things in themselves. It exists merely in the mind that contemplates them, and each mind perceives a different beauty.
>
> (Elledge, ed. 1961: II. 814)

Truth is different. It is objective. Reasons and arguments can be given for and against beliefs; and if the arguments are valid then rational people will be persuaded. The same is true of goodness and morality. Though there are areas of dispute, there are also fundamental moral principles which cannot be overturned if human society is to continue. Indeed the very fact that there are arguments about truth and morality shows that they are amenable to rational discussion; whereas beauty and taste are subjective and not open to debate. As Hume puts it:

> Truth is disputable; not taste: what exists in the nature of things is the standard of our judgement; what each man feels within himself is the standard of sentiment. Propositions in geometry may be proved, systems in physics may be controverted; but the harmony of verse, the tenderness of passion, the brilliancy of wit must give immediate pleasure.
>
> (Hume 1962: 171)

Either these things give delight to the recipient or they do not; there is about as much to be gained by presenting arguments as there is humour to be extracted by dissecting a joke.

Whereas centuries of logicians and epistemologists have developed criteria for the determination of truth, and ethicists have worked out criteria of moral behaviour, it is hard, if not impossible, to specify criteria for the determination of beauty. Beauty, therefore, is not sufficiently discernible by objective standards to play a central theological role. Quite apart from the strands of thinking in Christendom outlined in Chapter 1 that are suspicious of beauty, the subjective and relative character of beauty preclude it from any likelihood of bearing theological weight.

Feminists, in fact, may have additional reason to be sceptical of invoking beauty for theological purposes. Not only is beauty a matter of subjective taste, on this view, but the arbiters of this taste have regularly been men. Men, not women, have on the whole had the power to specify what should count as beautiful and what should not. In literature, art and music, the canon is constructed by men according to their tastes and desires. It is therefore not surprising that so few women find a place in the canon of great artists or composers. Usually they had neither the training nor the opportunity to produce great works; and even when they did, they were, with a few exceptions, marginalized by the men who policed the boundaries of the musical or artistic or literary canon. If beauty is to play a central role in theology or in religious life, might this not simply hand over yet more power to men?

This feminist scepticism is all the more pertinent because women themselves, or at least women's bodies, have often been treated by men as the paradigm of beauty, and then treated with contempt if they in some way fall short, or with either lust or suspicion or both if they measure up. So the 'beautiful' woman in western modernity is the woman who is attractive to men: young, able-bodied, slim, fair … Any search on the internet under 'beauty' brings up, not theological or aesthetic discussion of the topic (as is the case with 'truth'), but thousands of advertisements and items on the 'beauty industry', most of them focusing on how women can make themselves more sexually attractive to men. If beauty is in the eye of the beholder, and the beholder is usually male, feminists need to exercise great care in how beauty is appropriated in our thinking about religion, lest it serve to intensify the already dominant male gaze.

Nevertheless, without minimizing the importance of such feminist scepticism, I want to argue against such dismissal of beauty. To say that 'beauty is in the eye of the beholder' and assume that it can therefore not be of central theological significance is much too hasty. It is not my purpose to trace all the arguments in aesthetic theory regarding the subjectivity or objectivity of beauty; but I do want to say enough to show that dismissal of beauty on grounds of subjectivism is misguided.

In the first place, the supposed contrast between truth and goodness as objective, on the one hand, and beauty as subjective, on the other, is far from clear cut. It is true that philosophers and ethicists have developed standards or objective criteria for assessing truth claims and moral positions, though it is far from clear that those criteria are simply to be accepted. Indeed, they are contested at every turn by logicians and epistemologists. On the other hand, objective criteria of beauty have also been offered: until the Enlightenment, in fact, there were widely accepted standards of beauty (including harmony, proportion, integrity and clarity), which were taken to be objective (Bredin and Santoro-Brienza 2000; Beardsley 1966). With the Enlightenment, two things happened. One was that the alleged objective criteria of beauty were seen to be problematic as the importance of the perceiving subject came to the fore. The second was that a massive shift to epistemology took place. Philosophy became identified with the search for and evaluation of truth claims: with 'clear and distinct' ideas and indubitable foundations as, famously, in Descartes' *Meditations*. Although some philosophers – notably Hume, Kant and Hegel – continued to theorize about beauty, it received far less attention, even in their works, than did truth and belief; and many philosophers ignored beauty altogether. As a consequence, the disproportionate attention to truth and its criteria, and the relative neglect of beauty in modern philosophy, has made it easy to claim that there are objective standards for the former but not for the latter. But is that any more than a reflection of the effort that has been expended in trying to develop such standards? If philosophers and theologians were to spend even a fraction of the time developing aesthetic criteria, including their uses and limitations, that they routinely spend on epistemological criteria, the situation might be very different.

One way to approach the task is to think harder about what the claim to subjectivity comes to. The perception of beauty is often linked with the idea of taste. Now taste, it is said, is subjective, as can be seen when we think of taste in its literal sense, in connection with food. If I like spinach and you don't, that is the end of the matter and there is nothing more to be said. There are no criteria for taste, no arguments by which I could persuade you that spinach tastes good after all. And just the same applies to beauty. Some people like to listen to Mozart, others like Madonna. Some like Rembrandt, others like Picasso, many would never enter an art gallery at all. Some love the slant of light on hills and streams, the song of birds and the delicacy of wild flowers; but others are left cold by nature's beauties and would much rather go to a club or party than out for a long walk. It is all a matter of taste; it is not the sort of thing one can sensibly debate, even though everyone can have their own strong preferences.

But that argument is muddled, as can be shown by thinking a little more about spinach. When children say that they do not like spinach, or any other vegetables, it is a poor parent who takes the view that there is nothing more to be said and the child must be given burgers and fries. There is obviously a great deal more to be said: not least about health and nutrition and fitness. There are objective standards of nourishment; and parents try to help their children to develop their taste so that they will eat what is good for them and like it. It is true, of course, that this cannot usually be done by argument, which is very likely to be counterproductive. Typically, parents try to help their children by preparing the food in ways that the child will be able to deal with, progressively; and above all, they teach by example. The fact that development of taste cannot be acquired by argument does not show that taste is strictly subjective.

There are parallels with beauty, as well as differences. To note the parallels first: from the fact that our subjective likes and dislikes vary it does not follow that some things are not better for us than others, or more aesthetically nourishing, or even more objectively beautiful. It may only follow that we have never developed the taste for them. Our characters, in modernity, have not usually been built up by aesthetic sensibilities: we have fed our souls on the aesthetic equivalent of junk food and have never learned to appreciate anything better.[1]

Let me be clear. My argument up to this point does not prove that beauty is in fact objective, but only that an appeal to divergence of preference or taste does not automatically consign beauty to a realm of such utter subjective relativism that there is nothing more to be said. Even if it is in some sense true that 'beauty is in the eye of the beholder', it may be that the eye is myopic or untrained and cannot see or appreciate what is before it. I shall in fact argue later that the decline of developed aesthetic sensibility in western modernity correlates with increasing willingness to tolerate violence as a way of dealing with problems; or, putting the point in positive terms, that rebuilding our characters with beauty as a central value would also increase empathy and goodwill, essential for finding alternatives to violence. All of that comes later. The present point is only that taste, in beauty as in food, is not a natural given, but is a capacity that can be shaped and educated. In that respect it is more like a skill than like a physical quality, such as hair or eye colour.

Nor is this argument undermined by the vast differences in cultural sensibility. It is of course true that what is passed over without notice in one culture may count as exquisitely beautiful in another. But the same is true about food. There are vast differences in cuisine around the world: for many in the west a taste for grasshopper legs or frogspawn would definitely have to be acquired before we could treat them as delicacies. But that proves nothing, one way or the other, about whether or not grasshopper legs or frogspawn are good for us, let alone that nourishment is subjective. It only shows how large a role cultural situation plays in the formation of taste. The same is obviously the case in relation to beauty.

However, if the analogy with taste in food is to be sustained, then ultimately the question of criteria emerges after all. There are objective ways of measuring the nutritional value of food, independent of taste; and it is on the basis of these nutritional criteria that we can discriminate between wholesome food and junk food. But what criteria can we apply by which to measure beauty? How much sugar is there in a concerto, or salt in a sunset? What sorts of characteristics or values could we begin to generate that would give us, if not measurements or precise criteria, at least some objective basis for discrimination and appreciation? In the case of food, the criteria are derived from an empirical investigation into the body and its functions. What sort of empirical investigation could even in principle provide grounds or criteria by which we could justify a claim that a landscape or a work of art is beautiful? The analogy with food begins to seem strained.

Or does it? After all, people knew what to eat and how to select foods that were good for them long before biological science and nutritional measurements had been invented. Perhaps an entire nutritional science was implicit in people's development of taste in food, but it was not a precondition of good eating that such a science be consciously developed. Similarly, although there may be objective standards of beauty implicit in culturally developed taste, it is not the case that we can say nothing meaningful about beauty until we have established agreed criteria. In some respects, in fact, it is misguided to scurry around after criteria, as though we must first have objective standards before we can decide whether or not something is beautiful. We know in advance of any theory that sunrises and primroses and the song of the meadowlark are beautiful: if any theory seemed to suggest otherwise, we would throw out the theory, not the primroses. In this respect the task is less a matter of developing criteria to validate aesthetic judgements than to explain how it is that some people lack certain forms of aesthetic sensibility and to work out how that lack can be overcome. And we know in advance that, as with food, it will not be overcome by arguing about it.

One way to proceed, therefore, would be to try to work the other way around. What do we already know, how much can we already say, about beauty and our response to it? How far can we get towards objective criteria by proceeding this way; and how much (and for what) do such criteria matter? And what light does consideration of beauty shed on issues of gender construction and on the ugly violence that wracks the world?

What is beauty?

'Beauty' is a tricky term to define, as anyone who has been put on the spot knows. In this respect it is no different from other overarching terms, including 'truth' and 'goodness'. But this does not show that any of these terms are worthless: on the contrary, for the most part we know quite well how to use them. There are of course puzzling cases and contentious issues, but in ordinary life we have no difficulty understanding what is meant by saying that a sunrise is beautiful, or a Rembrandt painting, or a Bach concerto, any more than we have difficulty understanding what is meant by saying that a Marxist analysis of African poverty is true or that granting political asylum to people from Iraq is good. We may agree or disagree with any of these claims, but we know what the claims mean. To that extent it is clear that we understand the terms 'beauty', 'truth' and 'goodness', whether or not we can give precise definitions.

There have been those who have argued, partly from the fact that the concept of beauty throws up puzzles that are difficult to resolve and partly because of the way in which beauty can be cheapened into mere consolatory prettiness, that beauty is a term we should do without. Thus, for example, J.A. Passmore, in an article tellingly entitled 'The Dreariness of Aesthetics', says:

> I should suggest that there is something suspect ('phony') about 'beauty'. Artists seem to get along quite well without it; it is the café-haunters, the preachers, the metaphysicians, and the calendar-makers who talk of beauty ... 'Beauty' is always nice, always soothing; it is what the bourgeois pays the artist for ... In more professional circles, it is the refuge of the metaphysician finding a home for art in his harmonious universe, attempting to subdue its ferocity, its revelations of deep-seated conflict.
>
> (Passmore 1954: 50)

But such dismissal is too easy. In the first place, as we shall see more fully in Chapter 9, philosophers and theologians from Plato and Augustine through to Karl Barth would be surprised to hear that beauty is 'nice' or 'soothing': on the contrary, they spent much energy trying to avert its dangers. Second, however, 'beauty' is a term that we cannot do without. It captures something crucial to our existence. In contrast to the Gradgrinds of this world it points to values that are non-utilitarian and other than the free market economy. I shall argue later that it provides openings for alternatives to violence.

Ludwig Wittgenstein, in his later work, was fond of considering what it was to have a 'form of life' – a particular cultural formation or, more broadly, what it is to be human. In his view, the meaning of a term is not specifiable so clearly by precise definition, let alone by metaphysical essence, but by the way it functions in the everyday language of actual forms of life. What work does the term do? If we did not have the term, would we need to invent it (Wittgenstein 1969)?

In the case of beauty, it quickly becomes clear that we could not do without it. Unclear and puzzling though it may be, it is necessary both for philosophical reflection and for ordinary life to have a term like beauty, to stand alongside truth and goodness, without being reducible to either of them. As Mary Mothersill has argued, in partly Wittgensteinian terms:

> What makes the concept of beauty indispensable is the fact that there is a particular complex capacity, that of taking various items to be beautiful, which is central to our form of life. A description of a person who lacked that capacity would find its natural place, if anywhere, in the literature of psychopathology.
>
> (Mothersill 1984: 277)

The problems and insights into both the concept of beauty and the form of life in which it has its place should be sought, therefore, by considering its use, its function in our specific culture and our broader humanity.

How, then, is 'beauty' used? As the *Oxford English Dictionary* assesses its use, beauty is 'such combined perfection of form and charm of colouring as affords keen pleasure to the sense of sight', or 'that quality or combination of qualities which affords keen pleasure to other senses'. In secondary uses it can also refer to what affords intellectual or moral pleasure. The examples the Dictionary gives are, in the first case, the beauty of the human form or figure, and the beauties of nature and its creatures; or in relation to other senses, the beauty of poetry or music.

From this dictionary account of common usage of the term, I want to extract several issues which I will discuss more fully later. First, beauty has to do with the senses. It is perceived. It is therefore understood in relation to the body, to physicality. Whatever the contribution of intellectual assessment or moral evaluation, in the first instance beauty is perceived by bodily senses, especially sight and hearing, and thus depends more directly and immediately upon the body than does truth. We could give examples of truths that are strictly conceptual, such as mathematical theorems, but we could speak of disembodied beauty only in an extended and parasitic sense.

In its primary meaning, a beautiful thing is in some way physical, and accessible to the physical senses, whether a material object whose form and colour is perceived by the eyes or a piece of music whose notes are heard by the ear, or a scent that we can smell. Beauty is embodied, and depends upon bodies to be perceived.

This embodiment of beauty, in both the objective and the subjective senses, has a bearing on the topics around which this book revolves: gender and violence. If beauty is perceived by bodily senses, then the perceiving body is a gendered body. The eye that beholds beauty and the ear that hears it is gender specific. Moreover, one of the central examples of beauty is the human form, the body. Again, this is a gendered body. I suggest, therefore, that both in relation to the beautiful body and in relation to the body that perceives beauty, it is crucial to explore the interconnection with gender, and with embodiment more generally. I shall argue that a heightened emphasis upon beauty, and sensitivity towards it, is interconnected with greater appreciation of the human body, its gendered nature and its sexuality; and greater appreciation also of the material world more generally. If a sort of moral Puritanism leads to despising beauty, as discussed in Chapter 1, then heightened aesthetic sensibility leads to positive evaluation of the physical world, including the gendered human body. I shall discuss this in Chapter 9.

Moreover, if beauty is related to bodies, this relation stands in opposition to violence. That which we find beautiful we value, and want to preserve. It makes no sense to say that cowslips are beautiful and then to trample over them, or to delight in birds' song and wantonly destroy their habitat. The greater the degree and range of our aesthetic sensibility, the more we will care about conserving and fostering beautiful things. The more we discern the fragile beauty of gendered human bodies, the less we will condone violence against them. Sensitivity to beauty is in direct contrast to violent attitudes and actions, as I shall explore more fully later in this book.

A second, related theme that I wish to draw out of the dictionary account of 'beauty' is the theme of pleasure. Beauty is that which 'affords keen pleasure', whether to sight or hearing or all the senses combined. If we find something beautiful, we enjoy it. Nor do we need any additional reason for the pleasure: if I am asked why I enjoy walking in the hills and valleys of the Lake District, it is perfectly adequate to reply, 'Because it is beautiful'. Should someone press the question, 'But why do you enjoy what is beautiful?' it would show that they did not properly understand what the term 'beauty' means: how it is used in ordinary conversation. Because beauty is linked with pleasure and enjoyment, it attracts us, draws us towards it. We value and love it: this again is clearly related to a desire not only to experience it but to treasure and preserve it rather than allow it to be destroyed. The power of the pleasure of beauty is, I shall argue, to be fostered rather than to be feared, and it is a well-spring of resources for alternatives to violence.

The dictionary definition specifies that it is 'perfection of form or charm of colouring' in which (visual) beauty consists. Can this 'perfection' and 'charm' be more fully specified? We are back, here, to the question of objective standards or criteria for beauty. There have been theorists who have thought that such criteria could easily be stated. Edmund Burke, for example, argued in the eighteenth century that

> beauty is, for the greater part, some quality in bodies, acting mechanically upon the human mind by the intervention of the senses
>
> (Burke 1990: 102)

and arousing our pleasure and delight. Burke thought that the qualities of objects that are essential to beauty are smallness, smoothness, gradual variation, delicacy, clear and bright colours 'but not very strong and glaring' and, in the human form, 'the face must be expressive of such gentle and amiable qualities, as correspond with the softness, smoothness, and delicacy of the outward form' (107). Part of Burke's project was to make a distinction between the beautiful and the sublime, a distinction I shall revisit later. In doing so, he thought it entirely possible to specify what it is that beauty consists in.

In this he was not alone. As already mentioned, thinkers since the time of classical Athens had been concerned with the objective criteria of beauty, emphasizing in particular proportion (which Burke vigorously rejects), harmony, measure and order. But suppose an object meets all these criteria and yet a viewer finds no pleasure in it, does not see it as beautiful. Is it then not beautiful after all?

One possible response would be to reply that the object is indeed beautiful, even though some viewer does not appreciate it, just as certain objects are red or green even though some people cannot recognize colours. It is possible to be 'beauty blind' just as it is possible to be colour blind. The problem is with the perceiver, not with the object. It is true that some areas of aesthetic sensibility require education and are not automatic; but if someone is really unable to see the beauties of nature, the play of light, the scent of flowers, that person, it might be held, is seriously deprived of ability to perceive beauty. In such a case we do not ask whether flowers and trees are perhaps not beautiful after all; rather, we should see why and how the individual who cannot appreciate their beauty has been deprived, and how that deprivation could be remedied.

I think there is something in this response. Sometimes the failure to recognize beauty is to be located in a problem with the eye of the beholder, more complicated, to be sure, than simple visual problems that could be corrected with a new pair of spectacles, but nevertheless resting with the perceiver, not with the object. But note that to make that response it has been necessary to shift ground. The response is plausible if we think of concrete examples, specific instances of beautiful things, like flowers and trees. It might just barely be plausible, though much more debatable, if the examples were works of art: paintings or music, since here education and cultural location play so obvious a part. But it does not seem plausible at all if we think strictly in terms of the proffered objective criteria, whether Burke's or anyone else's. The most that could be said is that such criteria might be abstracted from a range of examples that we do in fact recognize as beautiful; but it would not be contradictory to say that some object met the criteria but was nevertheless ugly (see Ward 1992 for fuller discussion).

It follows that specification of criteria of beauty will always be parasitic upon, and more contentious than, recognition of actual objects of beauty. Two people could watch together the shifting colours and patterns of a sunset and agree that it is utterly beautiful, and yet have a hard time coming up with exactly what it is that makes it so beautiful or arguing with one another's efforts. In fact, arguing about what makes something beautiful can easily destroy aesthetic response, rather than enhancing it. The immediacy of beauty can be shared, as I shall discuss later; but such sharing is a sharing of perception and response, not a trading of reasons and arguments.

In summary, it is not necessary to be able to specify precise criteria in order to maintain that something is beautiful. The subjectivist–objectivist debate can rumble on in aesthetic theory, as it does in moral theory, but it need not be resolved before we can appreciate beautiful things or perform good acts. As Foucault has insisted, it is in many respects more important to understand function than essence: the crucial questions have more to do with what beauty *does* than with what it *is* in some precise ontological sense. Many puzzles remain; but to stay stuck on those puzzles or to assume that we cannot say anything intelligent about beauty until we have resolved them would be like saying that we can have no well-grounded moral principles unless we have resolved the complexities of ethical theory. Life is more important than theory. How does beauty live?

Nature and art

The term 'beauty', as it is commonly used, ranges over a wide variety of things: a landscape, a tree, a moonlit night, a human face, a kitten, a painting, a concerto ... the list is endless. One broad distinction between kinds of beautiful things is the distinction between those things that are made by humans and those that are not: the distinction between art and nature. Even this distinction is not as clear as it might seem. Is a human face that is framed by carefully styled hair and with tastefully applied cosmetics beautiful by nature or by art? What about a carefully planted garden, or a landscape produced by centuries of farming? Rather than clear boundaries, it may be more accurate to think of a continuum between nature and art, ranging from those things which in no way rely on human activity, like starlight on a clear winter's night, to those which are entirely human artefacts, like musical compositions.

This is not to say that everything in either nature or art, or their interaction, is beautiful. Nature produces deformities; and even perfect specimens of toads or cockroaches would appeal to the aesthetic sensibilities of only a small minority of people! In art, the intention might be quite deliberately *not* to produce something beautiful, perhaps making a political statement by its departure from usual aesthetic norms, as for example Picasso's *Guernica* and much else in modern art. Nevertheless it is fair to say, though with many qualifications, that the beauty of nature is primary, and art begins as an effort to copy or capture some aspect of that beauty, or in some way to comment on it or on its own history.

As I shall discuss more fully in the next two chapters, this idea that art in some sense tries to imitate nature has led to varying evaluations of art, beginning as early as the philosophy of Plato and Aristotle. Plato held (at least some of the time) that nature with its beauties was itself an imperfect material copy of an Idea or Form, which was perfect and immaterial. Art was therefore a copy of a copy. Now, in any copying, the further one is from the original, the more errors creep in. Art is therefore suspect: it is far removed from the perfection of the original Idea, and to be caught up in it is to subject oneself to the admiration or imitation of imperfection. Aristotle's view was different. In the first place, he did not share Plato's philosophy of non-material Ideas. In his view, what was primary was formed matter. Moreover, art, or any kind of imitation of what is good or beautiful, is the way in which such beauty and goodness is reproduced. Education is based on mimesis: we learn how to produce beautiful things by copying; we learn to be good by imitating those who are good. It is therefore important to choose our models with great care, but imitation is central to learning, and art contributes to human development.

Both of these views appear, with variations and tensions, in Christendom. Central to the creation story is the affirmation that God saw everything that God had made as 'very good': the Hebrew word implies that it was aesthetically pleasing, beautiful, as well as useful. Although beauty is not a dominant theme in biblical writing, it persists as an undercurrent. I shall discuss some aspects of it later: for now I want simply to note that the beauty of nature is seen as God's creation, and in that sense a manifestation or revelation of God, as a work of art reveals the artist. Human beings, moreover, are made in the image of God; hence, like God, humans seek to create what is beautiful in their arts and crafts. The point is that in Christendom the beauty of nature is primary, and the beauty of art is derived from it and ultimately dependent on it.

The term 'aesthetics' is much more recent. It derives from the Greek word *aísthesis*, which simply means sense perception. It was not until the eighteenth century that a German philosopher, Alexander Baumgarten, used the term 'aesthetics' to stand for 'the science of sensitive knowing', the most highly developed form of which he took to be the sense perception of beauty (Davey 1992: 40; Bredin and Santoro-Brienza 2000: 3). This direct perception of beauty was, according to Baumgarten, distinct from the sort of knowing which we experience in the natural sciences or in logic. We can have this direct perception of beauty, this 'aesthetic knowledge', in relation to natural beauty, but also in relation to the arts. Indeed it was the arts that came to be the focus of aesthetics, so that now the term 'aesthetics' sometimes refers primarily to works of art, especially music and painting. Journals or textbooks of aesthetics will take as their subject the theory or philosophy of art, rather than beauty more generally.

In this book, however, I shall retain the broader meaning. 'Aesthetic sensibility' refers, in my usage, to appreciation of beauty in both nature and art, since it is my view that sensitivity to beauty in either case calls for openness and response, and in turn evokes pleasure and stimulates creativity, as I shall show in the chapters that follow.

Chapter 9

Beauty and the body

The appeal of beauty to the physical senses makes it seem obvious that beauty and bodies are closely interrelated. Both the object and the subject of beauty are embodied; in other words, the beautiful thing is in some way material, whether as colour or shape or soundwave; and the one who perceives beauty does so by way of the physical senses. This being the case, it makes sense to suppose that we might understand both beauty and the body better by considering them together; and so I shall argue.

It is, however, contrary to a view of beauty which has had a very long run in western culture, beginning with Plato and extending far into Christendom. In Plato's famous discussion of beauty in the *Symposium*, for example, Beauty Itself is non-physical; and although the body of the perceiver plays an essential role, ultimately it is left behind. Both subject and object are disembodied.

According to the speech that Plato puts into the mouth of Diotima, the one who is to be initiated into beauty 'cannot begin too early to devote himself to the beauties of the body'. He (and in Plato's discourse it will always be 'he') rejects sexual association with women and chooses instead 'procreancy of the spirit', falling in love first with 'the beauty of one individual [boy's] body', from there to the loveliness of every lovely body. Next he will 'grasp that the beauties of the body are as nothing to the beauties of the soul', and will proceed via intellectual beauty to beauty itself, 'the open sea of beauty' perceived by the eyes of the mind, which confers immortality (Plato, *Symposium* 209a–212a). Plato is at pains to emphasize that the body plays no part in this vision of the beautiful itself, nor is ultimate universal beauty in any sense embodied.

> Nor will his vision of the beautiful take the form of a face, or of hands, or of anything that is of the flesh. It will be neither words, nor knowledge, nor a something that exists in something else, such as a living creature, or the earth, or the heavens, or anything that is – but subsisting in itself and by itself in an eternal oneness ...
>
> (*Symposium* 211a–b)

Although bodies are essential for initiation into beauty, they are left behind when the first stages are surpassed. Beauty Itself, in Plato's philosophy, is non-material, as indeed is all ultimate reality: an Idea perceived by the mind alone.

In the writings of Plotinus the tense relationship between bodies and beauty is explored further. Like Plato, Plotinus begins with the recognition that beauty is embodied, but ends by trying to transcend bodiliness altogether. Plotinus gives a summary of the objective characteristics of beauty, as popularly believed:

> Nearly everyone says that it is good proportion of the parts to each other and to the whole, with the addition of good colour, which produces visible beauty, and that with the objects of sight and generally with everything else, being beautiful is being well-proportioned and measured. On this theory nothing single and simple but only a composite thing will have any beauty. It will be the whole which is beautiful, and the parts will not have the property of beauty by themselves, but will contribute to the beauty of the whole. But if the whole is beautiful the parts must be beautiful too; a beautiful whole can certainly not be composed of ugly parts: all the parts must have beauty.
>
> (Plotinus, *Enneads* I. 6. 1)

But Plotinus could not accept this popular view. As he saw it, matter is not beautiful in itself; and therefore no mere rearrangement of matter could make it beautiful. Rather, beauty comes from the soul or Intellect; ultimately from God. It is this divine power which forms matter, and it is this formation, not the matter itself, which is beautiful.

> So the soul when it is purified becomes form and formative power, altogether bodiless and intellectual and entirely belonging to the divine, whence beauty springs and all that is akin to it ... For this reason it is right to say that the soul's becoming something good and beautiful is its being made like to God, because from him come beauty and all else which falls to the lot of real beings ... Everything else is beautiful by the shaping of soul, the beauties in actions and in ways of life. And soul makes beautiful the bodies which are spoken of as beautiful; for since it is a divine thing and a kind of part of beauty, it makes everything it grasps and masters beautiful.
>
> (*Enneads* I. 6. 6)

Exactly how the divine makes first the Intellect and then the soul beautiful, and how the soul can then act upon matter to give it form, has been a puzzle for scholars, but need not detain us here (see Rist 1967; Miles 1999). What is important is that ultimately beauty for Plotinus, as for Plato, is non-material.[1]

This being so, it will not be with the body and its senses that beauty is perceived. Indeed, in the 'ascent to the good', Plotinus echoes Plato's ideas in the *Symposium*, in which the body and its senses are gradually left behind or stripped off, 'just as for those who go up to the celebrations of sacred rites there are purifications, and strippings off of the clothes they wore before, and going up naked' (*Enneads* I. 6. 7). Thus, gradually, one will learn to see with the 'inner sight', a type of vision that can come only to those who 'shut [their] eyes, and change to and wake to another way of seeing' (I. 6. 8), a way that has altogether dispensed with the body.

> If you have become this, and see it, and are at home with yourself in purity, with nothing hindering you from becoming in this way one, with no inward mixture of anything else, but wholly yourself, nothing but true light, not measured by dimensions, or bounded by shape into little-ness, or expanded to size by unboundedness, but everywhere unmea-sured, because greater than all measure and superior to all quantity; when you see that you have become this, then you have become sight; you can trust yourself then; you have already ascended and need no one to show you; concentrate your gaze and see. This alone is the eye that sees the great beauty.
>
> (*Enneads* I. 6. 9)

Thus ultimately, for Plotinus and for the Neoplatonic tradition which owed so much to him, both subject and object of beauty are bodiless, 'for one must come to the sight with a seeing power made akin and like to what is seen' (ibid.).

I shall argue below that the attempt to make beauty bodiless makes non-sense of beauty: indeed that it is a gendered and violent nonsense, given that rationality was associated with men and bodies with women. It is also strongly at odds with a Christian understanding of incarnation. Before I do so, how-ever, I wish to pause a moment on Plotinus' idea that true sight must be made akin to what is seen, or, in standard Platonic formulation, that 'like is known only by like': it takes one to know one. This is the answer Plotinus would give to the idea that beauty is in the eye of the beholder. Of course it is, in the sense that the eye not formed to beauty will never perceive it, just as an evil person will not appreciate goodness. We take this for granted in ethics: why should it not be just as true of aesthetics?

> No eye ever saw the sun without becoming sun-like, nor can a soul see beauty without becoming beautiful. You must become first all godlike and all beautiful if you intend to see God and beauty.
>
> (Ibid.)

For Plotinus, this meant divesting oneself of the body, an idea taken up and modified in Christian asceticism. But although I shall oppose myself to the idea of disembodied beauty, I do not want to dismiss with it the Plotinian idea that aesthetic sensibility is not automatic: it requires dedication and training and becoming 'all beautiful', an idea largely lost in the theology of modernity which, if it treats beauty at all, seems to suppose that its perception is automatic or spontaneous. What 'becoming beautiful' involves and how it comes about will form the topic of later chapters.

'How late have I loved you': Augustine's affair with beauty

The Eternal Oneness, Beauty Itself, as spoken of by Plato and Plotinus, were taken up in Christendom as references to God; and the Platonic vision of beauty became the Christian Beatific Vision, reserved for the faithful in a heavenly life after death. In spite of the fact that this was standardly taken as the ultimate goal of the Christian life, and the greatest longing of the human soul, however, the idea of beauty and the importance of the education of specifically aesthetic sensibility lost ground, displaced by emphasis on the word, the creed and true beliefs, all of which were appropriated by men of the church as peculiarly their own province.

We can see the transition happening in Augustine. Augustine's acute sensitivity to beauty shines out in his writings; and often it is specifically embodied, material beauty to which he refers. He writes in *City of God*, for instance, of

> The manifold diversity of beauty in sky and earth and sea; the abundance of light, and its miraculous loveliness, in sun and moon and stars; the dark shades of woods; the colour and fragrance of flowers; the multitudinous varieties of birds, with their songs and their bright plumage; the countless different species of living creatures of all shapes and sizes, amongst whom it is the smallest in bulk that moves our greatest wonder – for we are more astonished at the activities of the tiny ants and bees than at the immense bulk of the whales. Then there is the mighty spectacle of the sea itself, putting on its changing colours like changing garments, now green, with all the many varied shades, now purple, now blue. Moreover, what a delightful sight it is when stormy ...
>
> (Augustine 1972: 1075 Bk xxii, Ch. 24)

And so he goes on, extolling the beauties of the physical world around him, and of God the creator of all this beauty, of whom the world's beauties speak to those who have learned to listen. In another place, where Augustine is commenting on Psalm 145, he says, 'The beauty of the earth is a kind of voice', a voice which one can hear only if one has learned to attend to it and be sensitive to the manifold beauties the earth contains (Augustine 1983: 659).

Sensitive though Augustine is to the beauties of the physical world, he is also always ambivalent. The world is a world of change and chance; it is infested with 'worm and mice'. How can that which is mortal and corruptible truly be beautiful? In Platonic terms, true Beauty, Being Itself, is eternal and changeless; yet Augustine recognizes that things are beautiful in spite of – indeed sometimes precisely because of – their fragile and transitory nature: he is much taken, for example, with the beauty of the play of light on water. Deeply attuned as he is both to the beauty of the world around him and to the beauties of music and the arts, however, he still speaks of earthly beauties as a 'snare' and a 'trap' in which his 'feet are still caught' until God sets him free from their entanglements (1961: 241; *Confessions* x. 34). What is it that Augustine so distrusts about bodily beauty, and why does he feel such anxiety at his own fervent response to it?

Historically, part of the reply of course has to do with Augustine's Platonism. But there are two reasons why we should not be content with this reply. The first is that Augustine was well able to reject or modify Platonism when it seemed necessary to him to do so, as for example in his adherence to the doctrine of the Incarnation (a doctrine which, consistently followed through, would offer a much stronger base for the bodily nature of beauty). The second reason is that attributing the difficulty to Plato only pushes the question a stage further back: why did Plato himself so distrust the body that he had to push beauty into some disembodied realm? Ultimately the same question applies to both men: given that both Plato and Augustine were intensely sensitive to beauty, and insisted that Beauty is ultimately a manifestation of (or even another name for) Ultimate Reality or the divine Creator, why did they remain so anxious about it, and in particular about its obvious bodily or physical nature? We can see how, once this distrust is in place and secured within a philosophical and theological framework, it would gradually take hold, so that the emphasis on beauty diminishes: thus for example the Protestant theology of modernity, dependent via Calvin, Schleiermacher, and others on the thought of Plato and Augustine, makes very little room for beauty in favour of an emphasis on the Word, and is at best inattentive, at worst sceptical of the aesthetic qualities of the flesh. But why this deep anxiety about the bodily nature of beauty in the first place?

Beauty as idolatry

Augustine's struggles with his attraction to beauty and yet his fear of it is often represented in terms of a concern with idolatry. Augustine was not the first early Christian writer to wrestle with questions of idol worship, but he was a major voice in constructing beauty in relation to idolatry. It is a construction that has had a long history in Christian thought, and even now continues to trouble Christian theologians: Karl Barth, to cite only one example, worries about the beauty of nature because, he says, 'always, when man has tried to read the truth from sun, moon and stars ... the result has been an idol' (Barth 1959: 52).

Augustine refers to idols in various ways in his writings. His particular concern is always with the way in which a created thing is given the worship due only to its Creator. Sometimes he discusses idols in relation to biblical stories like the golden calf (1961: 146; *Confessions* vii. 9). Sometimes he writes of the gods worshipped by the Romans or others as idols or demons, as contrasted with the true God of Christendom (1972: 86; *City of God* ii. 29; 1983: 477; *Psalms* xcvii. 10). These forms of idolatry, however, were never a particular temptation to Augustine himself, and though he refers to them, he does so without anxiety.

In the *Confessions*, however, when Augustine tells of his association with Manichaeism, he writes of idolatry in an altogether more engaged way. He explains that he was trying to come to an understanding of God, and as he did so, he got things badly wrong.

> My soul ... could find no rest ... [It] imagined for itself a god extended through all space to infinity. Thinking that this god was you, it had enshrined this idol in its heart and ... had made of itself a temple abominable to you ...
>
> (1961: 149; *Confessions* vii. 14)

This is the sort of idolatry that deeply troubles Augustine: the construction of a false conception of God, possibly made in all sincerity. In his account of his conversion the sequence of false conceptions and his gradual emergence to what he held to be the true God is a guiding thread of his story. His great concern is always his temptation to substitute the husk for the kernel: to take the manifestations of God in creation as though they were the divine essence. Beauty embodied in nature and art draws Augustine so strongly that his response, he worries, is idolatrous.

Even after his conversion Augustine is caught up in struggles of his conscience because of his enjoyment of beauty. He tells, for instance, as though he is ashamed of it, of his delight in church music if it is well performed.

> I admit that I still find some enjoyment in the music of hymns, which are alive with your praises, when I hear them sung by well-trained, melodious voices.
>
> (1961: 238; *Confessions* x. 33)

Augustine finds this problematic. He cannot just shut his ears to the music, since 'it is the setting for the words which give it life': here again we see the emerging priority of the word over the aesthetic. Moreover, the music itself stirs Augustine 'to greater religious fervour' than would the words alone.

> But I ought not to allow my mind to be paralyzed by the gratification of my senses, which often leads it astray. For the senses are not content to take second place. Simply because I allow them their due, as adjuncts to reason, they attempt to take precedence and forge ahead of it, with the result that I sometimes sin in this way ...
>
> (Ibid.)

This, for Augustine, is the nub of it. There is a strict hierarchy in which the immaterial – the words, the mind, God – take precedence over the material, the sensory, embodied beauty. When that hierarchy is disturbed, when correct ordering is not maintained, then the result is idolatry. And since beauty is that which most draws him forward, beauty is at the centre of his temptation. He laments:

> Though I say this and see that it is true, my feet are still caught in the toils of this world's beauty ... I am caught and need your mercy, and by your mercy you will save me from the snare ...
>
> (1961: 241; *Confessions* x. 34)

Augustine's insistence on right ordering, and his characterization of mistakes as idolatry, has been so widely taken up in Christendom that it is easy to take it for granted. I contend, however, that it is a rationalization; indeed that it is a rationalization that has gripped western Christendom precisely because it shares so strongly Augustine's anxieties, at the root of which are anxieties about gender, sexuality and otherness. To make that case, I begin with the obvious question: why should it be assumed that the beauty of bodies and of earthly things will in fact act as a snare, or induce anyone to worship them as though they were God? Does this bear any relationship to actual experience? Millions of people throughout the history of the west have found deep enrichment of their spirituality through the beauty of nature and the art, music and architecture of human creativity, but there is little evidence for the idea that music or buildings or the slant of light on hills has been worshipped, or that people have confused these things with God. Many people, indeed, feel that they experience the divine *through* these things, and value them all the more for that. It is not unusual for people to find more spiritual nourishment from a walk in the countryside than from a church service. But while this may be threatening to those with an investment in filling up churches, it is hardly a question of idolatry: the idea that because of the beauty of the primroses and the song of the skylarks I would begin to worship them as gods is, on the face of it, unlikely.

At his best, Augustine very well knows this. In the *Confessions* he describes his interrogation of the beauties of the natural world, asking the sea and sky and wind, 'But what is my God?' Each in turn replies, 'We are not your God'. So Augustine says:

> 'Since you are not my God, tell me about him. Tell me something of my God.' Clear and loud they answered, 'God is he who made us'. I asked these questions simply by gazing at these things, and *their beauty* was all the answer they gave.
>
> (1961: 212; *Confessions* x. 6, emphasis mine.)

Far from the beauty of nature causing Augustine to fall into idolatry, quite the opposite happens. The beauty of things is precisely what points him beyond the things themselves to the God who made them.

Now, this being so, two questions arise. First, if beauty is what leads Augustine to God, then why does he continue to be so suspicious of it? What is his problem? Second, why, in the face of what he experiences, does he characterize his potential problem with beauty as *idolatry*? Why does the language of idolatry spring so easily to his mind? At one level these are questions about the individual psychology and theology of Augustine. But they are worth investigating, because Augustine was vastly influential upon, and in that sense representative of, many aspects of the psychology and theology of western Christendom. Perhaps nowhere is this more the case than in relation to beauty. Therefore, if we can get closer to understanding both Augustine's suspicions, and his delineation of those suspicions in the language of idolatry, we will gain considerable insight into the unhappiness of the relationship between beauty and western theology.

Bodily anxiety: whose bodies?

In Augustine's actual confrontation with the beauties of the material world there is, as we have seen, no suggestion that he found himself confused between beautiful things and the God to whom their beauty points. This indicates that the idea that beauty acts as a distraction from God rather than a bridge to the divine is a rationalization that camouflages the true anxiety. The real anxiety, for Plato and Augustine and the tradition of western Christendom that followed them, is that not only is beauty deeply attractive, it is also paradigmatically bodily or physical, always closely related to sensuality and sexuality. Augustine was notoriously troubled about his sexuality, a trouble which he tried to resolve by conversion to celibacy, as recorded in his *Confessions*, and a trouble which he bequeathed to the history of western Christendom, with all its anxieties about the relationship between sexuality and spirituality. Beauty was such a problem for Augustine, I suggest, because it stood for all that tumultuous sexual passion. An encounter with beauty brought to the fore the carefully contained or repressed erotic dimension of his life, like a glimpse of a forsworn beloved, and challenged his commitment to continence all over again.

There is a telling choice of metaphor in the *Confessions* which reveals how closely Augustine associates the attraction of beauty with sexual attraction, and how dismayed he is by his response. One of the aspects of beauty to which his writings show him most susceptible is the beauty of light: its play on hills and valleys, its shimmering on water, its diffraction in the spectrum of colour. When he assesses his spiritual condition in relation to temptations of the senses, it is this which troubles him most, lest they 'take possession' of his soul. Light, he suggests, is like a seductress, a woman constantly finding new and subtle ways to entice him to evil.

> They [i.e. attractive colours] allow me no respite … For light, the queen of colours, pervades all that I see, wherever I am throughout the day, and by the ever-changing pattern of its rays it entices me even when I am occupied with something else and take no special note of it …
>
> (1961: 239; *Confessions* x. 34)

It is 'sweet and tempting, but dangerous for those whose love is blind'; it is something that 'beguiles' in dreams, an 'allurement' to be resisted (ibid.). Augustine uses various metaphors, jumbling them in a manner unlike his usual meticulously crafted prose, as though even a consistent use of the metaphor of the seductress would bring the erotic charge too near the surface of consciousness to bear. The real problem for Augustine is not that the beauties of nature tempt him to worship them as *gods*, but that they tempt him to be shaken in his resolve to continence. It is a sexual problem, not a religious one: or, better, it is a religious problem only because religion has been construed in terms of confused sexuality.

It is also misogynistic. When Augustine recognizes beauty as that which points him to God he does not use gendered metaphors; but when he worries about the temptations of beauty, then beauty is a queen of seduction and enticement. Women are problematic for Augustine because they stir his sexuality. His problems with his own sexuality are projected onto women, as though women themselves are the problem. And because beauty is conceptually and metonymically linked with women, their physicality and their erotic charge, beauty too is problematic, a source of ambivalence and anxiety.

All this was passed on to the western Christian tradition. Given the deep suspicion of the body, and especially of sexuality, in the development of Christian Platonism, the physical attractiveness of beauty, with all its affinities to erotic attraction, meant that while on the one hand beauty continued to draw men of aesthetic sensibility, on the other hand there was a deep distrust of this attraction, and therefore of beautiful things themselves. Moreover, since women were conceptually linked with the body, reproduction and death, while men were linked with the rational, godlike spirit, and women were held responsible for the sexual attraction and allure of which men were the hapless victims unable to control their own stirrings, the analogy between women and beauty was all too evident. In a misogynistic climate, where men felt deep anxiety about their bodies, and especially their sexuality, it is unsurprising that this anxiety also extended to beauty. The worry that beauty would lead to idolatry was a convenient rationalization, a displacement of sexual anxiety.

But why idolatry, exactly? Of all the forms of rationalization that could be chosen, why fix on idolatry as the focus of concern? What I want to suggest is that idolatry is chosen because it is just at this junction that anxiety about the body and sexuality intersects with the western concerns for radical monotheism discussed in Chapter 1. Beauty draws out a response of the physical senses to the physically sensuous, paradigmatically the beauties of the earth and its creatures. But if it has been determined that God is One, and radically separate from this material world, then beauty seems to point in the wrong direction, distorting unadulterated worship.

To see how this is so, it is helpful to circle back one more time to Augustine's debt to Plato. Both Plato and Augustine recognized that our first acquaintance with beauty and our regular experience of it is bodily experience. Although the idea of beauty may be extended to the intellectual, as when a mathematician speaks of a beautiful equation, that extension makes sense only because it is built upon an already existing idea of beauty that rests in physicality. Not only is beauty paradigmatically physical, it is also experienced by the body: our eyes, our ears, our senses of smell and touch are what enable us to experience beauty of nature and art. In short, beauty is perceptual. Its physical qualities appeal to our bodily senses.

The physical things that most attracted Plato were human bodies, in particular the bodies of adolescent boys. Plato had Diotima teach that the ascent to beauty begins by falling in love with one such beautiful body, then with many others like it. Augustine, ever more wary of the dangers of erotic attraction, went to earth and sea and sky, the play of light, and the fascination of living creatures, especially tiny ones like the bee and the ant. But the difference between Plato and Augustine is not just a different choice of initial objects. In Plato, the ascent to beauty is likened to 'mounting a heavenly ladder, stepping from rung to rung', each rung being another form of bodily or intellectual beauty, and each rung being left behind as the philosopher climbs. When at last he arrives at 'the open sea of beauty', he will have lost all interest in the beautiful people and things that enabled him to get there.

> Once you have seen it, you will never be seduced again by the charm of gold, of dress, of comely boys, or lads just ripening into manhood; you

will care nothing for the beauties that used to take your breath away and kindle such longing in you ...

(*Symposium* 211c–212a)

The body and its mortality are overcome, for such a man will 'be called the friend of god, and if it is ever given to man to put on immortality it shall be given to him' (ibid.). For Plato, beauty starts with the body, but ultimately bodies are not required. All that is physical, both about beauty itself and about our experience of it, is left behind, kicked away like the rungs of a ladder.

Augustine, too, starts with physical things; and his goal, too, is to go beyond them to the God who made them. But Augustine is more aware than is Plato that ultimately beauty cannot be abstracted from the physical. Beauty remains worryingly embodied, and our experience of it perceptual; and to say otherwise is to fail in gratitude to the God who created it. Most troubling of all is that even the experience of God is in some way sensual. Augustine's tension about this in the *Confessions* is palpable.

But what do I love when I love my God? Not material beauty, or beauty of a temporal order; not the brilliance of earthly light, so welcome to our eyes; not the sweet melody of harmony and song; not the fragrance of flowers, perfumes and spices; not manna or honey; not limbs such as the body delights to embrace. It is not these that I love when I love my God. And yet, when I love him, it is true that I love light of a certain kind, a voice, a perfume, a food, an embrace ...

(Augustine 1961: 211; *Confessions* x. 6)

Augustine struggles to internalize and spiritualize these sensory qualities, feeding his thoughts into the trajectory of the doctrine of 'spiritual senses', the idea of a set of non-physical senses parallel to the physical ones, that would have a long influence in medieval spirituality. He is always uneasy about the body and its involvement. But he cannot deny it, cannot kick it away as Plato does in the *Symposium*. He carried the tension to the end of his life. Even while the civilization he had known was collapsing, he wrote with deep appreciation of the beauties of creation and the blessings these beauties confer. Yet to the end of his life he *also* maintained a Platonic belief that ultimate beauty is incorporeal and unchanging, and that it will finally be encountered after death with the non-sensory eyes of the mind. As in Plato, ultimate beauty is displaced from the physical to the spiritual: in the case of Augustine the spiritual is represented in terms of the beatific vision of God in the heavenly realm. Nevertheless, there is in Augustine more ambivalence and less dismissal of the beauties of this world and our bodily experience of them.

Now for Augustine this tension created anxieties related to his psychosexual concerns, as I have already argued, but they also created anxieties about the nature of God and the relation of God to the world. Augustine's God is in many ways similar to Plato's One: God is incorporeal, unchanging, eternal Truth, Goodness and Beauty. There can be only one God. Yet Augustine is a Christian, and his God is therefore not simply the God of the philosophers but the God of the Bible, the God who is the creator of heaven and earth and all the beauties these contain. In the final three books of his *Confessions*, Augustine struggles to come to terms with this involvement of God in the physical universe. His commitment to the Platonic conception of the One means that he interprets divine eternity as timelessness (not as everlasting duration) and therefore is left with the unresolvable problems of what it might mean to say that God created time, and what God did before there was time: maybe God created hell for people who ask such impertinent questions (*Confessions* xi. 12)? It also means that he cannot accept the idea that God is in any sense material, or that the physical universe somehow shares in divine substance. There must be a clean division between God and the physical world. Nevertheless, that division is not between two eternally coexisting substances, one spiritual and the other material: this was the teaching of the Manichees, to which Augustine had adhered in his youth and from which he had freed himself with great effort.

It was this set of assumptions and commitments which shaped Augustine's articulation of the doctrine of creation, an articulation which goes well beyond scriptural pronouncement but which was to have measureless consequences for Christian theology. Creation must be *ex nihilo*, out of nothing.

> You created heaven and earth but you did not make them of your own substance ... But besides yourself, O God ... there was nothing from which you could make heaven and earth. Therefore you must have created them from nothing ... for there is nothing that you cannot do.
>
> (Augustine 1961: 284; *Confessions* xii. 7)

Having created heaven and earth *ex nihilo*, God then proceeded to shape it and fill it with plants and animals, as set out in the book of Genesis:

> For you, O Lord, made the world from formless matter, which you created out of nothing. This matter was itself almost nothing, but from it you made all the mighty things which are so wonderful to us. The sky above us ... the earth and the sea ... all the things of which our changing world consists ...
>
> (Augustine 1961: 285; *Confessions* xii. 8)

The Bible never says that God created the world *ex nihilo*, out of nothing. What the Bible does insist upon, however, is that there is only one God, and that all other contenders are false gods, idols. Taken together, these two ideas had momentous consequences for the way in which the beauty of the world, embodied beauty, could be understood. There are two main aspects of these consequences that I wish to draw out. The first concerns the content of creation: because of the radical separation between God and the world, the beauty of this world, which seems to indicate that the divine is construed precisely as temptation to idolatry. The second concerns the manner of creation: the divine *fiat*. Augustine makes much of the idea that God created the world by his *word*, by divine command. The word, the rational and verbal, takes precedence over (and command of) the tactile and material. Embodied beauty is displaced by words. Moreover, each of these carries a gendered charge. I shall discuss them in turn.

Radical monotheism and the idolatry of beauty

Once we see how important it was to Augustine and the Christian tradition to insist on a radical separation between God and the world, then it becomes easier to see why he would describe the beauties of this world as temptation to idolatry. Since earliest times, people have responded to the wonders of nature as manifestations of the divine: even today the beauty of nature is for many people a prime source of spiritual renewal. But for Augustine such a response is deeply problematic, even though he himself was drawn to it. The beauties of nature can reveal God, on his view of creation, only as a painting reveals the artist. We cannot encounter an artist in her painting except in a very extended sense: the artist is not *in* her painting. Yet it is commonplace to feel that God is in nature, that the divine can be encountered in nature, in a much fuller and more direct way than an artist can be encountered in her painting; that God continues to breathe and speak to us in nature, that nature is alive with God, shimmering with divine life.

This is exactly what scares Augustine. If the things of nature are not so radically separate from God after all, then bodies, beautiful bodies, sexual bodies cannot be so easily dismissed or regulated. They can attract; they can entice. The boundary between the bodily and the divine, between sexuality and spirituality, cannot be so rigidly drawn. For Augustine and many who come after him, this is deeply threatening. The boundaries must be policed; monotheism demands a sharp separation between God and all that is not God, paradigmatically the material world and its beautiful, sexually attractive bodies. To label as idolatry any response to the divine in beautiful bodies is one of the strongest rhetorical strategies available to counteract the threat.

The sharp separation between God and the world advocated by Augustine in his doctrine of creation *ex nihilo* continues to be maintained by many contemporary theologians, who see it as required by the idea of divine transcendence. It is still often assumed that if God is not to be reducible to the physical properties of the universe, then God must be some other substance, more than – other than – the universe. This idea of God as other – perhaps even as Wholly Other – means that the beauty of this world is at best only remotely related to God as its creator; it is not in any sense a direct manifestation, let alone incarnation of the divine, and is therefore not of much consequence theologically.

There are, however, huge problems with this construal of the doctrine of transcendence; and I shall suggest that it can be understood much better in a way that opens out in appreciation of beauty. The problems are manifold. In the first place, whatever Augustine might have thought, few theologians today would hold that the doctrine of creation *ex nihilo* should be taken literally as a theory of the origin of the cosmos, on a level with the Big Bang theory, say, or the Steady State theory. Whatever the doctrine of creation is, it is not an alternative scientific hypothesis.

More telling, however, from a theological perspective, is that a doctrine of creation out of nothing, which radically separates divine substance from material substance, God from the world, sets the divine over against the physical universe. The universe is what God is not, a place where God has no being. If God is wholly other than the universe, then the universe is wholly other than God. This is true not only of galaxies and physical particles but also of all forms of life, including human life. Even people, even their 'souls' – whatever is meant by that term – are part of creation, part of what God makes *ex nihilo*, and thus radically other than God.

Such a chasm between God and the world, including utter difference between God and the (created) human person, generates huge and, I believe, intractable problems. In the first place, it is hard to see how there could be divine action in the world. Providence, and answers to prayer, are equally problematic. Any divine action in the world would literally be intervention from outside it, a suspension of the laws of nature. It would be, literally, a miracle; though even the term 'miracle' would here be more of a label for a mystery than a solution of the problem of how or why God would set aside the course of nature which God had set in motion in the first place. Much theological ink has been spilled in an effort to overcome this problem; it arises directly from the insistence on the radical separation between God and the world generated by the idea of creation *ex nihilo*.

Second, and more important, if God is wholly other than the universe, then God cannot be encountered within it, either in prayer, in religious experience, or in the beauties of nature and in relationships with one another. This makes a nonsense of the lives and perceptions of religious people (including Augustine), who pray for and hold that they encounter the divine in the world in things large and small. Whether they are correct or not is not my present point. What I am arguing is that a doctrine of divine transcendence which would make a mockery of standard religious belief and practice can hardly be a doctrine in the service of Christendom.

One way of trying to deal with this problem, which occurs already in Augustine and becomes enormous in the Protestant theology of modernity, is a shift away from encounter with God through the world and emphasis instead on the word. The divine *fiat* of creation, the Word of God in the Bible and its exposition: these become the locus of religious faith: anything else is idolatry. I shall show later, however, that this shift cannot achieve its purpose. Words, language, are no more separate from the world than is beauty. It is as easy to fall into an idolatry of the word as an idolatry of the object. A shift to the word, away from the world, is a masculinist strategy that lends itself to violence. Or so I shall argue.

First, however, I wish to offer an alternative understanding of transcendence, to which beauty points the way. The traditional theological term 'transcendence', which has standardly been taken to require some sort of sharp distinction between God and the world, has usually been paired with 'immanence', the idea that God is somehow present within the world. On the face of it, these terms are mutually exclusive. They are often defined, as in the *Oxford English Dictionary*, simply as opposites of each other. In spite of this, it has usually been held in Christendom that God is both transcendent to and immanent in the universe, though how this could be so is not often explored. In practice, there has been much less effort to develop the doctrine of immanence and explore its meaning, while transcendence has been pushed in a direction which requires radical separation on pain of idolatry. Clearly, this will not do.

What I wish to show, however, is that if we take beauty seriously, we can come to a much more constructive account of transcendence and immanence.[2] Key to this account is the recognition, prompted by consideration of beauty, that transcendence is the opposite not of immanence but of reductionism.

As I have emphasized, beauty is embodied, physical. It requires sound waves, the colour spectrum, rays of light, solid matter in proportion or variation. It therefore also requires our bodily senses to perceive it. Nevertheless, beauty, while obviously having to do with such qualities as colour, harmony and proportion, cannot be reduced to them, as though something could be made beautiful by formula. The delicate beauty of a bank of primroses, or the slant of evening light on the fells, or the heart-stopping cadence of a cello sonata is something more than the material properties of these things. Even if we could give a complete list of these material properties, it would not follow that we had captured their beauty. It is always something more, something other than the list of characteristics. In theological terminology, it *transcends* that list.

But what is this 'more'? It is not another thing or property to be added to the list, as though, if we only had an exhaustive description, we could encapsulate a formula of beauty. Neither, however, is it some other thing or substance, some spiritual form or idea that is mysteriously compounded with the set of physical properties. Rather, it is more in the sense that the whole is more than the sum of its parts. Thus, for example, in one sense a painting just *is* the canvas and the patches of colour laid upon it by the artist; yet its beauty could never be described by setting out a catalogue of the shades of colour and their exact dimensions, nor would ever-greater completeness and precision of the list get us closer to describing the beauty of the painting. Beauty is not reducible to physical properties; in that sense it transcends the physical, even while being wholly immanent in it. Transcendence, thus, is the opposite not of immanence but of reductionism.

Precisely parallel considerations apply to our perception of beauty, which is likewise physical, wholly dependent upon our sense perception, but not reducible to it. It is possible for two people to hear exactly the same sounds, or see exactly the same canvas and patches of colour upon it, and yet one person experiences beautiful music or a beautiful painting and the other is left cold. We perceive the beauty of things through our physical senses; and yet a complete account of the neuro-physiological processes, even if it could be given, would not guarantee consciousness of beauty. There are many reasons for disagreement about whether or not something is beautiful, most obviously the cultural and individual histories of the people concerned. Yet the development of taste, mimetic and socially constructed as it is, cannot be reduced to a rearrangement of physical stimuli. To be conscious of beauty (and indeed to be conscious of anything else), to perceive it as beautiful, is more than a complicated set of physical properties.

But again, *what* more? What we do not need by way of explanation is reference to some additional substance, a 'soul' or 'mind' that is a different entity from the neuro-physiology of our bodies. The perception of beauty is more than the activity of our physical senses and central nervous system. But again, this 'more' is more in the sense that the whole is more than the sum of its parts: not a question of an extra entity or substance but of the emergence of new possibility with complexity. Again, transcendence is the opposite of reductionism, not of immanence.

This argument from beauty can be generalized to an account of what it is to be a person. To be a person is to be embodied; yet a person is somehow more than a body. In Christian theology, and in the philosophy of modernity shaped by it, this 'more' was often thought of as another substance: a soul or mind that inhabited or was somehow conjoined with the physical body of a person and would be separated after death. The question of how these separate substances were able to interact – how does the mind influence the body and vice versa – set much of the agenda of modern philosophy from Descartes onwards. The impasses to which the various attempts led suggest that the problem is badly structured; and in the twentieth century, starting with the work of Strawson (1959), Wittgenstein (1969) and others, it has become evident that the idea of the person (not her component 'parts') is the fundamental notion. A person is more than a body, but this does not mean that in addition to the physical parts of the body – arms, legs, internal organs – there is another, non-physical part called the soul. What it does mean is that the complexity that is a person is not reducible to a list of component parts. Love is more than chemistry; intelligence is more than neurological synapses; the appreciation of beauty is more than sense perception. To ask 'what more?' is not to ask for an additional physical or spiritual component. It is rather to see that a person must be described from the outset in non-reductionistic terms, so that emotion, intelligence and sensitivity are as fundamental to the concept of personhood as is physicality. This is of course the briefest of sketches of a complicated and still heavily contested area of modern philosophy. Nevertheless, it is enough to show that there is no need to make a choice between the equally unsatisfactory alternatives of materialist reductionism and body–soul dualism. A rich account of personhood preserves both immanence and transcendence without reductionism.

Now, it has regularly been held that the relationship between God and the world is in many respects analogous to the relationship between persons and their bodies. I suggest that if we retain the analogy while adopting the holistic account of persons prompted by consideration of the immanence and transcendence of beauty, it becomes possible to modify in constructive ways the radical monotheism which separates the divine from the world and rejects beauty as potential idolatry. On this analogy, God could be understood not as utterly other than the universe, but on the other hand not reducible to its material specifications, just as a person is not other than their body even though a physiological account of that body is inadequate as a description of the person. With this rich notion of personhood, the body is valued, indeed indispensable: it is not a hindrance to a 'soul' or 'spirit' which could somehow live independently of it after death. A person *is* her body, not in the sense that she is reducible to physiology but in the sense that there can be no self which is not a bodily self, a self which began with conception and birth and whose narrative is the narrative of a person in space and time. Nevertheless, a person transcends her body, not in the sense of being something different from the body – some other 'stuff' or substance – but in the sense of being irreducible to physiology. She is wholly immanent in her body: she is where her body is; she does what her body does. There is no extra 'bit', something additional to the body. And yet she transcends her body in the sense that much more can be said of her than can be said by medical science. In that sense she is more than – but never less than – her body. She is both immanent in and transcendent to her body, with no tension between the two ideas.

Just the same, I suggest, can be said of God and the universe. God is wholly immanent in the universe, its beauty is a manifestation of the divine; but because God is no more reducible to physics than a person is to physiology, God is also transcendent to the universe. Putting it another way, the universe *is* divine, not in the sense that God is reducible to atomic particles but in the sense that sacredness is one way of characterizing the universe, just as my thought and emotions are one way of characterizing me, even while these 'mental predicates', as they are sometimes labelled, are not separable from my bodily existence. A doctor, a psychiatrist and a lover each describe a person in very different ways, all of which may be simultaneously true; similarly a physicist, a theologian and a poet may describe God/the universe in different terms, all of which are appropriate for different purposes and in different contexts.

On this view, God is not some kind of divine substance, wholly other than the matter/energy of which the universe is composed, any more than we are souls or spiritual substance detachable from our physical bodies. A holistic view of a person is a richer and more coherent view than is body–soul dualism. Similarly, I am suggesting that a theology which refuses to divide God and the universe is a richer and more coherent theology than is the cosmic dualism which insists on radical separation between God and the universe, and can thus give no account of immanence or the manifestation of God in the beauty of the world.

I showed earlier how Augustine, with his acute sensitivity to natural beauty, was nevertheless anxious because he felt that he must keep a concept of a Creator who is wholly distinct from that beauty. Beauty is materially based, and God, in Augustine's Platonist thinking, is spiritual, a different substance from the substance of the universe which God created *ex nihilo*. No matter how beautifully the universe is configured, we cannot encounter God in it: its beauty is a snare and a trap.

But if the universe is not separable from God, then Augustine's anxieties need not arise. The beauty of the world around him, the beauty of bodies, of light, of the sea, of the tiny creatures like ants and bees that Augustine loved to watch and the music he loved to listen to *is* divine beauty. It does not pull away from the divine or compete with the divine; it is a manifestation of the divine. Although beauty is always physical – impossible without sound waves, the colour spectrum, rays of light – and always requires our bodily senses to perceive it, nevertheless it is not reducible to the physical. It is something more, not in the sense that it is another thing or an additional physical or spiritual substance but in the sense that we are more than our bodies. Beauty, in Christian theology, can be given its rightful place only if it is taken as a manifestation of the transcendence and immanence of God, a God not reducible to the materiality of the universe but not radically separate from it either.

Beauty and the golden calf

A theology which insists upon a radical separation between God and the world of natural and artistic beauty detaches God from the physical world of our bodies with their sensory perceptions and desires, may be the fulfilment of a masculinist dream of rational control, uncontaminated by feelings and sensibilities, but it is not a theology that can appreciate the spiritual nourishment of the experience of beauty. As the theology of modernity has insisted more and more upon transcendence understood as total otherness to the world, it has paid little attention to beauty. Instead, the focus has been on truths, on beliefs, on the creeds and the Word, all of which can be seen under the rubric of masculine rationality and control. Especially in Protestantism, as I pointed out in Chapter 1, beauty hardly figures in theological thought.

A partial exception, which nevertheless illustrates all this very clearly, is the massively influential theologian Karl Barth. When Barth writes briefly (for him!) about the glory of God in his *Church Dogmatics*, he acknowledges that God 'is beautiful, divinely beautiful, beautiful in his own way, in a way that is his alone, beautiful as the unattainable primal beauty, yet really beautiful' (Barth 1975 Vol. 2, Pt 1: 650). When he goes further in expounding what this means, however, he becomes very cautious, effectively withdrawing his claims for the significance of beauty. Barth makes, in fact, all the same moves and shows the same anxieties as did Augustine, but in the context of Protestant modernity.

In the first place, Barth is emphatic that the idea of transcendence requires radical separation between God and the world. He therefore insists on the doctrine of creation *ex nihilo*.

> Nor is it that the world is to be understood as an outflow, an emanation from God, as something divine which wells out of God like a stream out of a spring. That would really not be creation, but a living movement of God, an expression of himself. But creation means something different: it means reality distinct from God ... Creatively, reality means reality on the basis of a *creatio ex nihilo*, a creation out of nothing. Where nothing exists – and not a kind of primal matter – there through God there has come into existence that which is distinct from him.
>
> (Barth 1959: 55)

Because of this, Barth insists that beauty must never be given undue prominence. It can never be central to theology.

> Owing to its connexion with the idea of pleasure, desire and enjoyment ... the concept of the beautiful seems to be a particularly secular one, not at all adapted for introduction into the language of theology, and indeed extremely dangerous.
>
> (Ibid.: 651)

The idea of bodily attraction, which cannot be separated from the appeal of beauty to the senses, renders beauty unfit for theological use, even though Barth has also said that it is important to recognize beauty as an aspect of the glory of God. His sense of threat is acute. Like Augustine, Barth expresses his anxieties by using the rhetoric of idolatry.

> The Church attitude precludes ... the possibility of a dogmatics which thinks and speaks aesthetically. It is true, of course, that the object with

which it has to do has its characteristic and quite distinctive beauty which it would be unpardonable, because ungrateful, to overlook or to fail to find pleasing. But the moment dogmatics even temporarily surrenders to and loses itself in the contemplation of this beauty as such, instead of letting itself be held by the object, this beauty becomes the beauty of an idol ...

(Ibid.: 841)

Dogma, truth, the Word of God is what is paramount for Barth; and although he sometimes recognizes the importance of beauty, he does so only to undermine its theological impact. He insists that

attention should also be given to the fact that we cannot include the concept of beauty with the main concepts of the doctrine of God, with the divine perfections which are the divine essence itself ... It is not a leading concept. Not even in passing can we make it a primary motif in our understanding of the whole being of God as we necessarily did in the case of these other concepts.

(Ibid.: 652)

The concepts, that is, of God's holiness, wisdom, power, knowledge and eternity to which Barth has just devoted 650 pages. In about twenty pages Barth says all he has to say about divine beauty, mostly qualifying it in such a way that, while he does not actually deny it, he diminishes its meaning and significance in a way that overwhelmingly privileges the concepts of truth and doctrine. Having treated it here, he then hardly mentions it again in all the massive volumes of his *Dogmatics*. It does not so much as figure in the index.

Many modern theologians pay even less attention to beauty than does Barth. Although they may disagree with him in many other ways, there is a widespread tendency to emphasize (and argue about) truth and beliefs, and at the same time to ignore beauty. So general is this tendency that it is doubtful that many theologians even notice that it is happening, or feel a need to give an account of it. The privileging of truth over beauty is simply taken for granted.

However, quite apart from the enormous loss to spirituality that results from such displacement of beauty, there is the additional question of whether truth claims can actually enable us to understand the divine nature in a way that beauty allegedly cannot. One of the most insightful commentaries on this issue is written not by a professional theologian but by the composer Arnold Schoenberg in his opera *Moses and Aron*, skilfully analysed by Richard Viladesau in his *Theological Aesthetics* (1999). Like Barth, Schoenberg laboured over his work through the Nazi era, and it bears the marks of centuries of Jewish and Christian meditation. It takes its departure from the biblical book of *Exodus*, in which visual representation of God is forbidden.

The first two of the famous Ten Commandments prohibit making any statue or image of a deity.

> You shall have no other gods before [besides] me.
> You shall not make for yourself a graven image, or any likeness of anything that is in heaven above, or that is in the earth beneath ... you shall not bow down to them or serve them ...
>
> (Exodus 20.3–4)

But what did the Israelites do? At first, they entered into covenant with God. No sooner had Moses gone up the mountain for further instruction from God, however, than the Israelites demanded just such a graven image. Moses' brother Aaron asked them for their golden jewellery.

> He received the gold at their hand, and fashioned it with a graving tool, and made a molten calf; and they said, 'These are your gods, O Israel ... '

And worshipped the calf. It was this that brought Moses down from the mountain in haste, smashing the stone tablets of the law in his rage (Exodus 32). The punishment which followed was intended to teach the Israelites never again to make a visual representation of the divine beauty: any such attempt would be idolatrous.

As Schoenberg portrays this in his opera, Moses represents words, speech, law, whereas Aaron signifies the imagination and the sensory. According to Moses, no sensory image could do justice to the infinite God; no image could portray the divine who is beyond imagination.

> Thou shalt not make for thyself an image!
> For an image reduces, delimits, grasps,
> What should remain unlimited and unimaginable.
> An image wants a name:
> A name can only be taken from what is small;
> You should not worship what is small!
>
> (Schoenberg in Viladesau 1999: 42)

When Aaron produces the golden calf, Moses is outraged. How dare Aaron try to represent the unrepresentable in a statue, try to 'contain the Infinite in an image'? Moses destroys the golden calf; seeing it as idolatrous blasphemy. But then Schoenberg uses Aaron to point out that things are more complicated. Does not Moses have the tablets of stone, on which are written the words of God? Do not words, too, convey images of God, conceptual representations if not material ones? If we are to think of God at all, must we not do so in words, concepts and images, finite and inadequate as these inevitably are?

Moses' response is one of despair. He sees that he, too, in his words and mental concepts, is creating an image of God.

> Unimaginable God!
> Inexpressible, many-faceted idea!
> ... So I too have formed an image for myself: false,
>   as an image can only be!
> So I am stricken.
> So all that I thought was madness,
> And cannot and must not be spoken!
> O word, thou word that I lack!
>   (Schoenberg in Viladesau 1999: 47)

Moses smashes the tablets. Their images are conceptual, but they are images nonetheless, and as such they are as idolatrous as the golden calf.

Yet this ultimately will not do. As Schoenberg finishes the opera – itself an aesthetic representation – he shows that representations are all that humans have. Whether conceptual or sensory, they are finite, and cannot contain infinity; yet they are what we must use to communicate the ungraspable. If they are taken as adequate, then they are idolatrous; but if they are taken as windows for the mind and the imagination, they extend the human spirit. We cannot dispense with concepts, with truth, with verbal images of God, but neither need we abandon beauty and all the spiritual enrichment which it offers. The displacement of beauty is intertwined with the distortion of attitudes to the body and desire, sexuality and violence. Reclaiming beauty and its significance enables fresh approaches to the divine in the world and in one another, 'that of God in everyone', and shows how it can be cherished.

Chapter 10

Beauty, desire and need

Beauty attracts. At a most basic level, and without resolving puzzles of objective criteria, we can say that if we find something beautiful we are drawn towards it. We pause to watch a sunset or a rainbow; we walk in the woods to enjoy the colours of the autumn leaves; we listen gladly to music that we find beautiful; we take pleasure in beautiful objects or paintings. We are attracted to them and give them time and attention, not because we must but because we want to do so. What we find beautiful stimulates our desire.

That is exactly why Augustine and his followers are so afraid of beauty. At least since the time of Plato, desire has been characterized paradigmatically in sexual terms: desire is Eros. In Plato's mythological rendition, Eros is 'the follower and servant of Aphrodite', the beautiful, and 'is born to love the beautiful' (Plato, *Symposium* 203c). It is not simply that some forms of beauty, the beauty of human bodies, stimulate sexual desire. In Plato's representation, sexual desire is the pattern for *all* desire: Eros is modelled on sexuality. Not only so, but beauty, also, is thereby modelled as that which arouses Eros, understood in sexual terms.

'Sexual terms', moreover, are never gender neutral. In Plato's myth, Eros is masculine, and enacts masculine desire and masculine characteristics. Eros is aroused and tumescent; his longings are urgent, but, once satisfied, 'ebb away as fast' (203e). 'He is gallant, impetuous, and energetic, a mighty hunter, and a master of device and artifice' (203d). There is no representation here of female desire, or even acknowledgement of it, sexual or otherwise. Do women also have desires? If so, are they modelled upon male sexual desires, or could they be characterized differently? Indeed is it accurate to take sexual desire, male or female, as the paradigm of *all* desire?

Questions about Plato's representation of desire lead at once to questions about beauty. If beauty attracts, and if attraction is understood in terms of male sexuality, then what must be the nature of beauty? At a most basic level, and assuming (as Plato did not, but as Augustine and Christendom with him did) that heterosexuality is normative, beauty also will be understood in gendered terms. Beauty will be represented as female, attracting masculine Eros.

And so, indeed, we have found it in Augustine's anxieties about how beauty might bewitch and seduce him; might indeed entice him to idolatry. Moreover, it is obvious that even when beauty is spiritualized (and thus supposedly desexualized) ambivalences will remain: the beauty of God that attracts the soul is represented as active and 'masculine', while the souls of Christian men are represented as passive and female. All sorts of contortions and contradictions are generated by the gender assumptions, often unacknowledged, in the notions of desire and beauty.

I shall tease out some of these assumptions and their consequences for our concept of the divine later. First, however, it is important to see that many of Plato's ideas of desire and beauty are not simply relics of antiquity but are taken up in modernity and continue to shape our thinking. One of the most influential examples is that of Immanuel Kant, drawing on the work of Edmund Burke, who famously categorized beauty as feminine, and contrasted it with the sublime as masculine. According to Kant, it is obvious that women are more beautiful than men.

> The figure is finer, the features more delicate and gentler, and her mien more engaging and more expressive of friendliness, pleasantry, and kindness than in the male sex.
>
> (Kant 1960: 76)

Men, by contrast, are the 'noble sex', and identified with the sublime: the awesome, majestic and powerful. Moreover, as in Plato, it is (female) beauty that inspires (male) desire. Burke characterizes this as 'the *beauty* of the *sex*': 'the sex' is woman.

> Men are carried to the sex in general, as it is the sex, and by the common law of nature; but they are attached to particulars by personal *beauty*.
>
> (Burke 1990: 39)

The gender stereotypes are blatant: women are pretty creatures whose purpose is to serve men's desires and be good wives and mothers. They are to be sexually attractive for men's satisfaction and thus for the reproduction of humankind. Men, on the other hand, should cultivate their rationality and nobility, their capacity for mastery. As Kant puts it, in terms that clearly reveal his asymmetric gender assumptions, 'the principal object is that the man should become more perfect as a man [not, note, "as a husband"], and the woman as a wife [not "as a woman"]' (Kant 1960: 95). A woman, therefore, should not get involved in masculine education or other interests of men: 'A woman who has her head full of Greek ... might as well have a beard' (78). In all these comments, Burke and Kant are taking for granted the same constructions of gender in relation to beauty and desire that we have noted in Plato, without noticing that they are doing so. From these assumptions, furthermore, it is but a short step to the fashion and cosmetic industries that play so large a role in contemporary life, with their implications for everything from economics to entertainment. Women are constructed to see themselves as beautiful, as sexually alluring, and to purchase and use clothes and cosmetics which are marketed as promoting and enhancing such allure (see Hanson 1998; Balsamo 1996; Barthel 1988).

For Kant, not only are women more beautiful than men; they are also more drawn to beauty.

> Women have a strong inborn feeling for all that is beautiful, elegant, and decorated. Even in childhood they like to be dressed up, and take pleasure when they are adorned ... They love pleasantry and can be entertained by trivialities ...
>
> (Kant 1960: 77)

Kant does not notice that these comments actually conflict with his earlier Platonic representation of desire as masculine attraction to women as beautiful. Taken at face value, Kant's assertion that women are drawn to beautiful things, along with the stereotype that women are beautiful, would imply that women would desire one another. But Kant could hardly be interpreted as calmly envisioning a society of lesbians! Like many others, he simply reproduces gender stereotypes from an unexamined masculinist bias, even when he is writing about gender and ostensibly has a critical philosopher's eye upon it. So completely does he take gender constructions for granted that he does not notice the contradictions they generate for the very position that he is putting forward. (See Battersby 1995 for extended analysis of gender in Kant's account of beauty.)

In the light of the standard interconnection between the constructions of beauty and gender illustrated by Burke and Kant and exploited by the commercial interests of fashion and film, it is obvious that a feminist account of beauty and desire will require rethinking of both those terms and the relationship between them. How does beauty attract? Is that attraction best understood on the model of sexual desire? To the extent that erotic attraction is a paradigm for the attraction of beauty, *whose* eros are we talking about? Is this a reinscription of normative masculinist heterosexuality by the back door? What does all this say about beauty and desire? These questions cannot be avoided if beauty is to play a significant role in a theology focused on human flourishing as an alternative to violence, lest beauty be appealed to as nothing more than a consolatory evasion. Beauty and desire demand reconsideration from the roots up.

Desire and need

I want to begin that reconsideration by asking more about desire. What sort of desire does beauty evoke? I shall suggest several dimensions, and shall argue that, taken together, these considerations not only tell us something about beauty but also point to a reconfiguration of desire, a reconfiguration which destabilizes its connections with masculinism and with violence. In conventional theological terminology, they have a bearing both on theological aesthetics and on theological anthropology.

I have already referred to Plato's story of Eros as the lover of beauty, desire modelled on male sexuality. But there is more to Plato's rendition. In his account, Eros is the offspring of two parents, Resource and Need. Resource is the father, and from him Eros gets his characteristics of gallantry, energy and the rest. But his mother is Need: Eros, desire, is always born of lack.

> It has been his fate to be always needy; nor is he delicate and lovely as most of us believe, but harsh and arid, barefoot and homeless, sleeping on the naked earth, in doorways, or in the very streets beneath the stars of heaven, and always partaking of his mother's poverty.
>
> (Plato, *Symposium* 203c–d)

To be attracted by something, to desire it, is premised upon a sense of need, of lack. To want is to be in want. Moreover, in Plato's account, the desire is a longing to possess, to own. Plato puts this explicitly in relation to beauty. He has Diotima ask: 'What is it that the lover of the beautiful is longing for?' and Socrates replies: 'He is longing to make the beautiful his own' (*Symposium* 204d).

These two ideas, that desire is premised on a lack and that the fulfilment of desire is possession, have been largely taken for granted throughout western culture, in philosophy and psychoanalysis as well as in advertising and entertainment. To be attracted to something is to desire to possess it; desire indicates a lack or need which can be satisfied by ownership or consumption. Add to this the implicitly gendered construction of desire which I have already discussed, including its aggressive energy to get what it wants, and we have the ingredients of a consumer society structured according to masculinist erotic desire, in which needs are perceived as lack or inadequacy and are fulfilled by ownership, possession, whether it be computer toys, cars or women, to be acquired by violence if necessary and discarded or replaced if they do not, after all, fulfil the need. That many of these lacks are manufactured by cunning advertising strategies, and that men as well as women are both victims and perpetrators, is obvious. It is not the case that men are villains and women are victims. It is the case, however, that the gendered construction of desire premised upon lack, and fulfilment as possession, is all of a piece with a society built on consumption and violence.

What I wish to argue, however, is that Plato is wrong on both counts. Desire is not always a question of need or lack; neither is the fulfilment of desire necessarily possession. Indeed it is precisely reconsideration of beauty and desire which shows this to be so; and shows, therefore, a construction of desire and fulfilment that points to creativity and flourishing rather than to violence.

I begin with the question of possession. Plato said that the lover of the beautiful longs to make the beautiful his own, and in one sense this is obviously true. To find something beautiful is to be drawn to experience it, not just once but repeatedly, to become familiar with it, to love and cherish it. The beauty of the English Lake District draws me to it: I love the play of lights and shadows on the fells, the soft colours, the ripple and sparkle of lakes and becks, the wild flowers in the woodlands and the open spaces of the bare fell-sides. So I count myself lucky to be able to live in this area so that I can walk often on the many paths and tracks, and become familiar with their beauties as the seasons change. My favourite walks become part of my life: I am nurtured by them and have made them my own.

But what sort of ownership is this? Surely it is very far from being own-ership in any commercial sense: perhaps it is actually at odds with that sense of possession. The hills and valleys of the Lake District belong to me in the sense that their beauty has entered my soul, but not in the sense that the title deeds of the land are in my name in some land registry. I cannot buy or sell the hills; I do not possess them any more than do the many others who also walk the tracks and delight in their beauty. There is space and beauty enough for all.

Parallel things can be said about other forms of beauty: of painting or archi-tecture or music. To find a piece of music or a painting or a building beautiful is to want to experience it often, get to know it well, let it become part of one's life. It would be very odd to say, 'I found that symphony exquisitely beautiful and I never want to hear it again'. Things of beauty become our own through repeated exposure to them and deepening appreciation; but this is ownership in a very different sense from the possession that arises from monetary transac-tions. Neither is it in any sense exclusive. My delight in a piece of music is compatible with everyone else in the audience enjoying it too. Indeed, their enjoyment would be more likely to enhance my own than to diminish it.

The desire for possession that arises from the experience of beauty actually includes a desire to share it. If we are impressed by a symphony or a painting or a building we encourage our friends to see it too. There is indeed a sense in which beauty draws us to make it our own, to learn to know it deeply so that our lives and sensibilities are formed by it; but such ownership positively invites others to do the same. To want to walk in my beloved hills does not mean that I want others to stay away; to love a piece of music or a painting does not mean trying to keep it from others. Quite the reverse: beauty prompts us to try to share it, and is enriched, not diminished, by such sharing. Of course we want to share it only with others who will respond to the beauty too. If there is nothing better than sharing something beautiful with others who appreciate it, there is nothing worse than trying to share it with someone who is not interested, let alone with someone who is destructive. But what we hope for is that others will indeed respond positively, and that our responses will be mutually enriching.

What of the beauty of people? When Plato said that the desire evoked by beauty is a desire to possess, he was after all thinking in the first instance of people, not of landscapes or symphonies, and the sort of possession he had in mind was not commercial but sexual. It was the 'beauty of boys just ripening to manhood' that attracted Socrates/Plato, and the beauty of women that caused Augustine so much anxiety. Here too, however, 'possession' is not a question of exclusivity or ownership. I want my friends to know and like one another; it is a pleasure to introduce them, not to try to keep them apart. The intimacies of a partnership or marriage are, by mutual choice, reserved to that relationship alone, but even here the 'possession' is not ownership.

It is certainly true that this has not always been recognized. Historically, women were considered to be the property of men, an idea that undoubtedly lingers in masculinist fantasy. Claude Lévi-Strauss has famously argued that the exchange of women is the basis of civilization: fathers 'gave' their daughters to other men and received in return cattle or money or some other exchange value, and thereby alliances were forged and conflicts avoided. Nor was this notion of women as property confined to primitive cultures: one need only read the novels of Anthony Trollope to see how pervasive the idea still was in late nineteenth-century England. Even today a conventional wedding includes a ritual of the father of the bride 'giving away' his daughter to the groom, as though the woman is a piece of property being given by one man to another. It may be said that this is only a ritual; but to see the grip it still has on the imagination we need only consider how strange it would be if the marriage ceremony included instead the mother of the groom 'giving away' her son to the bride. The fantasy of women as possessions lives on; many men (and many women too) believe that men have a right to demand domestic and sexual services from their wives in a way that is not reciprocal. It is only in the last century that women have been considered persons in English law (rather than falling under the umbrella of father or husband) and only very recently that rape in marriage has become a legal offence.

But if feminism has taught us anything, it is that women are not chattels. No person can properly be owned by another. Any attempt at such ownership is called slavery; and slavery, whether marital or otherwise, is morally abhorrent, contrary to the human dignity of both slave and master. The desire for 'possession' of people evoked by the attractiveness of their beauty must be understood in other terms. I do not own my partner's body or soul any more than she owns mine: we belong to one another by mutual desire freely given and received. Moreover only an insecure or unhealthy relationship constructs the partnership as excluding other friendships, trying to keep one another in a cage. Although the intimacies of a sexual relationship are private to the partners concerned, there is much else in the partnership which is enriched by sharing it with others. Who is not proud to introduce their partner to family and friends?

What all these examples show, whether the beauty of the hills or of music or of people, is that while beauty attracts, it is not an attraction that is akin to desire for exclusive possession or ownership. There is something seriously wrong with a person who would try to keep a footpath closed to others or a painting from their sight (unless of course there was danger that they would destroy it), just as there is something wrong with a person who is jealous when their friends have other friends as well. The sort of possession which we can talk about in relation to beauty is not consumption. We do not eat beauty. Indeed the more we take it into ourselves and make it part of our being, the more we try to preserve it and make it available for others as well. Thus we find in the relationship between beauty and desire a multiple experience of nurture: beauty nurtures the one who experiences it, who in turn seeks to preserve and nurture beauty, and to share it with others so that they also are nurtured in a mutually enriching way. Response to beauty is a response that cherishes both that which is beautiful and that in ourselves and others which responds to beauty.

These considerations begin to point towards the way that beauty can be set against violence. The attractiveness of beauty draws us to experience it as much as we can, and therefore to try to preserve it rather than destroy it. I place my desk at a window so that I can see the hills and sky, and the thrush nesting in the rowan tree when I look up from my books. I take care not to damage the primroses and wild violets as I walk in the woodlands. Indeed it would be very strange if I were to say that I found all this beautiful and then deliberately closed the window shades or placed my desk so that I looked instead at a brick wall, or ground the heel of my boot into every primrose beside the path. The theft of a beautiful painting or the destruction of an ancient building causes distress. Similarly, when we see the beauty of their humanity in the eyes and face of one another we are prompted to cherish them, to do what we can to help them to flourish, whether those others are our dearest friends or strangers in particular need. This desire to cherish and protect the thing of beauty as its beauty enters my soul and shapes my sensibilities. It shapes me, therefore, in a manner that is directly opposite to destructiveness and violence.

Desire and lack

The other aspect of Plato's account of desire in relation to beauty was, as we saw, his idea that desire indicates a lack. I want what I do not have: I experience an emptiness and desire that it be filled. In Plato's myth, as we saw, Eros is represented as the child of Need. In the western intellectual tradition this idea of desire as premised upon a lack is, with a few exceptions, taken for granted. However, I believe that it is misguided, and that the conception of desire (and its connection to violence) must be reconfigured when it is considered in relation to beauty.

To show this, it is necessary to draw out two further aspects of the conventional connection between desire and lack. The first is gender. It is no coincidence that in Plato's myth Need is the *mother* of Eros, not the father. It is standardly the case in western thought that lack is represented in female terms, plenitude in male terms. Even in something as prosaic as heterosexual partnership, the male has been constructed as the provider, the female (with her children) as the one in need of provision. With the advent of psychoanalysis this conventional association of the female with lack was more explicitly theorized. In Lacanian terms, desire is founded on the loss of the (m)other. The fractured and fragmented self, torn by this loss, tries to hold itself together by aggressivity and violence, attempting to overcome its loss by mastery. Yet all the while, the (m)other for which the self yearns is itself configured as a lack, a 'hole' or receptacle for the (now obviously male) self (Lacan 1977: 8–29; Rose 1993).

As soon as these assumptions are openly stated, however, rather than allowed to remain implicit, they become much less obvious. Why should all desire be constructed upon male sexual fantasy or insecurity? I shall argue below that there are hugely important aspects of desire which can be much better understood as premised upon plenitude than upon lack, and for which male sexual desire is a very poor model indeed. It is, moreover, outrageous to configure women simply as lack, to reduce woman to her 'hole', to 'nothing' as Lacan does (Lacan 1982): it is a configuration which reveals much about masculinist attitudes to women and about male insecurities and anxieties, but it reveals nothing about the complex reality of women and of women's desires.

The second aspect of the conventional connection between desire and lack which I wish to draw out is that its gendered dimensions are interconnected with violence and death. Once again, this is brought out clearly in psychoanalytic theory, in which woman, the 'lack', is conceptually linked with death. As Freud presents it, for example, in his famous 'Fort-Da' game in 'Beyond the Pleasure Principle' (1984), desire seeks repetition, but repetition always looks to stasis and is ultimately connected to *Thanatos*, the death drive. As (male) desire yearns for the mother and tries to master her absence, part of the technology of mastery involves configuring the mother not only as lack but as death. Desire itself, since it is desire for the mother (transferred to the woman who replaces her), is deathly.

The configuration of woman with death long predates psychoanalytic theory. Throughout western Christendom runs the theme of the deadly, seductive woman whose prototype is Eve, remembered not as the mother of all who live but as the bringer of death to humanity. Thus, for instance, in the seventeenth century John Donne bemoaned the sexual arousal women caused him, 'since each such act, they say, diminishes the length of life a day' (in Hollander and Kermode 1973: 543): it was an attitude that had much in common with Augustine's sexual anxieties, discussed in Chapter 9.

But if women are standardly associated with death, men and masculine desire are associated with violence. In the 'Fort-Da' game played by Freud's grandson, Freud interpreted the little boy's manipulation of the reel and thread as the mastery of the absence of the boy's mother. In Lacan's account, that effort at mastery, the attempt to overcome the lack, is at the root of masculine aggressivity. As Lacan has it, desire is founded on the loss of the (m)other; and the fractured 'self' tries to hold itself together by aggressivity and violence (Lacan 1977: 8–29). The result, however, is inevitably an intensification of the lack, which in turn generates an escalation of violence. The aggressive response to need shapes the male psyche, and in so doing shapes all the configurations of masculine predominance: politics, economics, science, sports and philosophy among them. All these are fundamentally constructed as agonistic, as projections of an insecure defensive/aggressive male ego (Brennan 1993). It is no coincidence that they so readily utilize metaphors of war: arguments are 'attacked', 'defended', or 'shot down in flames'; elections are 'fought'; scientific or medical discoveries are presented as part of a 'battle' against disease or ignorance or weakness of any sort. Everyday language in western modernity is saturated with terminology of violence.

All of this seems a very long way from beauty. In Plato's presentation, as we saw, desire was aroused by beauty: beauty drew the beholder to long for what he did not have. But in the articulations of psychoanalytic theory by Freud and Lacan, there is little mention of beauty. Rather, the focus is on the notion of lack itself, and the aggression and violence that are generated to try to overcome the lack. The result of all this is in fact much more likely to be destruction and ugliness than the appreciation and enhancement of beauty.

What this indicates, I suggest, is that the notion of desire should be revisited. Desire itself must be understood differently. If beauty is taken as the starting point, then the fundamental assumptions that have shaped the concept of desire must be challenged, in particular the assumption that all desire is rooted in or at least analogous to male sexual desire, and that desire is premised upon a lack.

Desire, beauty and mimetic rivalry

The reconfiguration of the concept of desire that comes about from the standpoint of the centrality of beauty can be shown by a critical reconsideration of the work of René Girard. Girard accepts the premise that desire implies a lack – a premise which I shall challenge – but probes more closely than previous theorists had done the imitative dimension of lack. We want not simply what we lack, according to Girard; we want what someone else has, or, more accurately, we want what someone else *wants*. We learn to value things, and thus desire them, because other people value them: our values are culturally acquired from parents, teachers and peers. Lack itself is mimetic. Once basic physical needs for food and shelter and the like have been supplied, our further wants are established in relation to the wants of those around us, especially those we seek to emulate.

Girard argues, further, that this mimetic desire quickly generates mimetic rivalry, a rivalry that turns conflictual and violent. He gives an example:

> Place a certain number of identical toys in a room with the same number of children; there is every chance that the toys will not be distributed without quarrels.
>
> (Girard 1987: 9)

Although each child can have a toy just like each of the others', they will still fight over the toys because they will want the very toy another child has. Moreover, this will cause the child who has the coveted toy to cling to it all the more fiercely: mimetic desire is mutually reinforcing in escalating reciprocity. The resulting rivalry is at the basis of conflict.

> Violence is thus generated. Violence is not originary; it is a by-product of mimetic rivalry. Violence is mimetic rivalry itself becoming violent as the antagonists who desire the same object keep thwarting each other and desiring the object all the more. Violence is supremely mimetic.
>
> (Girard 1996: 12–13)

Girard proceeds from this point to elaborate his famous 'scapegoat' theory, and with it his views of the foundation of religion (Girard 1977; 1987): I have discussed this elsewhere (see Jantzen 2009: 25–32) and shall not pursue it further here.

Instead, I wish to ask how his concept of mimetic rivalry at the centre of desire fares when the desire in question is stimulated by beauty. Without for a moment wanting to minimize the frequently violent effects of mimetic rivalry, I shall argue, first, that beauty stimulates creative response in a manner incompatible with the assumption that desire is always premised upon a lack. Second, I shall argue that it is not always expressed in imitation, let alone in mimetic rivalry. On the contrary, the desires engendered by the experience of beauty are desires that foster empathy, generosity and alternatives to violence.

To begin these related arguments it is helpful to return to the basic experience of beauty: what is it like to listen to a superb performance of a cello concerto, or to watch the sun break through a wintry sky and light up the bracken-covered hillsides, or to see a person whose face and form bespeaks inward and outward radiance? What sort of desire do such experiences engender? I have already argued that the longings evoked by experiences of beauty, though sometimes involving the erotic, cannot be reduced to sexual desire, let alone to a desire for exclusive possession. On the contrary, we seek to preserve and cherish what we find to be beautiful, to experience it ever more deeply and to share it with others.

Now, one aspect of that longing, I suggest, is a longing to create. Those who listen to music are often inspired to try to make music themselves: one of the best incentives for learning to play a musical instrument is to hear it played beautifully by someone else. Similarly, it is no accident that in areas of great natural beauty, like the Lake District, the villages will contain shops selling artists' supplies and photography equipment. People who come and experience the beauty of the lakes and hills often want to reproduce it: to paint or photograph some particular aspect, partly to preserve the experience for themselves and partly to share it with others. Sometimes, in fact, the aesthetic and creative response has many layers, as, for example, learning to play the cello to participate in a Mahler symphony, which is itself a musical meditation on the beauties of the Alps in springtime.

Now, there is indeed a mimetic aspect (though not, I shall argue, mimetic rivalry) to this desire to create beauty in response to beauty. But there is much more to it than mimesis, contrary to Plato's views. According to Plato in the passages (like *Republic* iii) where he expresses suspicion of art, mimesis is purely repetitive, an effort at copying; and since the repetition can never be absolute, the copies deviate more and more from the perfect original. But Plato has, I believe, ignored a crucial dimension of the response to beauty and its expression in creative effort. Response to beauty does indeed stimulate creative desire, but that desire is not a desire simply to produce replicas. Replicas are for consumers: millions of mugs imprinted with Wordsworth's daffodils, trinkets that are at best pretty memorabilia, at worst dust collectors. The desire to create, however, is a desire simultaneously to preserve and to bring newness into the world, something original that will be a thing of beauty in its own right even while in some sense imitating what already exists and inspires it. This is true not only of abstract art and music. Representational art and even photography is an interpretation, a new perspective, a particular rendition. I am of course not claiming that all art aims to be beautiful. Art can also wake us up to the sordid and violent and oppressive: think, for example, of Picasso's *Guernica* or the string quartets of Shostakovich. What I am claiming, rather, is twofold: first, that the experience of beauty stimulates desire that is creative in its very nature, and second, that while this desire is indeed mimetic it cannot be reduced to the desire to merely replicate, but seeks to create something original.

This in turn shows how desire that is aroused by beauty is not simply founded upon lack. The human impulse to create, complicated though it may be by other needs, is, insofar as it is creative, necessarily an expression of resource, not simply of lack. Creativity is better understood as an outpouring of fullness than as an expression of need. Out of lack itself, newness cannot arise. Even in Plato's myth, desire is a child not only of Need but also of Resource: imagination and inner fullness overflow in the production of something new. The desire to create – a painting, a book, a garden, a child – is a desire arising as much out of inner resources and generosity stimulated by the experience of beauty as it is out of need, let alone emptiness: books and paintings and music cannot be created out of empty hearts and heads. It is true that we may speak of a 'need' to create, but this is not need in the sense of lack, but in the sense of desire so full of creative impulse and energy that it cannot be contained, must be allowed to express itself.

Creative desire – especially of humans – rarely receives attention in theological writing, even though it must surely count as one of the most significant elements of the *imago Dei* according to Christian belief, of 'that of God in everyone', as Quakers prefer to say. In Christian theological anthropology, human creativity must ultimately be grounded in the creativity of God. Now the Christian doctrine of creation, whatever else it means, indicates at least this much: that God did not create the world out of divine lack or need but out of generosity and the overflowing of divine resources. When Augustine insisted on the doctrine of *creatio ex nihilo* part of his point was that God created the world out of God's own plenitude and fecundity: subsequent theology (like Augustine himself) has emphasized the contrast between creating 'out of nothing' and creating from already existing material, and thus the radical division between God and the world, as I have already discussed. What has been lost sight of in this account of creation is the prior and fundamental point that divine desire in creation does not betoken need or lack, but an exuberance of plenitude rejoicing in creation. According to biblical accounts, God looked at the intricacy and variety of what he had made and exulted in it: he saw it to be 'very good/beautiful' (the Hebrew word, like its Greek counterpart, means both 'good' and 'beautiful').

Why did God create the world? Theologians who discuss this question tend to move quickly to discussions of deep moral purpose: Karl Barth, for instance, devotes virtually all of his massive volume on the doctrine of creation – some 1,700 pages in four-part volumes – to God's covenant with 'man' and God's providence and gift of freedom to people who are summoned to ethical responsibility in fellowship with God (Barth 1959). In spite of Barth's insistence on the absolute sovereignty of God, he shows little interest in God or God's desires or purposes except as they relate to humankind or human salvation. And yet, on his own terms, he would have to be the first to say that there is an exuberance of variety and beauty in the vastness of the universe and the abundance of its aesthetic delights that is far in excess of what comes into a Barthian 'doctrine of reconciliation'. Though all this abundance must surely have a bearing on Christian theology of God, Barth – like most modern theologians – ignores it.

The sheer delight and beauty of creation and God's joy in its making are given astonishingly little place even in Christian theology that emphasizes creation. A partial (and somewhat surprising) exception is John Calvin, who in his *Institutes* refers repeatedly to beauty. Calvin, taking his cue from Paul's comment in Romans 1.20 that God's nature 'has been clearly perceived in the things that have been made', says that

we cannot open our eyes without being compelled to behold him ...
Wherever you turn your eyes, there is no portion of the world, however
minute, that does not exhibit at least some sparks of beauty; while it is
impossible to contemplate the vast and beautiful fabric as it extends
around, without being overwhelmed by the immense weight of glory.

(Calvin 1957, Vol. 1: 57)

But rather than consider what this fecundity of beauty and delight might
indicate regarding God's desire and nature, Calvin immediately proceeds to
discussions of natural versus revealed theology: that is, whether God can be
known from the world and its creatures or whether scripture is necessary for
the knowledge of God. In making this the focus of attention, Calvin is of
course taking his place in an ancient debate that is still going on. Ever since
Thomas Aquinas (1975) proposed his famous 'Five Ways' of proving the existence of God from the existence and design of the universe, right up to contemporary discussions of theology and science (Peacocke 1993; Bonting 2005)
the question is whether and how God can be known from the existence of the
universe without reference to special revelation. These discussions, however,
are almost without exception couched in the language of ontology: it is the
being, not the beauty, of the universe (and of God) that is in focus, and when
it is held that God can indeed be known as the creator it is God's power and
mastery, not God's extravagant fecundity and the sheer excessiveness of the
created world that is to the fore.

It must be said that Calvin himself sometimes subverts this one-sided
emphasis and is alive to the beauties of creation. Indeed he argues in one passage from the abundant delightfulness of the things that God has created to
the legitimacy of human enjoyment. Not everything need be solemn; not
everything is utilitarian.

Has the Lord adorned flowers with all the beauty which spontaneously
presents itself to the eye, and the sweet odour which delights the sense of
smell, and shall it be unlawful for us to enjoy that beauty and that odour?
What? Has he not so distinguished colours as to make some more agree-
able than others? Has he not given qualities to gold and silver, ivory and
marble, thereby rendering them precious above other metals and stones?
In short, has he not given many things a value without having a use?

(Calvin 1957: II.32)

Like Augustine, Calvin quickly reverts to suspicion of the world and its beauties, anxious lest we should be seduced by them to abandon single-minded
pursuit of heaven. But at least for a moment Calvin is aware that there is
much more to the world than is strictly necessary; that God's abundance
overflows in the beauty of the world and betokens divine delight. (See also
Bouwsma 1988: 134–36.) In Christian theology, desire, especially originary

divine desire that expresses itself in creativity is not premised upon a lack, but upon the overflowing of plenitude.

But if this is the case in relation to God, must the same not be true of human creativity? A common response to beauty, I have argued, is to create something beautiful in turn; and although imitation is involved, the desire is not simply to replicate but to bring something new into the world. Once again this desire betokens inner resources stimulated to expression by encounter with beauty, not merely emptiness or lack. It thus serves as an important corrective to those theologies which place all the emphasis on human need and inadequacy, human sinfulness. Such theologians abound in modernity. Thus, for example, the Protestant Schleiermacher in his discussion of creation never mentions beauty or the delights of divine and human creativity, but emphasizes exclusively the 'absolute dependence' of humanity upon God that is generated by appreciation of the idea of creation (Schleiermacher 1928: 144). Similarly, the Catholic Karl Rahner represents 'creatureliness' not as bearing a creative likeness to the Creator but rather as 'radical difference from and radical dependence on God' (Rahner 1978: 77); and his central concern is with 'man' [sic] as a being threatened radically by 'guilt' (90). It is difficult to find, in modern theological writing, any discussion of the creativity of humankind, of delighted response to beauty and the spontaneity and joy it evokes. Yet in Christian theology's own terms, one would expect this to be a central theme, even though qualified by recognition of sin and need. Lack on its own cannot give rise to creativity, whether human or divine.

Yet if creative desire is not premised upon a lack, but upon fullness that overflows, then it follows that it cannot be understood solely in terms of mimesis or mimetic rivalry. As I have been arguing, the desire to create involves, by definition, the desire to bring newness into the world, not merely to replicate or imitate. Now, it is certainly true that mimesis plays a very large part, first of all in developing the skills necessary for creative expression to be satisfied rather than frustrated. All the creative impulse in the world will not enable me to paint a masterpiece if I have never learned to handle paints and brushes, or to make beautiful music on my cello if I have not developed the skill of playing in tune; and all these skills are learned mimetically, from teachers and masters of these arts who show us how. To learn, in this sense, is to learn to copy: to imitate and practise until we can replicate what our teachers do. Moreover, it is not only the skills themselves which are learned through imitation, but, more subtly, the values that underlie those skills. Our appreciation and understanding of everything from the varieties of wild orchids to the intricacies of a symphony is deepened if we experience it under the guidance of an enthusiastic expert who can communicate their own perceptions. Mimesis is fundamental not just for learning skills but for absorbing the values that make those skills desirable, including the value of creativity itself. Even the desire to create is absorbed mimetically. Mimesis is, in that sense, at the foundation of education and culture.

Indispensable as mimesis is to creativity, however, ultimately more is required than copying. I cannot produce a great painting by copying another one, even if I have the skill to copy it perfectly. Forgery is not creativity. Similarly I cannot write a great book by writing out word for word what even the greatest writers have published: this is plagiarism, not creativity. Unless I have something fresh in me to say (or to paint, or to express musically etc.), something original, I cannot create but only repeat. Creativity is more than mimesis.

It follows that it is also more than mimetic rivalry. Again, it is true that the creative works of others may quicken my own desire to create: I may be inspired by beautiful music to try to make beautiful music myself, or by my colleague's successful publication record to write a book too. Such mimetic desire can be based on admiration and emulation or on jealousy or the impulse to keep abreast of others, or a whole host of other, perhaps conflicting motivations. In this sense mimetic rivalry may play a part. But it can never be the whole explanation. It is impossible to write a good book or make beautiful music simply because someone I admire, or with whom I am in competition, has done so. It's no good saying, 'my colleague has written a brilliant book, so I will do so too', unless I have something of my own to say, something original. René Girard writes of mimetic rivalry as though it were the whole explanation of civilization, but it can never wholly explain creative desire, without which no civilization could exist.

In Girard's account, mimetic rivalry – by which he usually betokens the darker motivations of jealousy and envy, not admiration and a wish to emulate – lies at the heart of violence. If what I have been presenting is correct, however, then alongside mimetic desire, premised upon a lack, must be set creative desire, premised upon fecundity and the overflowing of plenitude. The desire that is activated by beauty to creativity stands against the destructive violence of mimetic rivalry. In less abstract terms, if I learn to respond to beauty, and wish to preserve and share it and create beauty in turn, I will deplore and work against violence and destruction. Desire inspired by beauty is desire for alternatives to violence, sensitivity to life and its creative outpouring.

It follows that a theology that has largely ignored beauty and creative desire, and concentrated instead on lack, sin and the violent rhetoric of salvation through the death of Christ and perpetual spiritual warfare, has much to answer for in the western civilization which that theology underwrites. The escalation of warfare, disregard of other peoples and their cultures, and wanton ecological unconcern are all of a piece with a theological symbolic in which the central ideas and even the language in which those ideas are couched are of death and destruction, evil and battle. A theology that shows little interest in the exuberance and excessiveness of divine creativity, the joy of divine desire in the outpouring of plenitude, will hardly have the resources to foster human creative desire. Instead, it will inevitably contribute to an increase of mimetic rivalry and violence.

Putting this the other way around, attentiveness to beauty and reconsideration of what it involves can point the way to alternatives to violence. The wide variety of creative outpouring, and the sensitivity which attention to beauty fosters, allow for a reconfiguration of desire based not upon deficiency and lack but upon fecundity. Such a consideration of beauty from a feminist theological perspective is long overdue, and is the task to which I turn in the following chapter.

Chapter 11

Flourishing

Towards an ethic of feminist theory

A common feature of many feminist philosophers, as well as philosophers in the Continental lineage, it can be argued, is their demand for utopian thinking and practice, 'the demand for a transformative practice of philosophy ... that would be capable of addressing, criticizing, and ultimately redeeming the present' (Critchley, 1998: 10). My concern in this chapter is not with the accuracy of this as an assessment of Continental philosophy, but rather with the underlying idea of utopian thinking and the transformative practice of philosophy. What does it mean to do feminist moral philosophy with notions of utopia and transformation as points of reference? What characteristics are necessary for moral philosophy to address, criticize and ultimately redeem the present – a present whose constitutive ingredients include massive inequalities of gender, 'race' and economic and cultural resources?

What I am after is the idea of a moral imaginary and how it is formed. The question of formation includes both the question of what its ingredients are and how it comes to be taken up as the imaginary of individuals and societies, at pre-reflective as well as reflective levels. I shall begin by trying to get a little clearer about what a moral imaginary is, starting with contrasts with what it is not and then showing its relationship to the practice of justice. I shall consider how the moral imaginary is formed and some of its present contours; and shall conclude by offering some suggestions for criteria for a transformative moral imaginary. Central to my article is the claim that I have argued elsewhere (Jantzen, 1998) and will sketch only in very general terms here, that the moral imaginary of the west is rooted in a preoccupation with gendered violence and death; and the suggestion that a transformative moral imaginary is grounded, rather, in flourishing and natality. What I have to say is necessarily in broad brush strokes and heavily programmatic: it is meant not as a 'final solution' – of which, in any case, I believe that feminists should be deeply suspicious – but as an agenda for further work.

What is a moral imaginary?

To become clearer about what I mean by a moral imaginary I shall begin with some contrasts. First, a moral imaginary is not a moral theory or a system of ethics. There has been considerable emphasis in western philosophy on developing moral systems, often taking the form of a foundational principle from which specific rights and wrongs, duties and responsibilities could be generated. A famous example is Kant's categorical imperative, demanding that one act upon what one would wish could be universal law, and do so though heaven and earth should fall: one's own moral purity is more important than the consequences for other people and the rest of the world. Sharply contrasting with this, but still a moral system of the same general sort, is the utilitarianism associated with John Stuart Mill, where the morality of any particular action is to be calculated on the basis of the greatest good for the greatest number of people. Utterly different though these two systems are, from the point of view of a moral imaginary they have a great deal in common. Both base themselves on a foundational principle that they take to be axiomatic, and then derive specific rules for action by rational deduction from that principle.

Feminist ethics, in all its many variations, usually begins from the premise that life isn't like that. Leaving aside the question of the abstract validity of either of these principles, it is simply not the case that ordinary people go about our moral lives generating or justifying our decisions about what we should do from overarching principles of this or any sort. Feminists frequently begin, as does normal moral thought, from some concrete situation – abortion, poverty, pornography, education – and if they invoke or generate wider ethical principles at all, they do so with direct reference to the specific issue in question.[1] In using this approach, moreover, some feminist ethicists have asked whether in fact the concept of care might be a better grounding for ethics than rights, justice or overarching principles.[2] Other feminists have shown that whereas care is a consideration too often omitted in traditional formulations of ethics, it will not be in women's interests to disregard justice, rights or impartiality, or to figure women as responsible for all the world's cares (see Benhabib, 1992; Bubeck, 1995). There have also been important discussions of moral agency and of conceptions of autonomy and responsibility in feminist ethics (see Friedman, 2000; Jaggar, 2000).

All of this work is enormously important for feminist ethics. Its significance for what I am after, however, lies less in the feminist writers' specific claims (which are in any case diverse) than in the way these writers disturb the often unconscious assumptions of much moral philosophy and thus reveal some-thing of the moral imaginary that underlies it. Thus, for example, Elizabeth Anderson (1993: 120), in her discussion of G.E. Moore's intuitionism as a theory of value, displays the extent to which his account unconsciously depends on the attitudes and values of the highly privileged

Bloomsbury Group. Again, Lynne Arnault, discussing Richard Hare's universal prescriptivism, points out how Hare's ideal of 'thinking like an archangel' works to prevent him from acknowledging material differences: his moral imaginary is one in which finitude, embodiment and gender are set aside (Arnault, 1989; Hare, 1981). The moral imaginary involves that which is taken for granted, the space – literal and figurative – from which moral thinking is done. It can be thought of in comparison with language: we are not consciously thinking of all the words we know, but we choose words from our common stock whenever we want to say something. Our language frames the possibilities of what we can say. Similarly, our moral imaginary frames what we can think in relation to moral attitudes and behaviour. If, for example, the space of the moral imaginary of our culture is inhabited only by men (and men who consider that they must 'think like archangels' at that), or if the women who inhabit it are there as servants or as sex objects but not as equal moral agents, then the principles and precepts that are generated, no matter how lofty they may sound or how logically they are derived, will be skewed.

So far, I have contrasted the moral imaginary, which may be pre-reflective, with moral theory, whether masculinist or feminist, generated usually by academics. But the moral imaginary, as I am using the term, is part of the wider cultural imaginary, and extends not only to moral theorists or academics but to society as a whole. In this respect it is akin to Pierre Bourdieu's idea of the habitus; and it is worth spending a little time on this notion, first in general, and then with particular reference to the moral imaginary. The habitus is the 'common-sense world' as it appears to, and is inhabited by, its participants. As human beings learn the language of their society and are socialized by it, so we acquire a sense of how to behave in all sorts of practical situations: what to wear on the beach or to a funeral, what things are good to eat and when and how (most English folk would have difficulty with roast beef for breakfast and muesli for tea); 'how things are done' in the multiple situations, trivial and complex, that make up our daily lives. It is this complex of tastes, preferences and learned behaviour patterns that make up the habitus, which then serves as the disposition to behave in ways congruent with it when confronted with practical choices (Bourdieu, 1998). In most situations in daily life we spontaneously know what to do; we have a sense of what is needed or appropriate and how to do it. When we don't – in a new job, say, or a new house, or with a new group of people – we feel cautious and perhaps a bit tense until we 'know the ropes'. Our spontaneous 'common sense' is not arbitrary; it derives from our socialization and the internalization of language and social rules and patterns. But while it is not arbitrary, neither is it mechanical. The habitus, rather, is the disposition from and by which choices are made, 'a spontaneity without consciousness or will' which generates 'reasonable' or 'common sense' behaviour that is neither mechanical nor unpredictable (Bourdieu, 1990: 55–56).

The habitus is what makes social life possible. Within a fairly limited range of possibilities, we know what sort of behaviour is expected in various social roles and contexts, even as we put our own distinctive personal style on the ways in which we fill these roles. Bourdieu writes:

> Habitus are generative principles of distinct and distinctive practices. But habitus are also classificatory schemes, principles of classification, principles of vision and division, different tastes. They make distinctions between what is good and what is bad, between what is right and what is wrong, between what is distinguished and what is vulgar, and so forth ... These principles ... become symbolic differences and constitute a veritable *language*.

> (Bourdieu, 1998: 8)

Thus 'habitus' is a wider category than the moral imaginary as I am using it, because habitus includes a whole range of customary practices and assumptions that are as amoral as having muesli for breakfast. But the moral imaginary can be thought of as one aspect of the habitus – the internalized norms and assumptions that give form and content to our dispositions to act and think. This means, moreover, that the moral imaginary is a wider category than figures of speech, symbols and myths, although it includes these. Michèle Le Doeuff (1989) has written of the philosophical imaginary, showing how the metaphors and figures of speech configure what can be thought; and Diana Meyers (1994) has done important work on the significance of figuration in our moral language. While I draw gratefully on their work, the moral imaginary as I am using the term involves, in addition, quite unmetaphoric ideas that configure our moral habitus: ideas of competition, for example, and violence and death, as I shall discuss further below.

The moral imaginary and social justice

Now, it seems to me to be self-evident that if the moral imaginary in fact shapes our moral beliefs and practices, then it should receive intense critical scrutiny by feminists. And of course in some respects it does, not least in feminist investigation of prejudice. 'Prejudice', after all, is 'habitus' by another name: the prejudgements that we make (and that form us), often without our being explicitly conscious of them, and that shape our actions and principles. These prejudgements become 'prejudice' in the pejorative sense when they are assumptions or prejudgements that place an implicit or explicit negative value on others, like Moore's Bloomsbury Group devaluing the moral intuitions of the less privileged, or Hare's would-be archangels devaluing material existence.

What I want to get at here, though, are not specific prejudices or prejudgements but the more underlying notion of the moral imaginary itself.

How is it formed? What are its contours? How can it be changed? Whose moral imaginary is it anyway? What are the relations between the individual and the social and the subgroups within the social in terms of the formation and function of the moral imaginary? How does gender come into it? There is more, here, than I can go into in this chapter, but these are questions which I think feminists should not ignore, because, although they are not about specific moral principles or actions, or the stuff of traditional moral philosophy, they have huge implications for social justice and transformative practice. The moral imaginary – the contours of our assumptions, prejudgements and dispositions – determines what is actually morally thinkable. Moral philosophers, politicians and policy makers share the same moral imaginary as the society of which they are a part; and thus any system they generate is likely to be a sophisticated articulation of that imaginary. If, as I believe, the western imaginary is deeply rooted in competition, death and gendered violence, then its policies and enactments will inevitably reflect and reinforce that imaginary.

The formation and transformation of the moral imaginary

To assess and intervene in the moral imaginary, and the wider cultural habitus of which it is a part, it is necessary to understand how it is formed as well as what its contours are: I shall discuss these in this section and the next. The formation of a cultural habitus is, as Le Doeuff and Meyers have pointed out, related to its narratives and symbols, its myths, jokes, figures of speech and cultural icons. To this list I would also add ordinary language, which may or may not include metaphor, in which we articulate our daily existence. I have in mind such verbal currency as 'competition', 'consumer choice', 'scientific', 'democratic', 'family values' and the like, all of which are expected to generate positive associations when used in, say, political speech. Tropes such as these inscribe and re-inscribe patterns of thought and behaviour that are normalized by the very fact that they come to be routine and conventional. But this observation only pushes the underlying question one step further back: where do these cultural figurations come from? How do they originate? Clearly, the central narratives, myths and icons of a society are usually generated by people already in that society, and 'catch on' as they do precisely because they give voice to that society's experience. But if these cultural figurations both form and arise out of the cultural imaginary, then what we have is a self-perpetuating circle. How, then, can it be transformed?

To begin to respond to that, I want to look more closely at how its initial formation can be understood, first in terms of psychoanalytic theory and then in terms of Foucauldian genealogy. Although Foucault is rightly regarded as in some respects an opponent of psychoanalysis, I believe that in relation to the formation of the moral imaginary, the two approaches can be seen as complementary rather than mutually exclusive, as I shall try to show.

Psychoanalytic formations

One need not accept all the misogynist baggage of Freudian–Lacanian psychoanalytic theory to find the idea of the unconscious and its formation through the repression of desires compelling. Psychoanalytic theory holds from that which comes to be 'other' to us: in the first instance from our mother. This separation will extend to all that seems dangerous or threatening to our subjectivity; moreover, anything that, at however unconscious a level, triggers that sense of threat will call forth our defences. Analogously (although psychoanalytic writers pay less attention to this), those things that reinforce our sense of selfhood will be eagerly appropriated. Both the threat and the reinforcement can of course be expressed in myths, symbols and narratives – in short, in the cultural figurations that help to form the habitus and shape our moral attitudes and behaviour. The more fragile the self-constitution is, the more vigorously it will have to be reinforced and defended against real or perceived dangers. A society like ours, therefore, where the white male is dominant, will be a society with a cultural and moral imaginary rife with racist, misogynist and xenophobic stereotypes. Even though at a conscious level racist or sexist behaviour may be sincerely deplored, the underlying cultural imaginary remains unreconstructed, and is played out in policy and practice and spontaneous reaction.

The importance of a psychoanalytic account lies in the fact that it shows how the cultural imaginary is related to the deep psychic needs of the individual or society. These needs are nothing less than the basis for self-definition, the constitution of self-identity. Accordingly, the symbolic structure that articulates the moral imaginary is not casual or coincidental: it is not pure happenstance that certain myths, stories, jokes, books, works of art and music are taken into the cultural repertoire whereas others fall by the wayside; nor is their acceptance necessarily an indication of their greater intrinsic worth. Moreover, if the cultural imaginary is formed to meet deep psychic needs, then changing it will be difficult. Indeed, if the habitus of a society is the structure of its self-formation, then an alteration to the habitus is potentially deeply unsettling, in a way analogous to a threat to an individual's self-perception. We should not be surprised if a challenge to the moral imaginary meets with every kind of resistance, from sheer physical force to sophisticated rationalization.[3] Like a neurosis, elements of an unhealthy moral imaginary nevertheless meet certain needs, and therefore will be clung to in every possible way.

Although a psychoanalytic model provides insight into the depth and strength and intractability of a moral imaginary, it does not really get us much further in understanding why it should have the particular contours that it does. *Why* is the moral imaginary of the west one that tolerates and even fosters massive social and economic inequalities, inequalities in which gender and race often play a major part? *Why* does it generate compliance with social policies that cause progressive environmental degradation? Once we agree that the cultural imaginary of the west has been formed by the violent self-constitution of powerful men over and against women and people of other races and creeds, then a psychoanalytic account is helpful in showing how this will play itself out in constant repetition, and be intractable to change. But why was that imaginary developed in such oppositional terms in the first place?

There would be those who would argue that the separation of a boy from his mother in the Oedipal phase necessarily results in self-formation by means of violence, which will ever thereafter have the gendered tones that contour the western habitus; and because other races and even the earth itself are feminized, they become stand-in (m)others who must be mastered for the preservation of subjectivity. Arguably, Freud, Lacan and even Kristeva sometimes write in these naturalizing, essentializing terms. If, however, as I would argue, our cultural imaginary is not universal or essential, but is a particular formation of western modernity, then the psychoanalytic model, although useful, is not enough. It can help us understand the depth of the grip of the cultural imaginary and why it is persistently reinscribed; but more is needed if we are to see where it came from or how it could be changed.

Foucault and the history of the present

The work of Michel Foucault has had enormous influence on scholars, including feminists, who are looking for a way to understand the cultural imaginary of western modernity – what in *The Order of Things* Foucault calls the *episteme* (Foucault, 1970: xxii). Foucault, in his various projects, showed how concepts and practices that we take for granted are nevertheless not ontologically fixed but socially constructed, Moreover, that construction is not always and everywhere the same: it has what he called a 'genealogy'. Thus, famously, Foucault wrote of a history of madness (and by implication, of rationality), showing how what has counted as madness has gone through significant shifts. He applied the same method of problematizing central ideas of the western imaginary to notions of health, punishment and sexuality, in each case showing how ideas that seem obvious or natural in one time or place seem highly questionable or absurd in another.

For Foucault the painstaking archival work that was necessary to develop these genealogies was not just academic brilliance for its own sake. Rather, he was posing 'the question of the present as a philosophical event incorporating within it the philosopher who speaks of it', as he said in an essay on Kant (Foucault, 1986: 89). It is we ourselves, our central ideas, our moral imaginary that must be problematized, brought to consciousness and held up to scrutiny, and thus shown to be rooted not in nature or biology or necessity but in the sedimentations of historical and social construction. As Foucault puts it in another essay, what he is trying to develop is a 'critical ontology of ourselves' as an attitude, an ethos, a philosophical life in which the critique of what we are is at one and the same time the historical analysis of the limits that are imposed on us as an experiment with the possibility of going beyond them (Foucault, 1984: 50).

In this way Foucault presents his genealogical method as a contribution to a transformative practice of philosophy: it is a method that helps to show what the contours are of the present moral and cultural imaginary and how those contours were formed and can, where needed, be re-formed. What this implies is that the onus for reconfiguring the moral imaginary is not left with those who are already too often its victims. It is certainly true that 'dissident speech' often arises out of the life experience of members of oppressed groups; and those who are in positions of economic and cultural privilege need to learn much from those who are not (see Meyers, 1994: 56f.). However, I suggest that Foucault's approach also invites those of us who are in privileged positions to problematize ourselves, to call into question our own moral imaginary. Paul Rabinow, following Foucault, has written of the need to develop an anthropology not of exotic others but precisely of ourselves, to become aware of how peculiar we are: we need, he says, to anthropologize the west: show how exotic its constitution of reality has been; emphasize those domains most taken for granted as universal (this includes epistemology and economics); make them seem as historically peculiar as possible; show how their claims to truth are linked to social practices and have hence become effective forces in the social world (Rabinow, 1996: x).

A fine example of what I mean is Richard Dyer's book *White* (1997). Rather than lay the burden of developing alternative and positive figurations of blackness on blacks, Dyer shows what an odd notion 'white' is as an image of a racial category. A person whose skin was actually white in colour would be very ill indeed: we who are classed as white are various shades of pink, cream, tan – 'flesh colour', as it is tellingly called. Yet we link up images of whiteness as a putative skin colour with cleanliness, with purity and with goodness: sin and evil are dark and black and dirty. When we stop to think of it, this is not only very odd but also morally chilling: the point is, Dyer *does* stop to think of it. He looks at how the imagery of whiteness works in the media, novels and film, and in the history of Christendom and colonialism, and destabilizes its taken-for-granted status and thus its grip on the imaginary. I am not suggesting (and neither is Dyer) that we should problematize whiteness without paying any attention to the dissident speech of blacks: certainly both are necessary. But what is important about the idea of problematizing ourselves is that it does not exoticize others or leave the whole burden of changing the moral imaginary on those who already bear the brunt of it.

Moreover, it enables us to see how our multiple positioning can be a help in transformative thinking. Most of us are simultaneously privileged and oppressed. All of us who are in academic life are culturally and economically privileged, some more than others. Yet, as women, we are members of what is still the 'second sex'. Our skin colour, sexual orientation, age and dis/abilities position us variously in relation to privilege. What Foucault's strategy and Dyer's example show is how it is not only insofar as we are oppressed or occupy places on the margin that we are in a position to develop dissident speech. Rather, it is precisely from our places of privilege that we have the responsibility of developing a transformative moral imaginary. We need to bring to consciousness the very things that shape us and too often shape us as oppressors; and in bringing them to consciousness, loosen their grip, destabilize their hegemonic status in the moral imaginary. When we begin to see the contours of our own moral imaginary, then we can also begin to see what some of the contrasts might be, what might be developed as transformative possibilities. I want to stress that this is not a question of dominant groups imposing our thinking – even our well-intentioned liberatory thinking – on those who are dominated: any helpfully transformative effort will require solidarity.[4] What I am after, rather, is our responsibility as privileged academics to use our thinking in ways that do not re-inscribe a moral imaginary of oppression, but rather in ways that open us to thinking and living to promote human flourishing.

Contours of the western imaginary

The central tropes that frame the imaginary of the west are so familiar to us that we have to work to notice them: they are part of our habitus, and as such shape our thoughts and actions even while remaining outside of our conscious focus. If we had time, I suggest that it would be enormously useful to consider, for example, the vocabulary of 'competition', 'freedom and free choice', 'family', 'democracy', 'science', 'opportunity for all', 'consumer' and many others, not so much in terms of the realities these terms may describe as the ways in which they are rhetorically used to promote certain attitudes and behaviours. Like terms of race and gender (with which they are intertwined), these are terms that shape our ways of thinking, often subliminally, and they are not without moral effect.

In the space that remains I propose to look more closely at just one such trope, which I believe has been of incalculable influence on the western imaginary, namely 'death'; and then to see what a transformative ethic might do with this trope. I want to be clear that I am here speaking of the way death functions in the imaginary: although that function is related to actual death and death-dealing, it should not be confused with it. The reason I speak in terms of a trope is that, although death is indubitably real, I suggest that, like sexuality, bodies and madness, death also is socially constructed and has a genealogy, which on another occasion I would like to elaborate. Death is a guiding motif in the construction of rationality, a rationality often characterized as freedom from the body and the delusions of the passions. Death is central to the construction of western science, which is premised on secularism, the banishment of divine life not only from the act of knowing (in the elimination of enthusiasm) but also from the universe, which is thereby rendered lifeless, even mechanistic, a complicated version of the Strasbourg clock beloved of Locke, Boyle and the early Royal Academy. The habitus of modernity is premised on the death of God, and this leads to ideas of the death of 'man', the death of the subject, the death of the author ... In popular and 'high' culture, in musical compositions, novels, paintings and sports writing, there is a continual preoccupation with death, often interlinked with love and sex.

The cultural portrayals of death show how closely death and gender are intertwined. This is, of course, not new to modernity, although it is given different emphasis. The womb and the tomb of Plato's cave or the anchorite's cell; the Christian insistence on a new birth not of flesh and blood as prerequisite for eternal life; the fear of female sexuality in medieval monastic writings and early modern witch hunts; the linkage of sexual love with death, so that women are regularly described in poetry as diverse as Donne's and Blake's as bearing children (not for life but) for death; ejaculation as a 'little death'; the interweaving of death and the female in the writings of psychoanalytic theory from Freud onwards: all these show that the genealogy of death in the west is a gendered genealogy, and one that has had disastrous consequences for women. The urgency to escape mortality, whether through immortal fame as a Greek – or Faustian – hero, through heaven after death, or through the attainment of some other world in outer space or in virtual reality, has been an obsession for men in the west, which did not disappear with modernity. The secular formations of gender and death are related closely to their precursors in Christendom, as a developed genealogy would show.

Moreover, it is this obsession with death, largely suppressed, that can be shown to be acted out in the violent and death-dealing structures of modernity. From militarization and death camps and genocide to exploitation and commodification and accumulation of wealth; from the construction of pleasure and desire to the development of terminator genes; from the violence on the streets to the heaven-obsessed hymnody of evangelical churches: preoccupation with death and the means of death and deathly combat is ubiquitous. It is a necrophilia so deeply a part of the western habitus that it emerges at every turn. Our language is full of metaphors of war, weaponry, violence and death, even in relation to aspects of life where violence should have no place: 'the war against homelessness', 'the battle with illness', 'fighting against child abuse'. Even philosophical argument is regularly constructed as a battle, in which only the winner's argument will survive.

Transforming the moral imaginary

If I am right in characterizing the deathly imaginary of modernity as a fundamental contour of our habitus, then it will not be changed simply by arguing against one or other of its effects or enactments. Here again, I suggest, the combination of genealogical and psychoanalytical approaches is important. Although a genealogy of death is indispensable in enabling a 'history of the present', enabling us to become aware of the dimensions of our deathly moral imaginary, by itself such a genealogy will not bring about transformation in the case of a society deeply invested in a habitus of death and unwilling to recognize at a deep level the problems which that habitus generates. However, these problems are coming more and more to the fore, in barbarically violent international and internecine conflicts, 'ethnic cleansings' and the degradation of the planet, to take only three examples: transformation is daily more urgent.

At this point we can once again have recourse to psychoanalytic theory. It is usually a step in any effective *individual* therapy that the client should come to explicit consciousness of the imaginary that has been shaping problematic responses and behaviours, and see as far as possible where those ideas came from. The same, I suggest, is true at a *cultural* level. Although a genealogy on its own is unlikely to change action, it is a crucial part of understanding the provenance of the habitus (and its changes and variants) and of recognizing how it configures behaviour. This then enables the question of whether we really want to continue to have our actions and thoughts controlled by these unconscious motivations or how we might find release from them.[5]

I suggest that using the therapeutic analogy for transformation of the moral imaginary brings to mind three related questions: what exactly is it that is being repressed in this gendered and ostensibly secular deathly habitus? What deep fear underlies the repression? How is that fear related to longing and desire: what are these desires? Only a patient and detailed investigation and analysis can develop adequate responses to these questions. Some preliminary considerations, however, present themselves. First, as Derrida has taught us, it is instructive to consider for any dominant discourse – in this case that of death – what it is that the discourse simultaneously silences and depends on.[6] As I have begun to argue elsewhere (Jantzen 1998: chapter 7), examination of the deathly symbolic from this perspective raises up the idea of *natality* – bodily birth – on which depends the very possibility of death. It is instructive that virtually every major philosopher of the western tradition at some point writes about death; almost none writes about birth. Moreover, it can hardly be doubted that birth is intricately involved with gender: every body who is born is gendered, and gender shapes the trajectory of natals. Although new reproductive technologies may make the generation of life possible in unforeseeable ways, everyone who has ever been born until now has been born of a woman.

Now, a moral imaginary of natality would necessarily be very different from a moral imaginary of death. Natals require care and protection to flourish. They rely on interdependence; and unless they are welcomed into the world, they will not survive. A moral imaginary that proceeds in terms of atomistic individualism simply could not get off the ground if we were thinking in terms of natality. Moreover, it is precisely the fact of natality that makes for possibility: natality is the condition of new life entering the world. It is therefore the condition of hope, and of future. A moral imaginary of natality is one that takes up the tough fragility of life, its hopefulness and its possibilities, its interconnectedness and the dependence of its flourishing on the whole web of life around it, not excluding the earth. All of this needs to be further developed, and I am not suggesting that it is without problems. What I do want to suggest, however, is that when we recognize the deathly imaginary that forms the history of the present, and begin to develop dissident speech, the imaginary of natality is a good place to begin.

A second consideration that the therapy analogy brings to mind is the question of displacement. A phobia about one thing (for example, spiders, dirt) is often actually a deeply unresolved complex about something else, to which the ostensible object of fear is related, but repressed precisely by attaching itself to a substitute.[7] What suggests itself, then, is that the obsession with death characteristic of the western habitus may be a displacement of something to which it is related but which renders it invisible in the symbolic structure. From what I have already said, an obvious candidate is natality, and underlying it the mother and female sexuality. The identification of the womb and the tomb is a trope in western representation, from Plato's myth of the cave to the medieval understanding of the monastery or anchor hold, from Francis Bacon's forcible 'wooing' of nature and the 'masculine birth of time' to William Blake's 'Daughters of Albion', and the lyrics of contemporary pop music. Could this be the real locus of the fear of death, the site that must be both silenced and controlled at all costs? And are the death-dealing structures of modernity and its master discourses attempts to silence and control the mother, and all the other (m)others that might bring this fear to mind: the earth, its beauty, its peoples, its unpredictable life?

Feminists have come to this recognition before, of course, from different starting points. What I am after here is that, if what we are dealing with is at the level of the moral imaginary, which is in urgent need of transformation, then these feminist insights must be brought to bear in order to generate dissident speech not just from the margins but from the centre of this habitus. We who are in academic life, although in some respects marginal, in other respects are beneficiaries of the vastly unequal system of wealth and power that the western imaginary has generated. We are therefore in a position to demand a transformative practice of moral philosophy, a moral philosophy capable of addressing, criticizing and ultimately redeeming the present, to develop therapeutic possibilities for a new moral imaginary of natality and flourishing.

Chapter 12

On changing the imaginary

Whatever their many differences, thinkers loosely categorized as 'postmodern' tend to be sharply critical of the trajectories that have shaped the west since its turn to 'modernity' from about the seventeenth century onwards. The general features of 'modernity' are easily rehearsed. Among other things there is the rise of science and the exaltation of empiricism as the foundation of knowledge; its tentacles in militarism and in technology; capitalism and commodification and utilitarianism; colonialism, slavery, the hegemony of the west and the exploitation of the rest; the destabilization of traditional social structures and the rise of individualism ... the litany could be extended. Of course much nuancing is necessary; of course it is not all bad. But one would need to be singularly unmindful of the effects of western modernity on the rest of the world's peoples, on the earth itself, and on the narrowing of the human spirit in the west, to think that the primary response to modernity should be celebration. Moreover one would need to be singularly optimistic to suppose that these effects will somehow right themselves in a new era called 'postmodernity' or 'the new millennium' without effort and without cost.

The point, however, is to change it: to change the world of modernity, and to change the imaginary which has rigidified into its death-dealing discursive and material structures. The world, to be sure, *is* changing, and with great rapidity. The ground shifts under our feet in relation to technologies, from informational and military hardware to genetically modified species. But these changes, arguably, are continuations of trajectories that already cut deep ruts through modernity. What is necessary is to find some way of thinking – and living – otherwise. If philosophy/theology does not engage with this problematic, the legacy of modernity, it is useless – or worse.

But how shall such thinking/living be done? By whom? And from what place? Should we perhaps wait for a great heroic poet heralding news of Being? But even if we thought that Being could become present, how would we recognize the difference between the demonic and the angelic messenger? Should we respond to the face of the other immediately before us – and the next one, and the next, until we turn away in exhaustion while the causes of human misery (which may rest in ourselves) remain unaddressed? Should we stop worrying about it, count ourselves lucky to be among the privileged, and play, erring, among the simulacra while we may? Heidegger once said, notoriously, 'Only a god can save us now.' But we had better not wait 'for the dead god of Nietzsche', whose absence is as hard to pin down as ever his presence was amongst the shifting signifiers, for this 'god is dead, and we have killed him', and the black sun is upon us. The allusions, of course, are to twentieth-century Continental thinkers who look for ways to deal with modernity, and point to their suggestions, and in some cases despair, for reconfiguration of its symbolic. Their writings merit sustained attention, especially, I think, in their hints and dismissals of the divine.

The invocation of the divine is indeed apposite: it leads, at least, to reconsideration of the features of modernity. For interconnected with all the characteristics of modernity is its secularism, achieved by the banishment of God from the world, at first into a 'heaven' to which one might aspire after death, and eventually out of consideration altogether for all practical or public purposes. The *saeculum*, which according to Christian thought was the time between creation and final judgement, became the present time, the time of God's absence. Eternity, and the divine who inhabits it, was something qualitatively different from the present order and irrelevant to the march of the millennia, which in the west are, ironically, dated (ostensibly) from the birth of Jesus.

There was no neat linear or logical progression about the banishment of the divine. At the same time as Locke was banning 'enthusiasm' (lit. 'God within') from rigorous epistemology, and Hume was mocking the idea of a miracle as divine 'tampering' with a law of nature, God was being invoked, by them and their compatriots, to justify civil religion, the appropriation of continents, slavery, genocide, the subordination of women and the exploitation of the 'lower' classes. Nevertheless, this God was a god in heaven, not on earth, and was increasingly removed from the public realm. Thus, more and more, religion was either rejected outright or confined to the private and domestic sphere. In either case, it was turned in large measure into a question of 'beliefs': it was no longer primarily the place of meeting between human and divine, the sacrament of divine presence, the holy place or saint or shrine or holy well in which heaven and earth were visibly fused in outward signature of grace: where, therefore, miracles might take place as between the two angels facing each other across the place of holiness.

All this has become at best 'poetic', where poetry itself serves no useful purpose unless as rhyming couplets to advertise McDonald's or to be placed with posters about what's on in the West End and the help-line for the Samaritans on the London underground. Yet, given the extent to which this process of secularization is interwoven with the discourses and practices of modernity, it is hardly possible to probe those discourses without revisiting the question of religion, a revisitation not separate from a revolution in poetic language, and indeed, I shall suggest, willingness once again to contemplate beauty (as distinct from the sublime and the unrepresentable). If this is what is involved, then it is very different from a return to endless assessments of 'proofs' for the existence of God, of the coherence of theism, of theodicy, and all the other tedious preoccupations of traditional Anglo-American analytic philosophers of religion. All these buy into, and thus reinforce, modernity's understanding of religion as a set of beliefs: they already have their reward. But perhaps we do need to ask what counts as religion, and who is doing the counting. What functions has religion served? Which technologies of power has it authorized, and what resistances can it generate? Moreover, all these questions must *also* be asked of secularism, religion's putative other.

As I shall explain later, probing these questions will not of itself change the imaginary. It will, however, generate a genealogy of religion/secularism which will show its place in the master discourses of modernity, the current cultural symbolic, and will also show, in an effective history of the present, how it came to be structured thus. The importance of such genealogies is largely taken for granted (at least among those open to Continental thought) in relation to many areas of discourse: sexuality, rationality and punishment, to name only three brought to the fore in the work of Michel Foucault. But if religion (as much as madness or sexuality) is to be understood not as a fixed or natural essence but as constructed, and with a genealogy, and interwoven in all the master discourses of modernity, then the urgency of re-examining it can hardly be overstated. Indeed it is all the more important because the unexamined assumptions of secularism have occluded consciousness of the ways in which a religious symbolic still permeates those discourses, as, for instance, in a preoccupation with other worlds, or the idea of a 'God's-eye view' from nowhere as the gold standard of rationality, or the warning against 'playing God' in genetic technology.

Such a genealogy of religion/secularism immediately indicates further dimensions. First among them is gender. As I have argued elsewhere, as long as Christendom considered religious experience potentially authoritative not merely over the private life of the experiencer, but over the whole polity, then there were very strict controls, along gendered lines, over who could legitimately claim to be the recipient of such experiences. Once religion became a private matter, these controls were largely dropped; anybody could count as a mystic, when a mystic did not count for much. But this should not mislead us into thinking that the secularism of modernity was less oppressive to women. Feminists who turn with relief from the misogynistic structures of Christendom find misogyny re-inscribed in the secular structures of modernity, though often under a veneer of liberalism reminiscent of the churches' avowals of the value of women: in both cases the menial jobs without which the structures would collapse are largely women's work, and this remains the case even when a few women are priests, scientists or executive directors.

Feminists are aware, of course, that the master discourses of modernity oppress women. Feminist philosophers have been showing how rationality (putatively neutral) has been constructed on masculine lines; how science (putatively objective) has worked against the insights and interests of women; how politics and economics (putatively free and democratic) have been developed in ways that foster competition, aggression and an adversarial approach which has often actively excluded women or been uncongenial to women, or, perhaps even worse, encouraged women to develop those same attitudes and responses until they have (as it was said of Mrs Thatcher) more balls than the boys. I am not suggesting that there is any one-to-one gender mapping, let alone biological essentialism. Nevertheless, many feminists assume that by discarding religion we have at least rid ourselves of one misogynist structure, even if there are plenty left to be going on with. That there is systemic oppression of women (and others) in the material and discursive practices of Christendom is not in doubt. However, if my suggestion for a genealogy of religion in the west (largely though not only of Christendom) is correct, then it follows, first, that it is mistaken to see secularism and religion in essentialist terms; second, that secularism and religion are not therefore binary opposites; and third, that it is thus too simplistic to assume that secularism is the obvious choice for feminists (or for any progressive thinkers). What I believe emerges instead is that the construction of both religion *and* secularism in modernity leaves the two in mutual entanglement, not least in what count as rationality and value, and that this is closely entwined with questions of gender.

This becomes more apparent by the introduction of the notion of death. I use the term 'notion' because, although death is indubitably real, I suggest that, like sexuality, bodies, madness and, indeed, religion, death is also socially constructed and has a genealogy. Death is a guiding motif in the construction of rationality, a rationality often characterized as freedom from the body and the delusions of the passions. Death is central to the construction of western science, which is premised on the banishment of divine life not only from the act of knowing (in elimination of enthusiasm) but also from the universe; which is thereby rendered lifeless, even mechanistic, a complicated version of the Strasbourg clock beloved of Locke, Boyle, and the Royal Academy. The philosophy of modernity is premised on the death of God; and this leads to the death of 'man', the death of the subject, the death of the author ... In popular and 'high' culture, in musical compositions, novels, painting and sports writing, there is continual preoccupation with death, often interlinked with love and sex.

The cultural portrayals of death show how closely ideas of death and gender are intertwined. This is of course not new in modernity, though it is given different emphases. The womb and the tomb of Plato's cave or the anchorite's cell, the Christian insistence on a new birth not of flesh and blood as prerequisite for eternal life, the fear of female sexuality in medieval monastic writings and early modern witch hunts, the linkage of sexual love with death so that women are regularly described in poetry as diverse as Donne and Blake as bearing children (not for life but) for death, ejaculation as a 'little death' and the interweaving of death and the female in the writings of psychoanalytic theory from Freud onwards, all show that the genealogy of death in the west is a gendered genealogy, and one which has had disastrous consequences for women. The urgency to escape mortality, whether through immortal fame as a Greek – or Faustian – hero, through heaven after death, or through the attainment of some other world in outer space, has been an obsession for men in the west which did not disappear with modernity; it went through meta-morphoses into secular (but no less gendered) forms. Indeed the secular forms of modernity are, in relation to gender and death, related very closely indeed to their precursors in Christendom, as a developed genealogy would show.

Moreover, it is this obsession with death, largely suppressed, which can be shown to be acted out in the violent and death-dealing structures of moder-nity. From militarization and death camps and genocide to exploitation and commodification and the accumulation of wealth, from the construction of pleasure and desire to the development of terminator genes, from the violence on the streets to the heaven-obsessed hymnody of evangelical churches, pre-occupation with death and the means of death and the combat with death is ubiquitous. It is a necrophilia so deeply a part of the western symbolic that it emerges at every turn: our language is full of metaphors of war, weaponry, violence, and death, even in relation to aspects of life where violence should have no place: 'the war against homelessness', 'the battle with illness', 'fighting against child abuse' ...

The term 'necrophilia' is appropriate: for although the preoccupation with death presents itself as a dread or fear, literally a phobia, Freud has shown how such phobias, as obsessions, are simultaneously a love or desire for the very thing so dreaded. In fact Freud believed that *Thanatos*, a death drive, was as strong as Eros, and closely linked with it. Whereas he held that it was a universal of human nature, I would argue that it is a gendered construction of western modernity, with precursors in Christendom and in ancient Greek thought. It is at least abundantly clear that a gendered obsession with death saturates the western symbolic and is actualized in the continuing destructive-obsessive practices of modernity.

Now, if I am correct in characterizing the deathly symbolic of modernity (and indeed postmodernity) as rooted in and reinforcing necrophilia/phobia; if I am correct, that is, in treating it as an obsession or psychic disorder of the social realm, then it will not be changed by arguing against it. Although many traditional philosophers of religion and theologians continue to write as though Freud and Lacan had never lived, such an approach, in my opinion, lacks integrity. For all the problems of psychoanalytic theory – and from a feminist perspective there are many – its recognition that the structures of social and individual existence both act out and reinforce the cultural sym-bolic, complete with its (gendered) repressions, means that rational analysis of the ills of modernity, and rational solutions to them (even if they can be found), will not effect a cure. The symbolic of western modernity is inseparable from the repressions and compulsions which form its underside. That being the case, appeals to rationality will not bring about the desired change, any more than it would help to tell a person in the grip of a neurosis what it is that they are repressing. Such strategies only bring out stronger resistance, ever more clever rationalizations, deeper anger and control.

This is not to say that careful analysis, genealogies, archaeologies and deconstructions are useless; it does, however, mean that it is necessary to think through what their use is and what it is not. As I have said, it is not likely to be effective in the case of a society deeply invested in the symbolic of modernity and unwilling to recognize at a deep level the problems which that symbolic generates. However, these problems are coming more and more to the fore, in barbarically violent international and internecine conflicts, 'ethnic cleansings', and the consequences of global warming, to take only three examples; and there are those who are seeking ways of thinking otherwise. Now, it is usually a necessary step in any effective *individual* therapy that the client should come to explicit consciousness of the ideas that have been shaping problematic responses and behaviours, and see where those ideas came from. The same, I suggest, is true at a *cultural* level. Although rational argument on its own is unlikely to change action, it is a crucial part of understanding the provenances of the symbolic (and its changes and variants) and of recognizing the responses it generates. This then enables the question of whether we really want to continue to have our actions and thoughts controlled by these unconscious motivations or how we might find release from them. It is worth reiterating that even this will be useful only for those who acknowledge that there is a problem, however. Those who refuse that recognition, or displace the problem onto others – 'underdeveloped countries', 'welfare scroungers', 'climatic forces' – will only try to strengthen their controlling grip.

I am not arguing that the psychoanalytic model of neurosis and therapy is in every respect applicable to the social order, let alone that it is the only model. The analogy must be complexified, for example, by attention to ideologies and their function; and also the dynamics of resistance within any power structure. Nevertheless, although the analogy must be qualified and supplemented, I believe that it is a useful one in probing the cultural symbolic of the west, formed as it is by the triangulation of death, gender and religion/secularism, especially if we are asking how this symbolic and its underlying imaginary could be transformed. I suggest in particular that using the therapeutic analogy brings to mind three related questions, questions which are heightened by the development of a critical genealogy. What is it exactly that is being repressed in this gendered and ostensibly secular necrophilic symbolic? What deep fear underlies the repression? How is that fear related to longing and desire: what are these desires?

Only a patient and detailed investigation and analysis can develop adequate responses to these questions. Some preliminary considerations, however, present themselves. First, as we have learned from the deconstructive strategies of Derrida, it is instructive to discern, in a dominant notion like necrophilia (or speech, or rationality, or indeed religion), what it is that this discourse simultaneously silences and depends upon: what it constructs as its binary opposite. This is not to say that it really is its opposite, of course; indeed, part of the point of the deconstructive strategy is to dismantle such putative binaries. However, it is significant to lift up what has been suppressed, to see how this changes the picture. As I have begun to argue elsewhere, drawing on the work of Hannah Arendt and Adriana Cavarero, examination of the necrophilic symbolic from this perspective raises up the idea of natality: bodily birth, which is hardly ever taken seriously in the western philosophical tradition and yet upon which depends the very possibility of death, not only as a philosophical category but also in reality. Moreover, that birth is intricately involved with gender can hardly be in doubt. Every body who is born is gendered, and gender shapes the trajectory of natals. And although new reproductive technologies may make the generation of human life possible in unforeseeable ways, everyone who has ever been born until now has been born of a woman.

This leads to a second preliminary consideration. Necrophilia presents itself as obsessive anxiety about death, and virtually ignores birth, which is repressed at the level of the symbolic. Now, one of the things that the therapy analogy brings to mind is the question of displacement. A phobia about one thing (e.g., spiders, dirt) is often actually a deeply unresolved complex about something else, to which the ostensible object of fear is related but represses precisely by attaching itself to a substitute. Thus in Freud's account of Little Hans, the boy's phobia about horses was a disguised complex about his father and masculine sexuality. What suggests itself, then, is that the obsession with death characteristic of the western symbolic may be a displacement of something to which it is related but which renders it invisible within the symbolic structure. From what I have already said, an obvious candidate is natality, and underlying it the mother and female sexuality. Could this be the real locus of fear of death, the site which must be both silenced and controlled at all costs? And are the death-dealing structures of modernity and its master discourses attempts to silence and control the mother, and all the other (m)others which might bring this fear to mind: the earth, its beauty, its peoples, its unpredictable life? Again, the suggestion calls for careful working out; but if what we need is a changed imaginary, then I think we ignore it at our peril.

If for the moment we assume that it is along the right lines, then this raises another consideration. Is it not the case that a phobia, if it is expressive of an unresolved complex, indicates not only deep fear and dread but also unacknowledgeable longing and desire? If that is so, or even partly so, what desire lies deep within the symbolic of necrophilia/phobia? Freud took the death drive at face value: he postulated *Thanatos* straightforwardly as a desire for stasis. However, I believe that a genealogy of western necrophilia reveals not so much a desire for death as stasis, but a desire for death as entrance to other worlds: immortality, whether understood in religious or secular terms. It is a desire to escape from gendered bodies (and indeed the gendered earth) by regimes of control. But underlying that, as Freud also sometimes recognized, is there not a repression of longing for lost unity – and lost unity precisely with the maternal? The identification of the womb and the tomb is a trope in western representation from Plato's myth of the cave, to the medieval understanding of a monastery or an anchor hold, from Francis Bacon's forcible 'wooing' of nature and the 'masculine birth of time' to William Blake's 'Daughters of Albion, and the lyrics of contemporary pop music. Moreover it is a commonplace of psychoanalytic theory that the infant longs for unification with its mother, and enters the (masculinist) social and linguistic symbolic only by repressing that unassuageable loss. Now if, as I would argue, that symbolic is necrophilic, then the complex which underlies it is at least in part an unacknowledged longing for the maternal, a longing repressed by death-dealing strategies of control.

In many respects these ideas are not new; they are the stock-in-trade of a considerable body of feminist writings, even if I have juxtaposed them in a slightly different way. But the question returns: how shall this necrophilic symbolic be changed, even if it is complexified in the ways I have mentioned? Again, the analogy with therapy may prove useful. When a client has begun to recognize not only the problems generated by their feelings, responses and behaviours, but also the underlying fears and desires, these then become available for deliberate reappraisal and choice: not choice in the abstract or once and for all, but steady, quotidian reorientation. Similarly, when society recognizes the genealogy of death on which it is premised, and its underlying fears and desires, then choices open up for natality, new beginnings which reorient responses and attitudes and revalue otherness, whether of gender, sexuality, 'race,' or species, or indeed the planet itself and the material universe.

These considerations are further sharpened by reintroducing the third side of the triangulation, namely the genealogy of religion/secularism, which is at every turn interrelated with gender but also with the symbolic of death and other worlds. In modernity religion and secularism are regularly presented as opposites, as for example in the putative conflict between religion and science. However, I have already suggested that in many respects religion and secularism in modernity are on common ground, in particular in banishing God from the world and from knowledge, in the emphasis on beliefs and their justification, and in their focus on practicality or utilitarianism which easily slides into commodification: all these, again, can be shown to be interlinked with preoccupation with death and with 'conquering' death, whether in this world or some other.

What I suggest, therefore, is that we should look not so much for what secularism by itself is repressing, or religion by itself; but rather we should ask what is being silenced by the common ground shared between them. And here I want to urge that a very important consideration is beauty. If we compare the centrality of beauty in the religious writings of late antiquity and the medieval mystics and theologians with its virtual absence in contemporary Christian theology and philosophy of religion, the contrast is startling. In pre-modern writing there were many who placed beauty squarely in the centre of such a conversion of the imaginary: 'Late have I loved you, O Beauty, so ancient and so new, late have I loved you!' wrote Augustine (*Confessions* x. 27); and it was the discovery of this Beauty and this love that released him to his real longings and helped him find a way forward in his tangled-up sexuality. Augustine, to be sure, struggled with the relationship between this Beauty and his sensory experiences, often relegating the former to the strictly spiritual, as though Beauty can have nothing to do with the body. He bequeathed his struggle, on this as on sexual matters, to medieval thinkers in the west, who were often torn, as he was, between *concupiscentia ocularum*, ocular desire for beauty that diverts from spiritual concern, and a recognition that in painting, architecture, music, illumination of manuscripts and the physical world itself the soul can be drawn to the wonder of God.[1] With the Reformation, however, and the emphasis (at least in Protestant countries) upon the Word, visual representation was often taken to be less important, even idolatrous;[2] and belief replaced beauty as the mode of access to the divine. The emphasis on beliefs and their justification in Protestant theology and philosophy of religion almost completely obscures consideration of beauty and its centrality in inspiring and focusing longing and desire.[3]

In the secular counterpart of religion in modernity, the march of technology and the military-industrial-information complex has little room for beauty, which is relegated (with mystical experience) to the private realm, not of public importance. It is of course true that there is great interest in 'fine arts', as well as intense holiday pressure on the countryside; but here again we find the features of modernity, of slipping into commodification and being a private 'leisure' activity, not part of the serious business of everyday life. It could be argued that, contrary to what I am suggesting, modernity in fact shows a heightened awareness of beauty, as evidenced by the establishment of museums, national parks, art galleries and concert halls. Welcome as these are, however, I would argue that the very need for them partly proves my point: if areas of the countryside were not set apart for conservation they would be gobbled up as building sites; but we do not have to worry about the converse, that fac-tories or motorways will be destroyed because of increasing demand for unspoiled country. Similarly, art and artefacts are gathered into museums and galleries partly to conserve them, partly to render them commodities for cul-tured consumption; but it would be hard to argue that before the existence of museums people were less involved with beautiful things or cared less about their preservation.

Beauty is, of course, also a candidate for genealogy, and can not be discussed as a natural or universal essence. In modernity beauty has been linked with the feminine, as in the writings of Burke and Kant, and with the emotional; whereas sublimity was seen as masculine, awe-inspiring and ultimately rational. Again, there has been considerable attention focused on the sublime, perhaps precisely because it has been constructed as rational and masculine, whereas (feminized) beauty was more easily dismissable as mere prettiness.[4] Thus Derrida, in *The Truth in Painting*, discusses the claim that 'the sublime cannot inhabit any sensible form' (Derrida 1987: 131), and therefore, unlike beauty, cannot be presented or occur in natural configuration. The unrepresentability of the sublime is taken even further by Lyotard, who valorizes the sublime precisely as the feeling of incommensurability, the shock of impossible juxtaposition, linked with desire, but desire best glossed as violent (Lyotard 1984: 78; 1989: 196–211). Beauty and its attracting power is ignored or dismissed as naive consolation. Throughout the modern and postmodern discourse on the beautiful and the sublime, the interconnections with gender and death require careful investigation; clearly they are ubiquitous.

One of the reasons why it is so interesting to lift up beauty for reconsideration is the way in which it links longing and desire with natality, and both with the divine. Elaine Scarry, in her book *On Beauty and Being Just*, points out that recognition of beauty 'seems to incite, even to require, the act of replication' (Scarry 1999: 3). If we see a beautiful landscape (or person, or painting) we paint a copy, if we can, or take photographs, or write a poem or an entry in a journal, or send a postcard to a friend describing the beauty we have experienced. We long not only to retain the experience of the beautiful but also in some way to recreate it. Yet the recreation is not just mindless copying (unless it is mere commodification: a thousand bookmarks and mugs printed with Wordsworth's 'Daffodils'), but can often be a creation of beauty in itself, as a Mahler symphony creates a musical rendition of light upon a mountain. Thus beauty demands the enactments of one of the central features of natality, which, above all else, is the potential for newness, fresh beginnings, while at the same time requiring its own preservation. Scarry points out how often we remark of a beautiful thing: 'I never saw/heard/etc. anything quite like it': it both presents itself as newness and also leads to fresh creativity. 'The beautiful thing seems – is – incomparable, unprecedented; and that sense of being without precedent conveys a sense of the "newness" or "newbornness" of the entire world' (22). As Simone Weil wrote: 'The love of the beauty of the world ... involves ... the love of all the truly precious things that bad fortune can destroy. The truly precious things are those forming ladders reaching toward the beauty of the world, openings on to it' – and Weil immediately speaks of books and education, along with the kestrel hovering in the air currents, as having the potential to develop in us such openings (Weil 1951: 180).

But putting this another way, is there not here an indication that attending to beauty could help to change the imaginary? If the necrophilia of modernity is an obsession, to be understood as I have suggested as a collective neurosis, then even if we accept this diagnosis, I have pointed out why rational argument and analysis will not get us out of it. Only by catching glimpses of a better way, of delight, of freedom and joy can those struggling with neuroses find the courage and incentive to liberate themselves from the structures of control and claim instead that which meets their true desires. To change the necrophilic symbolic of modernity and its discursive and material practices, might it not be an effective strategy to seek, in the counter-discourses of natality which give the lie to the omnipotence and fearfulness of death, the beauty that draws us spontaneously to yearn towards it?

And yet, even if this is partly right, it cannot be the whole story. For if it is true that attending to beauty could change the imaginary, surely it is equally true that, unless our imaginary changes, we will not attend to beauty. Part of my point, after all, has been that in modernity beauty – and certainly an acknowledgment of longing for beauty – has largely been crowded out of the world into museums and galleries and national parks, into the margins of private or leisure existence. Neither is it any use pretending that anyone seeking to address this situation, no matter how progressive in their thinking, is somehow outside of the necrophilic symbolic, in a pure place, free of the compulsions and repressions which that symbolic enacts in the master discourses and practices of modernity. We cannot just step outside the broad contours of the scientific or legal or economic or philosophical conceptualizations of western modernity, even if we want to. We bring ourselves along to any consideration and action; and we – any who read and write and seek to intervene in the languages and civilization of western post/modernity – are always already formed, for good and ill, by its symbolic.

Thus those of us who want to help effect changes in the death-dealing structures of thought and practice are the first to stand in need of re-formation, of learning how to think – and be – otherwise. And so we are back to the questions with which I began: who, and from what place, can intervene in the imaginary? Yet this sort of circle is of course not new, either in hermeneutics or in psychotherapy; and in both cases it is frequently found that while one might return again and again to the same old questions, one is not asking them from quite the same old place or in quite the same old way. The previous considerations have, I hope, somewhat altered the perspective on these questions. Indeed, though the questions are the same, some resources have begun to emerge which help enable a response.

Some things are obvious. First, we cannot think otherwise just by deciding, perhaps as a resolution for the new millennium, that from now on that is what we are going to do. But what we can do is to set ourselves the task of deliberately problematizing the present and its symbolic. Moreover, once we are alert to thinking about the multiple ways in which religion, gender and death have been triangulated in the changing formation of the western symbolic, we can work to develop genealogies which bring them to light and thus enable us to understand the present in different ways. This will ensure that we will never be able to think about it in the same way again, just as we can never go back to the old ways of thinking about madness or sexuality or carceral regimes once we have read Foucault. And in this work we can try to uncover what has been silenced, listen to the voices which can often be discerned in the margins, retrieve the dangerous memories that tell of other ways of thinking and being. All this requires patience and investigation; and in the research on which I am embarked I make a start at a gendered genealogy of necrophilia and at attending to alternative voices, voices of natality and beauty which can still be discerned and retrieved, even if not unambiguously.

Yet while I believe that such mental re-education is enormously important, the idea of the centrality of beauty suggests something further. There is something highly ironic (if not actually disingenuous) about those of us who are paid good salaries and retained in posts of respect and esteem by academic establishments to set ourselves up as people who will lead the way in thinking/being otherwise. Our identities, not to mention our livelihoods and our daily tasks and expectations, are shaped by these institutions of modernity. While there is a long and precious tradition of academic freedom which must be zealously guarded, it is also true that respectability, publication and professional advance are never without criteria set from within the academic world; and indeed it is probably better that they are set there than by some external body which would be all too prone further to commodify and package what counts as thought. Inevitably, our thoughts and even the possibilities of our thoughts are shaped by where we are and whom we wish to please, whose respect we need to gain or retain. How, then, shall *we* think otherwise?

The pre-modern monastic impulse, especially the early movement by men and women into the solitude and silence of the desert, for all its many problems, did recognize the need, and provided the opportunity, to place oneself outside conventional structures and expectations, and to develop a self-discipline geared toward contemplation of the divine Beauty as a central good. At its worst, asceticism degenerated into self-hatred, misogyny, fear of sexuality, irrelevance and utter pettiness. But at its best it enabled a gradual transformation in which core desires could be recognized and enhanced, desire for beauty, goodness, the divine; while the fears and attachments that stood in as the displacement of these desires could gradually fall away. Such an *ascesis*, or 'therapy of desires', worked not by trying to argue people out of a destructive symbolic but by fostering the longing for beauty and its creative newness. Nor was this desire premised on a lack, but on a plenitude, whose fullness, however, deepened and reduplicated desire.

From any perspective, and certainly from a feminist's, an exploration of such *ascesis*, not merely as an idea but as a way of living, has enormous problems. And yet, if we dismiss it altogether, as has largely been the case in modernity, do we not lose more than we gain? Putting it another way, is it not urgent that we – academics – find or construct places where we become again vulnerable to beauty? – beauty that incites to creativity, which must on no account be lost? What is holiness in postmodernity? That is the underlying question of my research.

Notes

Preface

1 Some discussion of the unpublished later volumes can be found in Jeremy Carrette's essay, 'In the Name of Life', in *Grace Jantzen: Redeeming the Present* ed. Elaine Graham (Ashgate, 2010.)

Introduction

1 In a later chapter I shall look further at this idea of salvation and its centrality to traditional Christendom, and shall argue that it is not as obvious as it may seem.

Chapter 1

1 For extensive retellings of the tale and critical analysis, see Betsy Hearne (1993).
2 Whether women's meetings were a way of diluting or enhancing gender equality is a matter of debate: see Trevett (1991); Mack (1992).

Chapter 2

1 Or superseded by. See my account of Plato's developing philosophy of beauty in Jantzen (2004): 193–221.
2 Besides Farley himself, see, for example, Sherry (2002); Begbie (2000); de Gruchy (2001); Crockett (2001); Viladesau (1999); and the work by and on Hans Urs von Balthasar's *Theological Aesthetics* (1982). I have discussed these books in 'Beauty for Ashes: Notes on the displacement of Beauty' (Jantzen 2002).

Chapter 5

1 I gratefully acknowledge the financial support of the John Rylands Trust for this research. Most of the Quaker documents consulted are contained in the Midgely Collection of the John Rylands Library. For the general reader, many of the women's writings have recently been republished in Garmen *et al.* (1996). Additional works of Margaret Fell are reprinted in T.H.S. Wallace (ed.) *A Sincere and Constant Love* (1992).
2 Cf. John Bunyan *Pilgrim's Progress* (1965).

3 Cf. Hill (1971): 78–88.
4 Cf. Hill (1970).
5 Cf. Baxter (1659).
6 Fox, ed. Nickalls (1952): 35–8. The date given for this occurrence in the *Journal* is 1649; but this material was not in the early manuscripts and was added later, possibly by Fox himself, or perhaps by William Penn or Thomas Ellwood, who edited the *Journal* after Fox's death.
7 Cf. Filmer (1949); Locke (1960).
8 See also T.L. Underwood (1997).
9 A famous example is that of Mary Dyer and her friends. See Plumpton (1994).
10 In the late seventeenth century, Britain and the Netherlands were competing 'for monopoly in the buying and selling of black slaves'. See St Clair Drake (1990), II: 269.

Chapter 7

1 By 'necrophilia' I mean obsession with death and other worlds, whether that is expressed in focus of attention or in refusal to contemplate it (phobia); I do not mean the strictly technical sense of sexual fantasies about dead bodies.
2 I am much indebted in this, discussion to the work of Peter A. Schouls (1980; 1992).

Chapter 8

1 The idea of *Bildung* and the aesthetic development of taste and character owes much to Gadamer, especially his *Truth and Method* (1989). But see also my critique of Gadamer from a feminist perspective (Jantzen 2003).

Chapter 9

1 It is also, therefore, a means for Plotinus of escape from unpleasant political realities, as I have argued in Jantzen 2004: 348–53.
2 I have argued this in detail in previous writings (Jantzen 1984; 1997) but not with reference to beauty.

Chapter 11

1 To illustrate this claim, see Debra Shogun (1993) and Elizabeth Frazer *et al.* (1992).
2 For feminists presenting an 'ethic of care', see Carol Gilligan (1982), Nel Noddings (1986) and Joan Tronto (1993).
3 One might even speculate that this is part of the reason for the deep suspicion of Continental thought in circles of analytic philosophy; often before serious engagement with its (highly diverse) texts, the very idea of transformative thought is already threatening.
4 Moreover, this solidarity will have to be at material as well as intellectual levels: although I am writing here of intellectual interventions, I do not mean to suggest that thinking is all that is needed.
5 It is sobering to remember, however, that even this will be useful only for those who acknowledge that there is a problem. Those who refuse that recognition, or who displace the problem onto others – 'underdeveloped countries', 'welfare scroungers', 'climatic forces' – will only strengthen their controlling grip.

6 It regularly constructs this as its binary opposite. This is not to say that it really is its opposite, of course; indeed, part of the point of the deconstructive strategy is to dismantle such putative binaries. However, it is significant to lift up what has been suppressed, to see how this changes the picture.

7 Thus, in Freud's account of Little Hans, the boy's phobia about horses was a disguised complex about his father and masculine sexuality.

Chapter 12

1 Cf. Miles (1985).

2 Cf. Jay (1994), chapter 1.

3 This is to a large extent also true of Catholic theology in modernity, with, however, the monumental exception of Hans Urs von Balthasar (1982). Cf. Riches (1986).

4 Cf. de Bella (1989).

Bibliography

Ambler, R. (2001) *Truth of the Heart: An Anthology of George Fox*, London: Quaker Books.

Anderson, Elizabeth (1993) *Value in Ethics and Economics*, Cambridge, MA: Harvard University Press.

Aquinas, Thomas (1975) *Summa Contra Gentiles*, 5 volumes, trans. Anton C. Pegis, Notre Dame: University of Notre Dame Press.

Arnault, Lynne S. (1989) 'The Radical Future of a Classic Moral Theory', in Alison M. Jaggar and Susan R. Bordo (eds), *Gender/Body/Knowledge: Feminist Reconstructions of Being and Knowing,* New Brunswick, NJ: Rutgers University Press.

Augustine (1961) *Confessions*, trans. R.S. Pine-Coffin, London: Penguin.

—— (1972) *Concerning the City of God against the Pagans*, trans. Henry Bettenson, Harmondsworth: Penguin.

—— (1983) *Expositions on the Book of Psalms*, ed. A. Cleveland Coxe, Nicene and Post-Nicene Fathers Vol. VIII, Grand Rapids, MI: Erdmans.

—— (1984) *Augustine of Hippo: selected writings*, ed. Mary T. Clark, New York: Paulist Press.

Balsamo, Anne (1996) *Technologies of the Gendered Body: Reading Cyborg Women*, Durham, NC: Duke University Press.

Barbour, Hugh (1964) *The Quakers in Puritan England*, New Haven: Yale University Press.

Barth, Karl (1959) *Dogmatics in Outline*, New York: Harper and Row.

—— (1975) *Church Dogmatics*, 4 volumes, ed. G.W. Bromiley and T.F. Torrance, Edinburgh: T. & T. Clark.

Barthel, Diane (1988) *Putting on Appearances: Gender and Advertising*, Philadelphia: Temple University Press.

Battersby, Christine (1995) 'Stages on Kant's Way: Aesthetics, Morality, and the Gendered Sublime', in Peggy Zeglin Brand and Carolyn Korsmeyer (eds), *Feminism and Tradition in Aesthetics*, University Park, PA: Pennsylvania State University Press, pp. 88–114.

Baxter, Richard (1659) *The Holy Commonwealth*, London: n.p.

Beardsley, Monroe C. (1966) *Aesthetics from Classical Greece to the Present: A Short History*, Tuscaloosa and London: University of Alabama Press.

Begbie, J.S. (2000) *Theology, Music and Time*, Cambridge: Cambridge University Press.

Benefiel, Margaret and Phipps, Rebecca (2001) "Quakers and Social Transformation", Janet K. Ruffing, RSM (ed.), in *Mysticism and Social Transformation*, Syracuse, NY: Syracuse University Press, pp.124–42.

Benhabib, Seyla (1992) *Situating the Self: Gender, Community and Postmodernism in Contemporary Ethics*, New York: Routledge.

Bernard of Clairvaux (1977–80) *On the Song of Songs* Vols I–IV, trans. Killian Walsh, OCSO, Cistercian Fathers Series 40, Kalamazoo, MI: Cistercian Publications.

Bettleheim, Bruno (1989) *The Uses of Enchantment: The Meaning and Importance of Fairy Tales*, New York: Vintage.

Bonting, Sjoerd L. (2005) *Creation and Double Chaos: Science and Theology in Discussion*, Minneapolis, MN: Augsburg Fortress.

Bourdieu, Pierre (1990 [1980]) *The Logic of Practice*, trans. Richard Nice, Cambridge: Cambridge University Press.

—— (1998 [1994]) *Practical Reason: On the Theory of Action*, Cambridge: Cambridge University Press.

Bouwsma, William J. (1988) *John Calvin: A Sixteenth Century Portrait*, New York and Oxford: Oxford University Press.

Braithwaite, William C. (1955) *The Beginnings of Quakerism*, 2nd edition, Cambridge: Cambridge University Press.

—— (1961) *The Second Period of Quakerism*, 2nd edition, Cambridge: Cambridge University Press.

Bredin, Hugh and Santoro-Brienza, Liberato (2000) *Philosophies of Art and Beauty: Introducing Aesthetics*, Edinburgh: Edinburgh University Press.

Brennan, Teresa (1993) *History after Lacan*, London and New York: Routledge.

British Yearly Meeting of the Religious Society of Friends (Quakers) (1995) *Quaker Faith and Practice*, 2nd edition, London: the Yearly Meeting of the Religious Society of Friends (Quakers) in Britain.

Brown, Peter (1988) *The Body and Society: Men, Women and Sexual Renunciation in Early Christianity*, New York: Columbia University Press.

Bubeck, Diemut (1995) *Care, Gender and Justice*, Oxford: Clarendon Press.

Bunyan, John (1965) *Pilgrim's Progress*, Harmondsworth: Penguin.

Burke, Edmund (1990) *A Philosophical Enquiry into the Origin of our Ideas of the Sublime and Beautiful*, ed. Adam Phillips, Oxford: Oxford University Press.

Burrough, Edward (1659) *The Great Mistery of the Great Whore Unfolded*, London: n.p.

Byrne, Peter (1989) *Natural Religion and the Nature of Religion*, London: Routledge.

Calvin, John (1957) *Institutes of the Christian Religion*, 2 volumes, trans. Henry Beveridge, Grand Rapids, MI: Eerdmans.

Carrette, Jeremy and King, Richard (2005) *Selling Spirituality: The Silent Takeover of Religion*, London: Routledge.

Code, Lorraine (1991) *What Can She Know? Feminist Theory and the Construction of Knowledge*, Ithaca, NY: Cornell University Press.

—— (1995) *Rhetorical Spaces: Essays on Gendered Locations*, New York: Routledge.

Cranston, Maurice (1957) *John Locke. A Biography*, London: Longman.

Critchley, Simon (1998) 'Introduction', in Simon Critchley and William R. Schroeder (eds), *A Companion to Continental Philosophy*, Oxford: Blackwell.

Crockett, C. (2001) *A Theology of the Sublime*, London: Routledge.

Damrosch, Leo (1996) *The Sorrows of the Quaker Jesus: James Naylor and the Puritan Crackdown on the Free Spirit*, Cambridge, MA: Harvard University Press.

Davey, Nicholas (1992) 'Baumgarten, Alexander' in David E. Cooper (ed.), *A Companion to Aesthetics*, Oxford: Blackwell, pp. 40–42.

de Bella, Peter (1989) *The Discourse of the Sublime: History, Aesthetics and the Subject*, Oxford: Blackwell Publishers.

de Gruchy, J.W. (2001) *Christianity, Art and Transformation: Theological Aesthetics in the Struggle for Justice*, Cambridge: Cambridge University Press.

Derrida, Jacques (1987) *The Truth in Painting*, trans. Geoff Bennington and Ian McLeod, Chicago: University of Chicago Press.

Descartes, R. (1969) *Descartes: Philosophical Writings*, trans. Elizabeth Anscombe and Peter Geach, containing Discourse on Method [1637], London: Thomas Nelson & Sons.

Dollimore, Jonathan (1998) *Death, Desire and Loss in Western Culture*, New York: Routledge.

Drake, St. Clair (1990) *Black Folk Here and There*, 2 volumes, Los Angeles: University of California Press.

Dyer, Richard (1997) *White*, London: Routledge.

Eco, Umberto (1986) *Art and Beauty in the Middle Ages*, trans. Hugh Bredin, New Haven: Yale University Press.

Elledge, Scott (ed.) (1961) *Eighteenth Century Critical Essays*, 2 volumes, Ithaca, NY: Cornell University Press.

Farley, Edward (2001) *Faith and Beauty: A Theological Aesthetic*, Aldershot: Ashgate.

Fell, Margaret (1992) *A Sincere and Constant Love: An Introduction to the Work of Margaret Fell*, ed. T.H.S. Wallace, Richmond, IN: Friends United Press.

—— (1995) *Quaker Faith and Practice*, London: The Yearly Meeting of the Religious Society of Friends [Quakers] in Britain.

Filmer, R. (1949) *Patriarchia and Other Works by Robert Filmer*, ed. P. Laslett, Oxford: Blackwell.

—— (1960) *Patriarchia and Other Works by Robert Filmer*, ed. Peter Laslett, Cambridge: Cambridge University Press.

Fiorenza, Elisabeth Schüssler (1983) *In Memory of Her: A Feminist Theological Reconstruction of Christian Origins*, London: SCM.

—— (1993) *Discipleship of Equals: A Critical Feminist Ecclesialogy of Liberation*, London: SCM.

Foucault, Michel (1970) *The Order of Things: An Archaeology of the Human Sciences*, New York: Random House.

—— (1984) 'What is Enlightenment?', in P. Rabinow (ed.), *Foucault Reader*, New York: Pantheon.

—— (1986) 'Kant on Enlightenment and Revolution', trans. C. Gordon, *Economy and Society* 15 (1), p. 89.

Fox, George (1657a) *Ground of High places, and the end of high places*, Earlham School of Religion Digital Quaker Collection, http://esr.earlham.edu/dqc/biblio.html.

—— (1657b) *Priests' fruits made manifest*, Earlham School of Religion Digital Quaker Collection, http://esr.earlham.edu/dqc/biblio.html.

—— (1831) 'Distinction Between The Two Suppers of Christ', in *Works of George Fox (Volume 6)*, Earlham School of Religion Digital Quaker Collection, http://esr.earlham.edu/dqc/biblio.html.

—— (1952) *Journal of George Fox*, ed. John L. Nickalls, London: Religious Society of Friends.

Frazer, Elizabeth, Hornsby, Jennifer and Lovibond, Sabina (eds) (1992) *Ethics: A Feminist Reader*, Oxford: Blackwell.

Freud, Sigmund (1984) 'Beyond the Pleasure Principle', in *On Metapsychology*, trans. J. Strachey, The Penguin Freud Library Vol. II, Harmondsworth: Penguin.

Friedman, Marilyn (2000) 'Feminism in Ethics', in Miranda Fricker and Jennifer Hornsby (eds), *The Cambridge Companion to Feminism in Philosophy*, Cambridge: Cambridge University Press, pp. 205–24.

Gadamer, Hans-Georg (1989) *Truth and Method*, trans. Joel Weinsheimer and Donald G. Marshall, New York: Continuum.

Garmen, Mary, Applegate, Judith, Benefiel, Margaret and Meredith, Dorothea (eds) (1996) *Hidden in Plain Sight: Quaker Women's Writings 1650–1700*, Wallingford, PA: Pendle Hill Publications.

Gilligan, Carol (1982) *In a Different Voice: Psychological Theory and Women's Development*, Cambridge, MA: Harvard University Press.

Girard, René (1977) *Violence and the Sacred*, trans. Patrick Gregory, Baltimore: Johns Hopkins University Press.

—— (1987) *Things Hidden Since the Foundation of the World*, trans. Stephen Bann and Michael Metteer, Stanford: Stanford University Press.

—— (1996) *The Girard Reader*, ed. James G. Williams, New York: Crossroad.

Graham, Elspeth, *et al.* (1989) 'Introduction' to *Her Own Life: Autobiographical Writings by Seventeenth-Century Englishwomen*, London: Routledge.

Gwyn, Douglas (1986) *Apocalypse of the Word: The Life and Message of George Fox*, Richmond, IN: Friends United Press.

—— (1995) *The Covenant Crucified: Quakers and the Rise of Capitalism*, Wallingford, PA: Pendle Hill Publications.

—— (2000) *Seekers Found: Atonement in Early Quaker Experience*, Wallingford, PA: Pendle Hill Publications.

Haller, William (1938) *The Rise of Puritanism*, New York: Columbia University Press.

Hannay, Margaret (ed.) (1985) *Silent but for the Word: Tudor Women as Patrons, Translators, and Writers of Religious Works*, Kent OH: Kent State University Press.

Hanson, Karen (1998) 'Dressing Down Dressing Up: The Philosophic Fear of Fashion' in Carolyn Korsmeyer (ed), *Aesthetics: The Big Questions*, Oxford: Blackwell, pp. 59–71.

Haraway, Donna (1991) *Simians, Cyborgs and Women: the Reinvention of Nature*, London: Free Association Press.

Hare, Richard (1981) *Moral Thinking: Its Levels, Method and Point*, Oxford: Clarendon Press.

Harrison, Peter (1990) *'Religion' and the Religions in the English Enlightenment*, Cambridge: Cambridge University Press.

Hearne, Betsy (1993) *Beauties and Beasts*, New York and London: Greenwood Press.

Hill, Christopher (1965) *Intellectual Origins of the English Revolution*, Oxford: Clarendon.

—— (1970) *God's Englishman: Oliver Cromwell and the English Revolution*, Harmomdsworth: Penguin.

—— (1971) *Antichrist in Seventeenth Century England*, London: Penguin.

—— (1972) *The World Turned Upside Down: Radical Ideas During the English Revolution*, Harmondsworth: Penguin.

Hobbes, Thomas (1968) *Leviathan*, ed. C.B. MacPherson, Harmondsworth: Penguin.

Hobhouse, Stephen (1927) *William Law and Eighteenth Century Quakerism*, London: George Allen and Unwin.

Hollander, J. and Kermode, F. (eds) (1973) *The Literature of Renaissance England*, Oxford: Oxford University Press.

Hume, David (1962) *Enquiries Concerning the Human Understanding and Concerning the Principles of Morals*, ed. L.A. Selby-Bigge, 2nd edition, Oxford: Clarendon Press.

Ingle, H. Larry (1994) *First Among Friends: George Fox and the Creation of Quakerism*, New York and Oxford: Oxford University Press.

Israel, Jonathan I. (2001) *Radical Enlightenment: Philosophy and the Making of Modernity 1650–1750*, Oxford and New York: Oxford University Press.

Jaggar, Alison (2000) 'Feminism in Ethics', in Miranda Fricker and Jennifer Hornsby (eds), *The Cambridge Companion to Feminism in Philosophy*, Cambridge: Cambridge University Press, pp. 225–44.

Jantzen, Grace M. (1984) *God's World, God's Body*, London: Darton, Longman and Todd.

—— (1995) *Power, Gender and Christian Mysticism*, Cambridge: Cambridge University Press.

—— (1997) 'Feminism and Pantheism', *The Monist* Vol. 80 No. 2, pp. 266–85.

—— (1998) *Becoming Divine: Towards a Feminist Philosophy of Religion*, Manchester: Manchester University Press and Bloomington, IN: Indiana University Press.

—— (2002) 'Beauty for Ashes: Notes on the Displacement of Beauty', *Literature and Theology* Vol. 16 No. 2, pp. 427–49.

—— (2003) 'The Horizon of Natality: Gadamer, Heidegger and the Limits of Existence' in Lorraine Cole (ed.) *Feminist Interpretations of Hans-Georg Gadamer*, University Park, PA: Pennsylvania State University Press, pp. 285–306.

—— (2004) *Foundations of Violence: Volume 1 of Death and the Displacement of Beauty*, London and New York: Routledge.

—— (2009) *Violence to Eternity, Volume 2 of Death and the Displacement of Beauty*, London and New York: Routledge.

Jay, Martin (1994) *Downcast Eyes: The Denigration of Vision in Twentieth-Century French Thought*, Berkeley: University of California Press.

Jones, Rufus M. (1914) *Spiritual Reformers in the Sixteenth and Seventeenth Centuries*, London: Macmillan.

—— (1971 [1923]) *Studies in Mystical Religion*, London: Macmillan.

Jones, T.C. (ed.) (1989) *The Power of the Lord Is Over All: The Pastoral Letters of George Fox*, Richmond, IN: Friends United Press.

Kant, Immanuel (1960) *Observations on the Feeling of the Beautiful and Sublime*, trans. John T. Goldthwaite, Berkeley: University of California Press.

Kunze, Bonnelyn Young (1994) *Margaret Fell and the Rise of Quakerism*, Stanford: Stanford University Press.

Lacan, Jacques (1977) *Écrits: A Selection*, trans. A. Sheridan, London: Tavistock.

—— (1982) 'God and the *Jouissance* of The Woman', in Juliet Mitchell and Jacqueline Rose (eds), *Feminine Sexuality: Jacques Lacan and the École Freudienne*, London: Macmillan.

Laslett, Peter (1960) 'Introduction' to John Locke, *Locke's Two Treatises on Government*, Oxford: Oxford University Press.

Law, William (1969) *The Spirit of Prayer and The Spirit of Love*, London: James Clarke & Co. Ltd.

Leclercq, Jean (1989) *Women and St Bernard of Clairvaux*, Cistercian Studies Series 104, Kalamazoo, MI: Cistercian Publications.

Le Doeuff, Michèle (1989) *The Philosophical Imaginary*, London: Athlone.

Locke, John (1958) *The Reasonableness of Christianity*, ed. I.T. Ramsey, Stanford: Stanford University Press.

—— (1959) *An Essay Concerning Human Understanding* 2 volumes, ed. Alexander Campbell Fraser, New York: Dover, and Oxford: Oxford University Press [1689; 4th edition, 1700.]

—— (1960) *Two Treatises of Government*, ed. Peter Laslett, Cambridge: Cambridge University Press.

—— (1693) [1989] *Some Thoughts Concerning Education*, ed. John W. Yolton and Jean S. Yolton, Oxford: Oxford University Press [5th edition, 1705.]

Lyotard, Jean-François. (1984) *The Postmodern Condition: A Report on Knowledge*, trans. Geoff Bennington and Brian Massumi, Manchester: Manchester University Press.

—— (1989) 'The Sublime and the Avant-Garde', in Andrew Benjamin (ed.), *The Lyotard Reader*, Oxford: Blackwell Publishers.

MacHaffie, Barbara J. (ed.) (1992) *Readings in Her Story: Women in Christian Tradition*, Minneapolis: Augsburg Fortress.

Mack, Phyllis (1992) *Visionary Women: Ecstatic Prophecy in Seventeenth Century England*, Berkeley: University of California Press.

McCann, Edwin (1994) 'Locke's Philosophy of Body' in Vere Chappell (ed.), *The Cambridge Companion to Locke*, Cambridge: Cambridge University Press.

McGinn, Bernard (1991) *The Foundations of Mysticism*, Volume I of *The Presence of God: A History of Western Mysticism*, New York: Crossroad.

—— (1994) *The Growth of Mysticism*, Volume II of *The Presence of God: A History of Western Mysticism*, New York: Crossroad.

McGregor, J. F. M. and Reay, B. (eds) (1984) *Radical Religion in the English Revolution*, Oxford: Oxford University Press.

Meyers, Diana Tietjens (1994) *Subjection and Subjectivity: Psychoanalytic Feminism and Moral Philosophy*, New York and London: Routledge.

Miles, Margaret (1985) *Image as Insight: Visual Understanding in Western Christianity and Secular Culture*, Boston, MA: Beacon Press.

Miles, Margaret R. (1999) *Plotinus on Body and Beauty: Society, Philosophy and Religion in Third-Century Rome*, Oxford: Blackwell.

Moore, Rosemary (2000) *The Light in Their Consciences: Early Quakers in Britain 1646–1666*, University Park, PA: Pennsylvania State University Press.

Mothersill, Mary (1984) *Beauty Restored*, Oxford: Clarendon Press.

Naylor, James (1661) *Milk for babes: and meat for strong men*, Earlham School of Religion Digital Quaker Collection, http://esr.earlham.edu/dqc/biblio.html.

Noddings, Nel (1986) *Caring: A Feminine Approach to Ethics and Moral Education*, Berkeley: University of California Press.

Nuovo, J. Victor (ed.) (1997) *John Locke and Christianity: Contemporary Responses to 'The Reasonableness of Christianity'*, Bristol: Thoemmes Press.

Nuttall, Geoffrey F. [1946] (1992) *The Holy Spirit in Puritan Faith and Experience*, Chicago: University of Chicago Press..

Passmore, J.A. (1954) 'The Dreariness of Aesthetics', in William Elton (ed.), *Aesthetics and Language*, Oxford: Blackwell.

Peacocke, Arthur R. (1993) *Theology for a Scientific Age*, 2nd edition, Minneapolis, MN: Augsburg Fortress.

Plato (1961) *The Collected Dialogues of Plato*, ed. Edith Hamilton and Huntington Cairns, Princeton: Princeton University Press.

Plotinus (1966f) *The Enneads*, 7 volumes, trans. A.H. Armstrong, Loeb Classical Library, Cambridge, MA: Harvard University Press, and London: William Heinemann Ltd.

Plumpton, Ruth (1994) *Mary Dyer: Biography of a Rebel Quaker*, Boston: Branden Publishing Co.

Poovey, Mary (1998) *A History of the Modern Fact: Problems of Knowledge in the Science of Wealth and Society*, Chicago: University of Chicago Press.

Punshon, John (1984) *Portrait in Grey: A Short History of the Quakers*, London: Quaker Home Service.

Quaker Women's Group (1986) *Bringing the Invisible into the Light: Some Quaker Feminists Speak of Their Experience*, London: Quaker Home Service.

Rabinow, Paul (1996) *Essays on the Anthropology of Reason*, Princeton, NJ: Princeton University Press.

Rahner, Karl (1978) *Foundations of Christian Faith: An Introduction to the Idea of Christianity*, trans. William V. Dych, London: Darton, Longman and Todd.

Riches, John (ed.) (1986) *The Analogy of Beauty: The Theology of Hans Urs von Balthasar*, Edinburgh: T. & T. Clark.

Rist, John M. (1967) *Plotinus: The Road to Reality*, Cambridge: Cambridge University Press.

Rose, Jacqueline (1993) *Why War?* Oxford: Blackwell.

Sawday, Jonathan (1995) *The Body Emblazoned: Dissection and the Human Body in Renaissance Culture*, London: Routledge.

Scarry, Elaine (1999) *On Beauty and Being Just*, Princeton, NJ: Princeton University Press.

Schleiermacher, Friedrich (1928) *The Christian Faith*, Edinburgh: T. & T. Clark.

Schouls, Peter A. (1980) *The Imposition of Method: A Study of Descartes and Locke*, Oxford: Oxford University Press.

—— (1992) *Reasoned Freedom: John Locke and Enlightenment*, Ithaca, NY and London: Cornell University Press.

Shapin, Steven (1994) *A Social History of Truth: Civility and Science in Seventeenth Century England*, Chicago: University of Chicago Press.

—— (1996) *The Scientific Revolution*, Chicago: University of Chicago Press.

Sherry, Patrick (2002) *Spirit and Beauty*, 2nd edition, London: SCM.

Shogun, Debra (ed.) (1993) *A Reader in Feminist Ethics*, Toronto: Canadian Scholars' Press.

Springborg, Patricia (1997) 'Introduction' to *Mary Astell: A Serious Proposal to the Ladies*, London: Pickering and Chatto.

Strawson, P.F. (1959) *Individuals*, London: Methuen.

Taylor, Charles (1989) *Sources of the Self: The Making of Modern Identity*, Cambridge: Cambridge University Press, and Cambridge, MA: Harvard University Press.

Trevett, Christine (1991) *Women and Quakerism in the Seventeenth Century*, York: The Ebor Press.

Tronto, Joan (1993) *Moral Boundaries: A Political Argument for the Ethic of Care*, New York: Routledge.

Underwood, T.L. (1997) *Primitivism, Radicalism, and the Lamb's War: The Baptist–Quaker Conflict in Seventeenth-Century England*, New York and Oxford: Oxford University Press.

Viladesau, Richard (1999) *Theological Aesthetics: God in Imagination, Beauty and Art*, Oxford and New York: Oxford University Press.

von Balthasar, Hans Urs (1982) *The Glory of the Lord: A Theological Aesthetics*, 7 volumes, Edinburgh: T. & T. Clark.

Ward, Andrew (1992) 'Judgement, Aesthetic' in David E. Cooper (ed.), *A Companion to Aesthetics*, Oxford: Blackwell, pp. 243–49.

Weil, Simone (1951) *Waiting for God*, trans. Emma Craufurd, New York: Harper and Row.

William of St Thierry (1980) *The Golden Epistle: A Letter to the Brethren at Mont Dieu*, trans. Theodore Berkeley, Cistercian Fathers Series No. 12, Kalamazoo, MI: Cistercian Publications.

Wittgenstein, Ludwig (1969) *Philosophical Investigations*, trans. G.E.M. Anscombe, Oxford: Basil Blackwell.

Wolterstorff, Nicholas (1994) 'Locke's Philosophy of Religion', in Vere Chappell (ed.), *The Cambridge Companion to Locke*, Cambridge: Cambridge University Press.

—— (1996) *John Locke and the Ethics of Belief*, Cambridge: Cambridge University Press.

Woolhouse, Roger (1994) 'Locke's Theory of Knowledge' in Vere Chappell (ed.), *The Cambridge Companion to Locke*, Cambridge: Cambridge University Press.

Wordsworth, W. (1984) *William Wordsworth: The Major Works*, ed. Stephen Gill, Oxford: Oxford University Press.

Index

aesthetic sensibility, 127, 138, 140;
  decline in, 11, 124; education, 129,
  135; shaped by Christian teachings, 19
aesthetic theory, 59
aesthetics, 131; theological, 157
Anabaptists, 5
anchorite's cell, 179, 181, 185, 189
Anderson, Elizabeth, 171
Anselm of Canterbury, 40
apocalyptic expectations, 28–29, 46, 80.
  See also Kingdom of God:
  Armageddon, 49, 84; damnation and
  destruction of this world, 82;
  environmental concerns and, 47;
  violence in, 48–49
Apology (Barclay), 89
Arendt, Hannah, 188
Aristotle, 44, 130
Arnault, Lynne, 172
art and artefacts, 19, 24, 39, 41, 49. *See
  also* creativity: art galleries, 190, 192;
  beauty of art as derived, 130–31
artistic expression, 19
ascesis, 193
asceticism, 44–45, 49, 193; beauty
  denied, 23, 42, 46; hostility to body
  and pleasure, 42; renunciation of
  women, 24
Astell, Mary, 76, 110; *Serious Proposal,*
  110
atonement, 39, 84
Augustine, Saint, Bishop of Hippo, 31–32,
  50, 52, 126, 145, 190; ambivalence
  towards beauty, 42, 48, 135–36, 139,
  142, 154–55; anxieties about gender,
  sexuality, and otherness, 24, 138–41,
  159; beauty is embodied, material,
  135, 142; celibacy, 139; *City of God,*
  33, 135; concern with idolatry, 136–38;

Confessions, 30, 136–37, 139–40,
  142–43; doctrine of creation (creation
  ex nihilo), 143–44, 149, 165; Platonist
  thinking, 149; sensitivity to beauty, 12,
  24, 135–37

Bacon, Francis, 46, 181, 189
Baptists, 29, 63
Barbour, Hugh, 79
Barclay, Robert, *Apology,* 89
Barth, Karl, 51, 126, 137, 165; *Church
  Dogmatics,* 150–51
Bathurst, Elizabeth, 90, 113; Choose Life
  message, 91; *Truth Vindicated,* 89;
  Truth's Vindication, 78
Baumgarten, Alexander, 131
Baxter, Richard, 79
Beatific Vision, 42, 61, 135, 142
beauty, 49, 51, 125–27, 184. *See also*
  sublime: absence in modern Christian
  theology, 19–20, 139, 150–51, 190;
  absence in philosophy of religion, 190;
  adornment (women's), 48, 156; as
  alternative symbolic, ix, xii, 169;
  ambivalence in Christendom, 10,
  21–22, 42; analogy with taste, 123–24;
  anxiety about, xii, 3, 23–24, 159;
  attentiveness to, 28, 44, 169; Barth's
  view, 150; Calvin's references to, 165;
  central place for life and living, ix, 34;
  creativity and, 58, 163; deferred to a
  future life, 42, 46–49; denial of (*See*
  denial of beauty); dismissal, 121;
  displacement, 22, 93, 97–98, 135, 144,
  151 (*See also* beauty and belief; word
  (the word, the rational and verbal));
  distraction from God, 139; divine, 151;
  early church views of, 50; early
  Quaker views of, 22–23, 61; embodied,